THE BASKETBALL ABSTRACT

Dave Heeren

PRENTICE HALL
Englewood Cliffs, New Jersey 07632

Prentice-Hall International (UK) Limited, *London*
Prentice-Hall of Australia Pty. Limited, *Sydney*
Prentice-Hall Canada Inc., *Toronto*
Prentice-Hall Hispanoamericana, S.A., *Mexico*
Prentice-Hall of India Private Limited, *New Delhi*
Prentice-Hall of Japan, Inc., *Tokyo*
Simon & Schuster Asia Pte. Ltd., *Singapore*
Editora Prentice-Hall do Brasil, Ltda., *Rio de Janeiro*

PRINTED IN THE UNITED STATES OF AMERICA

10 9 8 7 6 5 4 3 2 1

Library of Congress Cataloging-in-Publication Data

Heeren, Dave.
    The basketball abstract / by Dave Heeren.
      p.   cm.
    ISBN 0-13-069170-4
    1. Basketball—United States—Statistics. 2. National Basketball
Association—Statistics. I. Title.
GV885.55.H44 1989   88-28942
796.32′3′0973—dc19   CIP

ISBN 0-13-069170-4

PRENTICE HALL
BUSINESS & PROFESSIONAL DIVISION
A division of Simon & Schuster
Englewood Cliffs, New Jersey 07632

Acknowledgments

My thanks to Randy Mell and Robert Stern
for suggesting this book,
to Chris Lazzarino and Paul Heidelberg
for encouraging it,
and to Art Van Voolen
for making it possible.

Contents

SECTION III
CHARTS   **195**

Introduction

This happened on a radio sports talk show last spring. It was early in the NBA playoffs, so I was asked by the host of the show to identify a team I considered to be a dark horse.

In the pontificating spirit of Howard Cosell, I replied, without hesitation, the Utah Jazz.

When the Jazz proceeded to upset the Portland Trail Blazers and then played the Los Angeles Lakers to a dead heat that was decided only by a home-court advantage, it made me look pretty smart.

The truth is I had no idea the Jazz were that good.

Like most everybody else, I figured the Jazz were about as good as their regular-season record—ninth best in the NBA—and that they probably would be bounced out of the playoffs in the first round by Portland.

TENDEX disagreed.

No, TENDEX is not the code name of a computer. It's a statistical system that can be used to measure relative strengths of basketball players, teams, and coaches.

The day I guested on the radio program I had spent a lot of time arguing with TENDEX. I had computed the NBA team ratings, TENDEX, and when the Jazz were rated on a level with the Lakers and the Boston Celtics, above every other team in the league, I didn't believe it. I rechecked the statistics several

times before concluding that either TENDEX was wrong or I was.

After some cogitation it occurred to me that maybe TENDEX was more objective than I was.

That's the trouble with most of us sports fans: We lack objectivity. I have received telephone calls from fans throughout the United States who want me to change the TENDEX formula, and they always contend that their suggestions will make the system more accurate. But after the conversation continues for a while, it becomes evident that the real reason they want to make changes is to improve the ratings of their favorite players.

We all have our opinions, our favorite players and teams. There is nothing wrong with that. It's what makes us good fans, and as such we can always figure out how to manipulate statistics in the best interests of our favorites.

TENDEX is not a fan and plays no favorites. It simply computes, and there it is, like it or not. I didn't like what it computed about the Utah Jazz, but that didn't disturb TENDEX in the least. Utah's rating turned out exactly the same every time it was computed.

TENDEX pretty much covers the court, as using far as it is possible to do so. It incorporates points, assists, rebounds, blocked shots, steals, turnovers, missed field goals and free throws, minutes played, and a game-pace factor in a formula that is based on the fact that the average ball possession is worth one point. The formula is analyzed in the first chapter of this book, but for now it is enough to admit that there are a few things even TENDEX can't figure.

There is man-to-man defense, for one thing. If this were measurable, you could probably add 100 percentage points to the ratings of Michael Cooper, Dudley Bradley, and T.R. Dunn.

There is role-playing, for another. Byron Scott improved his TENDEX rating by about 100 points during the ten games Magic Johnson missed last season. This came about because, with Johnson out, Scott's role changed and he had more opportunity to handle the basketball. If Johnson were to retire tomorrow, Scott would probably be regarded as an all-star player before the 1988–89 season ended.

A third factor that is difficult to compute is an individual's impact on his team. With a league-wide average of .500, there were only three players last season who had TENDEX ratings of .800 or better—Michael Jordan (.887), Charles Barkley (.829), and Larry Bird (.824).

But the mere fact that they were rated in this order did not prove they should be regarded as having this order of value to their respective teams. There is no doubt in my mind but that Bird was a much better player than Barkley, and there are statistics, not included in the TENDEX formula, that show why. The most significant of these stats is that the last three low-post players who played full seasons as teammates of Barkley all suddenly improved their TENDEX ratings by 100 points after being traded to other teams. This is because Barkley is a space-hogger: He is a dominator who does not bother to notice whom he is dominating. As often as not the victim is one of his teammates. Bird is the opposite kind of player: He keeps out of his teammates' way when the situation calls for it, but when he has the ball he involves them in the game with such effectiveness that he makes them better players.

Even though Jordan and Bird both were manhandled by a double-teaming Detroit defense in the playoffs last spring, there is little question but that they are the best players in basketball. Because of Barkley's tendency to focus everything around himself, often to the detriment of his team, he probably should be rated behind Bird, Jordan, Akeem Olajuwon, Magic Johnson, and John Stockton.

The Bird-Jordan argument is not that simple to resolve. Jordan certainly had the better individual statistics last season, but over the course of the two players' careers it can be demonstrated that Bird has made a greater positive impact on the winning percentage of his team. It began with Boston improving by 32 games (from 29–53 to 61–21) in Bird's rookie season and has held true to the present, even when the relative strength of Bird's and Jordan's teammates has been considered.

TENDEX is the basis for most of this book. It is not infallible, but in the course of its refinement during the past 25 years, it has become a comprehensive system for evaluating basketball teams, players, and coaches.

It can also be used for rating college players and as the foundation for a basketball draft game similar to Rotisserie Baseball. These features are included in this book.

But no matter how sophisticated and far-ranging a statistical system may become, let's not give up our prerogatives as fans. I may have given in (grudgingly) to TENDEX concerning the Utah Jazz, but please indulge my fancy if I stick to the belief that Larry Bird is a more valuable basketball player than Michael Jordan.

Dave Heeren

SECTION I

THE NBA:
AN OVERVIEW—
1946–1987

1

Hen Peckin'

*I*t's hard to believe this actually happened 30 years ago. I was covering a basketball game at the University of Delaware field house, which was little more than an oversized gym.

One thing you should know about the Delaware Blue Hens: In football, they are regular banty roosters, upsetting teams from bigger, more prestigious universities; in basketball, they are chicken salad, fit for consumption by the Lafayettes and Drexel Techs. As long as memory serves, it has been this way.

The visiting team that day was "upsetting" Delaware by 15 or 20 points late in the game. Bored, I began doodling on a scorepad, and from doodling somehow got into tinkering with statistics.

At that time only the most rudimentary statistics were kept—field goals attempted and made, free throws attempted and made, rebounds, and assists. Delaware had an all-conference forward who averaged 20 points a game, but it became evident after a few minutes of figuring that he was not the team's best player, at least not for that particular game.

The basic statistics for Delaware's top two players that day were:

	FG	FT	R	A	P
Joe All-Conference	7–15	7–10	2	2	21
Charlie Underrated	5–8	4–6	9	4	14

From these stats came a formula that could be called FIVEDEX, a primitive ancestor of TENDEX. The FIVEDEX formula consisted of points, plus rebounds, plus assists, minus missed field goal attempts, minus missed free throw attempts.

The results were:

	P	+ R	+ A	− MFG	− MFT	= FIVE
Joe	21	+ 2	+ 2	− 8	− 3	= 14
Charlie	14	+ 9	+ 4	− 3	− 2	= 22

In a game story for the student newspaper I mentioned that statistical analyses showed Charlie to have been Delaware's standout player in that game, even though stories that appeared in Philadelphia and Wilmington daily newspapers referred to Joe as having "led" the Blue Hens' losing effort with 21 points. At that time I had no idea that this little formula eventually would evolve into a comprehensive system for evaluating basketball players.

After graduation from Delaware I became a publicity assistant for the New York Knicks and it was in the old Madison Square Garden that the next addition was made to this system during the 1961–62 season.

In the NBA at that time the only statistics that were kept other than the basic five were personal fouls and minutes played. It was tempting to include personal fouls as negatives, along with missed shots; but for reasons that will be explained in Chapter 4, I decided that personal fouls are neutral statistics, neither good nor bad, and therefore should not be included.

Minutes played, however, are important. If blue cannot be compared with green, then neither should a basketball player who plays only 20 minutes of a game be compared statistically with one who plays 40 minutes. They should be rated only on the basis of their performance for the amount of court time they have.

For example, although this didn't actually happen, let's say that Joe played only 14 minutes while Charlie played 33 in the Delaware game. Dividing the FIVEDEX statistic by minutes played, this would reverse the ratings and move Joe ahead of Charlie:

	FIVE	÷	MINS	=	SIX
Joe	14	÷	14	=	1.000
Charlie	22	÷	33	=	.667

This method of computing a basketball rating is like computing a batting average in baseball, with basketball minutes played being comparable to baseball at bats. Obviously, the baseball player who collects 100 hits in 300 at bats (.333) is a better hitter than the one who goes 150 for 600 (.250), even though the former has fewer hits.

The 1961–62 season was one of the most exciting in NBA history. A new wave of superstars had entered the league. Bob Pettit was in his eighth season, Bill Russell his sixth, Elgin Baylor his fourth, Wilt Chamberlain his third, and Oscar Robertson and Jerry West their second. Walt Bellamy was a rookie.

These seven players rewrote the record book that season, and even today Chamberlain's TENDEX rating of 1.037 achieved that year stands as the highest ever by an NBA player. Bellamy (.929), Robertson (.892), and Pettit (.884) also had ratings in 1961–62 that rank among the all-time best.

Chapter 7 of this book will deal with the all-time best players, but at this point one thing should be said about Chamberlain: He averaged 48.5 minutes per game during 1961–62, playing every minute in 79 of Philadelphia's 80 games, including overtime. To do that and to play to the level he did was amazing. Most players lose their fine edge of effectiveness when they have played too many minutes. Basketball is different from baseball in this respect, because in baseball a player such as Cal Ripken can make headlines by playing every inning of every game for several seasons. In baseball there is a lot of sitting and standing around. In basketball the players are constantly on the move and tire easily.

After 1961–62, 12 years passed before the NBA expanded its statistics to include the ones that became the seventh and eighth in the TENDEX formula. In 1973–74, steals and blocked shots were tabulated for the first time. The tabulation of turnovers, the ninth of the ten statistics, was introduced in 1977–78.

By this time I had learned that a ball possession was worth almost exactly one point, and it has continued that way to the present. To hit, precisely, the mark of one point per ball possession during the 1988–89 season, a team would have to score on one-third of its three-point field goal attempts, one-half of its two-point field goal attempts, and average one point every time one of its players goes to the free throw line. The actual two- and three-point field goal averages will come very close to these ratios, falling slightly below them. Also on the negative side will be turnovers in which the ball is lost without a shot being taken. But the negatives will be counterbalanced by free throws and three-point plays. Most teams will average about 1.5 points for every two-shot trip to the free throw line, and they will also score several three-point plays (field goal + free throw) per game.

With the one-point ball possession as the new theoretical basis for the system, the new equation becomes:

$$P + R + A + B + S - T - MFG - MFT + MIN = NINEDEX$$

This is points, plus rebounds, plus assists, plus blocked shots, plus steals, minus turnovers, minus missed field-goal attempts, minus missed free throw attempts, divided by minutes played, equals a player's performance rating.

If a ball possession is worth a point, then so is a rebound that gains control of the ball. Recently, I saw a statistical system in which the analyst had computed that offensive rebounds were more important than defensive rebounds because the team that gets an offensive rebound, close to the basket, has a better-than-average chance to score.

There is no disputing this arithmetic—offensive rebounds often do lead directly to easy baskets—but the analysis is faulty even so. This is because a defensive rebound prevents an offensive rebound.

No, this is not simplistic circular reasoning. It is only when a defensive team fails to block its opponents and maintain its advantage under the boards that the offensive team becomes able to rebound. When this happens, it follows that the offensive team will rebound and gain the scoring advantage.

The trade-off is then obvious: A defensive rebound prevents an offensive rebound and vice versa. There is therefore no innate difference in value between offensive and defensive rebounds. The team that wins the overall battle for rebounds—on the offensive boards, the defensive boards, or both—will have more ball possessions and more opportunities to score.

Also worth one point is an assist that converts a normal one-point possession into an easy two-point basket. A steal is worth a point because it gains possession, while a turnover is minus-one because it loses possession. A missed field goal attempt is minus-one because it loses possession (unless the ball is regained by an offensive rebound, which is counted as plus-one to offset the minus-one of the missed shot). A missed free throw attempt is minus-one because it forfeits an easy point that should have been scored on an uncontested high-percentage shot.

The only questionable item in this formula is the blocked shot. The truth is that not every blocked shot results in a turnover. In fact, probably less than half of them do. It could therefore be argued that a blocked shot is not worth one point. There are two arguments on the other side, however. The first is that there is an unmeasurable intimidation factor involved with a blocked shot; the second is that there is a lot of defensive work that goes unrewarded for every blocked shot that is achieved. No rating points are given for near-blocks or altered shots. Taking all things into consideration, a blocked shot is probably worth at least one point to the defensive player's team. NBA statistics show that opponents of the league's best shot-blocking teams usually have low field goal shooting percentages.

There was still one more factor necessary for rounding out the TENDEX system, and it was while computing the final statistics for the 1982–83 season that I discovered it. That season, Alex English of Denver computed as the NBA's best player according to the formula using nine basic statistics. Although English was an excellent player, his lofty rating disturbed me because I did not think he was the best in the league. The problem was that he played for a team that did so much running that it accumulated more offensive statistics than any other team in the league, which in turn inflated the ratings of every player on the team, English included.

The missing factor was game pace.

But how can you compute something as elusive as game pace?

An elementary way would be by comparing the total points scored in games played by each team in the league. In Denver, games that season (counting the Nuggets and their opponents) averaged 245.8 points per game, while at the opposite end of the scale the New York Knicks plodded along at 197.5. This meant that New York was playing the game at a pace 20 percent slower than Denver, so of course Alex English had better stats than New York's Bernard King. But when this 20 percent factor was included, English and King came out with almost identical ratings. Several other players in the league wound up ranking ahead of both of them.

With the sophisticated system I was developing, however, making game pace exclusively dependent on points did not seem adequate. The problem was how to compute game pace on the basis of the essential statistics within the system.

It turned out to be rather simple.

By now I had learned that the average NBA player, counting regulars and reserves, had a rating of almost exactly .500. To be categorized as a star, a player had to average .600. For a superstar the standard was .700.

If the norm was .500, it followed that the pace of a game played by two teams with average players should be twice .500 or 1.000. Here is how to calculate a team's game pace for an entire season: Compute a rating based on the team's season totals for the nine statistics in the formula. Then compute a rating based on the same totals for the team's opponents for the 82-game season and add the two ratings.

Let's use the NBA champion Los Angeles Lakers of 1986–87 as an example. The Lakers' overall rating on the basis of the nine-statistic formula was .585, while the rating of the Laker's collective opponents in games against the Lakers was .495. Therefore, game pace for the Lakers, one of the league's running teams, was .585 + .495 = 1.080.

The Lakers played the game at a faster pace than most teams, so in order to compare their individual statistics with those of other teams that did not do as much running, and therefore had fewer ball possessions than the Lakers, it was necessary to divide the rating of each Laker player by the team's game pace (1.080).

The general formula became:

$$P + R + A + S + B - T - MFG - MFT + MIN + GP = TENDEX$$

Earvin (Magic) Johnson of the Lakers was the league's Most Valuable Player during the 1986–87 season, so let's use his statistics for that season as an illustration and compute his rating by plugging them into this equation.

Johnson scored 1,909 points, pulled down 504 rebounds, handed out 977 assists, stole the ball 138 times, and blocked 36 shots. The total of these five positive factors was 3,564.

On the negative side, he missed 625 field goal attempts (including three-pointers) and 96 free throw attempts. He also turned the ball over 300 times, for a minus total of 1,021.

Johnson's overall total including positives and negatives was 2,543. Dividing that by the number of minutes he played (2,904) yielded a rating of .876. Dividing that by the Lakers' game pace (1.080) gave the final TENDEX rating of .811, which justified Johnson's MVP award and placed him on our list of the all-time best players in the NBA (see Chapter 7).

2

Choosing Up Sides and Playing the Game

A few years ago the University of Kentucky's basketball team played an inferior team the Wildcats were expected to defeat by 40 or 50 points. This was before the rule was adopted limiting a college basketball team to 45 seconds of possession time, and the underdog team was able to frustrate Kentucky by holding the ball for long periods of time without taking a shot.

Although Kentucky won the game, the score was something like 20–13 and the Wildcats complained bitterly about the sportsmanship of their opponents. Underlying the complaints was the fact that the individual statistics of Kentucky players, which they had expected to bloat, were instead deflated by the slow pace of the game.

The TENDEX system, with its game pace factor, adjusts for a game that is intentionally slowed down. Comparatively speaking, a player who scored six or seven points in this game probably would have scored 25 or 30 in a game played at a normal pace. But the Wildcats' statistician apparently didn't try to pacify them

with a game pace adjustment, because they weren't happy with the outcome, even though they won.

Players are not the only ones who relish statistics. Fans do as well. I remember as a young man going into depression when my favorite athletes were injured or in slumps, even though the teams they played for may have been winning at the time. In baseball, I idolized Mickey Mantle. In basketball, I rooted for Carl Braun of the Knicks and tried to learn to shoot with a graceful style similar to his. The $E = MC^2$ of my existence consisted of Mantle's slugging statistics, Braun's scoring average, and comparisons between them and other players.

Using the TENDEX system, some intricate comparisons can be made.

Beginning with the fact that an average professional basketball player has a TENDEX rating of .500, computations can be made by position. Listing all of the NBA's players at each position for the past seven seasons shows approximate norms:

- Centers .550
- Power forwards .525
- Quick forwards .500
- Point guards .475
- Shooting guards .450

NBA scouts' knowledge of the fact that bigger players have more of an impact on the game than smaller players is the reason that such outstanding guards as Michael Jordan and Ron Harper have been selected later in recent drafts than less talented big men such as Sam Bowie and Brad Daugherty. It sometimes seems as if NBA teams overdo the big-man syndrome. Seldom is it done, but wouldn't it make sense for a team to draft a dominating guard ahead of a big man who had the potential to be just a little better than average?

A player such as Jordan, who plays both guard positions, could rate 75 to 100 TENDEX points lower than a center and be as effective a player, considering his positional standard (In reality, there is no active NBA center who rates 75 points ahead of Jordan; in fact, no center rates ahead of him at all).

The differences on the rating scale do not mean that centers are innately better basketball players than power forwards, or that power forwards are better than quick forwards, and so on. The distinguishing factors are closeness to the basket and ball-handling. Centers and power forwards play closer to the basket than smaller players and, with their size advantage, are able to pull down more rebounds and put up more easy shots. Point guards have higher ratings than shooting guards because they handle the ball more and therefore have more opportunities to become involved in the offense.

The way to develop an outstanding team is to acquire at least one superstar (TENDEX rating .700 or better), support him with players of average or better-than-average ability at the other four starting positions, and blend in two or three reserves with enough versatility to play different positions with effectiveness.

Do this and you have what basketball pundits refer to as chemistry. For an example, let's use approximate ratings of the Los Angeles Lakers at the halfway point of the 1987–88 season:

Player, Position	Rating	Standard	Plus/Minus
Abdul-Jabbar, center	.530	.550	−.020
Green, power forward	.520	.525	−.005
Worthy, quick forward	.520	.500	+.020
Johnson, point guard	.730	.475	+.255
Scott, shooting guard	.540	.450	+.090
Reserves	.460	.500	−.040
TOTALS	.532	.500	+.032

It should be noted that even though the Lakers' reserves are listed with a minus .040 rating, they are not weak reserves because most reserves rank below positional norms. This is to be expected. If they were above average, they would be starters. What this means in practical terms is that a team must have starters with above-average ratings; otherwise, it is sure to be a losing team, because its reserves certainly will not be better than the starters. To win, a team must have starters, like the Lakers have, who overall are considerably above the standard for their positions. The backcourt of Johnson (superstar rating .730) and Scott provided the Lakers with a high standard. Their frontcourt of Abdul-Jabbar, Worthy, and Green was only average at the time these ratings were computed.

Starters will generally play two-thirds of the time, reserves the remaining one-third. So the reserves' impact on a team is only about half as great as the impact of the five starters, and the combined ratings of all reserves is equivalent to 2½ starters.

The Laker's rating of .532 may not seem much above the average of .500, but it is about equal to the Boston Celtics as the best in the league. It is 6.4 percent above the NBA average. In a routine game in which 110 points are scored by the winning team, a 6.4 percent difference is equivalent to about seven points. This means that, assuming the Lakers' defense was average at this time, they were seven points better than a .500 team on a neutral court, three points better on the road, and 11 points better at home.

We are using a standard four-point home-court advantage, because over the course of a full NBA season research shows that the average margin of victory is four points for the home team.

You probably have a pretty good idea by now how to rate players according to the TENDEX system, but why bother to rate them at all? What does it mean to say that a player has a rating of 1.000 or .500?

The simplest answer to these questions is that a player with a rating of 1.000 is worth one point per minute to his team. If he plays 40 minutes, scores 40 points and does not do another thing, positive or negative, he is a 1.000 player.

On the other hand a player such as Kiki Vandeweghe, who is weak in many phases of the game, could score 40 points in a game and wind up with a rating for that game of something like .500. Vandeweghe's overall rating is only a little above .500, despite a high scoring average. A player with a .500 rating is worth one point to his team for every two minutes he spends on the court, regardless of the actual number of points he scores.

The opposite of this is a player such as Bill Russell, who often scored only 10 or 12 points in a game but did so many other things well that his rating frequently approached 1.000.

In a game in which the pace was an even 1.000, let's say Russell played 40 minutes, shot 5-for-8 on field goals, 3-for-5 on free throws, pulled down 25 rebounds, passed off for five assists, blocked five shots, stole the ball once, and committed four turnovers. Plugging in to the TENDEX formula, we have:

$$P + R + A + B + S - T - MFG - MFT =$$
$$13 + 25 + 5 + 5 + 1 - 4 - 3 - 2 =$$

$$SUM \div M \div GP = RATING$$
$$40 \div 40 \div 1.000 = 1.000$$

With an efficient boxscore anyone could compute the rating for any player in any game and find out who, in fact, are the standout players, not just who the leading scorers and rebounders are. So the next step is to put together a boxscore that is more workable than the ones in current use.

3

Keeping Score

*O*ne of the best things about baseball is the boxscore. I don't know about you, but I can sit for hours poring over boxscores from baseball games.

There is a good reason for this: From a boxscore you can learn almost everything important that happened in a baseball game, including much of the play by play. You can learn more from the boxscore than you can from reading a game story.

Not so in basketball, but it could be so. NBA boxscores could be made as comprehensive as baseball boxscores by following the pattern of the TENDEX system.

You don't need TENDEX to know that the most important statistics for a basketball player are his minutes played, rebounds, assists, and points. Without the court time, he can't accumulate the other statistics. A player whose total of points, rebounds, and assists matches or exceeds his minutes on the court probably has played an excellent basketball game.

So we start with these four statistics, labeled M-R-A-P, at the top of the boxscore.

With the old-fashioned boxscores listing only field goals and attempts, free throws and attempts, points, and in some cases, personal fouls, it is no wonder that basketball writers

come up with "high-point" leads for most of their stories. It's almost automatic: "Joe Buckets scored 21 points last night to pace the Boston Celtics . . . blah . . . blah . . . blah . . ."

Perhaps with a new-style of boxscore, writers would begin emphasizing all-around play, not just scoring. If after a game they were handed an official boxscore showing matchups and listing all major statistics, they might produce more leads like this one: "Bill Russell pulled down 25 rebounds, blocked five shots, and held Wilt Chamberlain to 19 points last night in leading the Boston Celtics . . . blah . . . blah . . ."

Although it probably doesn't matter in what order the players are listed in the boxscore, it seems logical to start with the highest-rated position (center) and list them down to the lowest. According to TENDEX, the way the positions compute are center, .550; power forward, .525; quick forward, .500; point guard, .475; and scoring guard, .450.

Regardless of the order in which the positions are listed, it is important that the order be the same for both teams. This way you can tell what happened in matchups simply by glancing back and forth at the parallel names for the two teams.

Player A may have scored 30 points and retrieved ten rebounds; but if Player B, who was being guarded by Player A, scored 40 points and pulled down 20 rebounds, with all other statistics being equal, Player A did not play a good game. Offensive performances always should be considered relative to matchups. Individual offensive statistics don't always win a basketball game, but the team that wins the most matchups by the biggest margins almost invariably will win.

After the main section of the boxscore comes a line showing the score by quarters. Then, in paragraph form below the linescore, the other significant elements of the game should be listed. These are three-point field goals, blocked shots, steals, turnovers, and missed shots. This is done in a way similar to the baseball boxscore's listing of errors, double plays, players left on base, extra-base hits, stolen bases, and sacrifices.

In order to conserve space, missed field goal and free throw attempts can be combined into one missed-shots statistic. Not having a breakdown of whether the missed shots were two- or three-point field-goal attempts or free throw attempts takes nothing away from the reader. A missed shot is a minus-one statistic, no matter what kind of shot it is. If a player shoots 8-for-10 from the field, but only 2-for-10 from the free throw line, he scores more points than one who goes 2-for-10 from the field and 8-for-10 from the foul line, but his point total already is listed in the top part of the boxscore. The total of missed shots for both players is ten, which is a minus-10 in this rating system.

The way the boxscore traditionally has been done, combining two- and three-point field goal attempts in one statistic, you can't tell if a player had a good shooting game from the field anyway. Let's say that Player A went 4-for-11 in field goals while Player B went 5-for-10. At first glance it looks as if Player A shot poorly while Player B shot well. But let's say that all of Player A's attempts were three-pointers, while all of Player B's were two-pointers. This means

that Player A scored 12 points with his 11 shots while Player B scored ten points with his ten shots. Player A actually had the better shooting game. A good shooting player is one whose total of points equals or exceeds his total of shots.

In the TENDEX boxscore, three-point field goals are taken care of by listing how many of them were made by individual players. This is the first item below the line score. The average fan is interested in knowing who makes these shots, just as the baseball fan wants to know who hits home runs.

At the bottom of the boxscore are listings for team fouls, fouled out, officials, time of game, and attendance.

Team fouls give an indication of how the game was officiated. Often this statistic will reveal that intimidated referees were putting the home team on the free throw line twice as often as the visiting team, a significant factor indeed. As I write this I have before me a boxscore of a game played in Los Angeles in which the New York Knicks were charged with 66 personal fouls but the Lakers were assessed with only 27. Los Angeles is a tough place for a road team, and it isn't only because of the skills of the Laker players.

Individual personal fouls are not included in the TENDEX boxscore because personal fouls are essentially neutral statistics. There are "good" fouls as well as "bad" fouls, so the mere fact that a player commits a certain number of personal fouls does not tell anything about the caliber of defense he played in the game. Personal fouls are to be discussed in more detail in the next chapter.

The fouled-out category is different: If a player fouls out, it often has an impact on the game. Although it is my opinion that no player should be disqualified from a game because of personal fouls, as long as the rules permit disqualifications they should be listed in boxscores. The team that loses one or more players because of personal fouls very likely will lose the game.

Here is a sample TENDEX boxscore:

BOSTON					LOS ANGELES				
	M	R	A	P		M	R	A	P
Parish C	36	11	3	15	A-Jabbar C	32	6	3	14
Lohaus	12	2	0	0	Thompson	16	7	2	11
McHale PF	37	10	2	25	Green PF	32	9	2	12
Roberts	11	3	0	4	Rambis	16	8	2	7
Bird QF	41	9	8	29	Worthy QF	35	6	3	16
Daye	7	1	2	4	Tolbert	13	2	0	5
DJohnson PG	39	5	7	11	EJohnson PG	39	7	14	24
Sichting	9	0	4	3	Cooper	24	5	5	14
Ainge SG	33	4	5	17	Scott SG	33	3	3	15
Lewis	15	1	4	6					
Totals	240	46	35	114		240	53	34	118

Boston	32	31	29	22—114
Los Angeles	35	28	27	28—118

Three-Point Field Goals—Bird 3, Ainge 4, Green 1, Cooper 3.

Blocked Shots—Parish 2, McHale 2, Bird 1, DJohnson 1, Abdul-Jabbar 2, Worthy 1, Cooper 1, Scott 1.

Steals—Parish 1, McHale 1, Bird 2, DJohnson 1, Ainge 2, Green 3, Worthy 3, EJohnson 2, Cooper 2.

Turnovers—Parish 2, McHale 2, Bird 4, Daye 2, Ainge 3, DJohnson 4, Abdul-Jabbar 3, Green 3, Rambis 2, EJohnson 5, Worthy 3, Cooper 3, Scott 2, Thompson 3.

Shots Missed—Parrish 10, Lohaus 1, McHale 9, Roberts 1, Bird 12, Daye 2, DJohnson 10, Lewis 2, Ainge 8, Sichting 2, Abdul-Jabbar 5, Thompson 8, Green 5, Rambis 6, EJohnson 11, Worthy 6, Tolbert 6, Cooper 8, Scott 7.

Team Fouls—Boston 37, Los Angeles 22.

Fouled Out—Parish, McHale.

Referees—Smith, Jones, Brown.

T—2:14. A—10,324.

A few publications use comprehensive box-scores similar to this one, but rarely does a basketball boxscore appear in print that is both statistically comprehensive and uniform in style to clarify matchups. In the sample box, let's see how the statement holds true that winning the matchups results in winning the game. Using the TENDEX formula, excluding game pace, which is the same for both teams anyway in a particular game, let's compute the matchups of starting players. The basic equation is:

$$P + R + A + B + S - T - MFT - MFG + MIN = RATING$$

Missed free throw attempts and missed field goal attempts are combined into one MS (missed shots) category in the boxscore and the center matchup is:

	P	+	R	+	A	+	B	+	S	−	T	−	MS	=
Parish	16	+	11	+	3	+	2	+	1	−	2	−	10	=
A-Jabbar	14	+	6	+	3	+	2	+	0	−	3	−	5	=

	SUM	÷	MIN	=	RATING
Parish	20	÷	36	=	.555
A-Jabbar	17	÷	32	=	.531

Take a few minutes to compute the other matchups of the starting players and then check them with the listings at the end of this chapter. You should find it to be a simple exercise in arithmetic and an interesting way to convert cold statistics into meaningful ratings. It's challenging to do it yourself.

There are a few cases in which problems occur with matchups, even as they are listed in boxscores. You can't always tell who wins the center matchups, because some teams do a lot of double-teaming against opposing centers while others do not. The Celtics traditionally have done more double-teaming than most teams. In the great Russell–Chamberlain matchups for example, it often came down to Wilt against practically the entire Boston team.

Another example of a misleading matchup is the one in which a player does not defend against his counterpart on the opposing team. After one bad experience when Bob Cousy attempted to guard the bigger and stronger Oscar Robertson, the Celtics rarely gave the Robertson defensive assignment to Cousy for more than a minute or two at a time. It usually went to a bigger guard such as John Havlicek or Sam Jones, even though Robertson, like Cousy, was a point guard.

But in most cases the matchups are true to position, and in most cases the team that wins most of them by the biggest margins will win the game.

In our hypothetical Boston–Los Angeles game, if you just glance at the individual statistics you could be deceived into thinking the Celtics won the game because the way it works out is that they won most of the matchups. Results of the five major matchups are: Parish over Abdul-Jabbar, .555 to .531; McHale over Green, .784 to .562; Bird over Worthy, .805 to .571; Magic Johnson over Dennis Johnson, .795 to .282; and Ainge over Scott, .515 to .394. The Celtics win four of the five.

However, Magic Johnson's 513-point advantage over Dennis Johnson compensates for about 80 percent of the losses the Lakers experienced in the other four matchups. The rest of the difference was made up by reserves. In this game, the Laker reserves played exceptionally well with a rating of .507 for 69 minutes of playing time (roughly equivalent to two starters). The Celtics' reserves, on the other hand, managed only a .444 rating for 54 minutes.

4

Hollering Foul

*T*here have been only a few major fights during NBA games in recent seasons, but plenty of players have been ejected from games. There have been more ejections from NBA games than from NFL football, NHL hockey, and major league baseball combined, even though there are more violent incidents in each of the other three sports than in pro basketball.

In the NBA, the seasonal average of ejections for the past few years has exceeded 500. Most of the ejected players did nothing more reprehensible than playing the best basketball they knew how.

And for this they fouled out.

It's time for somebody to holler foul about the archaic personal foul rules. Basketball is the only professional sport that penalizes players for good hard-nosed play by ejecting them. In many games the strategy is not focused on playing good basketball but on getting the other team's best players in foul trouble. Often there is more playacting going on than actual playing as players flop all over the floor trying to draw fouls.

Consider these comparable situations in other sports:

- If Dan Marino throws six incomplete passes, does the referee toss him out of a football game?

- If Roger Clemens misses the strike zone with six straight pitches, do the umpires send him to the showers?

- If Wayne Gretzky loses six faceoffs, is he forced to spend the rest of the game in the penalty box?

Ridiculous? Of course.

But if an NBA player commits six personal fouls, he's out. And quite often videotape replays show that one or two of the fouls that resulted in his ejection occurred in the minds of the referees only and that, in other cases, they were "good" fouls that prevented the opposing team from scoring easy baskets.

So what you have in essence is a player being disqualified from a game either because of an official's blunder or because he played hard and well.

Remember the Elvin Hayes incident? During the 1978 playoffs, the championship series between Washington and Seattle reached the seventh game. Rick Barry, whose Golden State team had not qualified for the playoffs that season, was announcing the game for television and was doing his usual candid job. He pointed out that one of the officials had a short temper and that he was especially apt to make hasty foul calls against Hayes, whom he did not like because Hayes did a lot of complaining about his calls.

Hayes, who had been the series' outstanding player to that point, picked up his fourth foul during the third quarter and argued the call before his coach took him out of the game. The same official whistled him for his fifth and sixth fouls in quick succession after he reentered the game early in the fourth quarter. Replays showed that Hayes had not committed either of the final two fouls. On one of them there was no physical contact at all.

But Hayes was out of the game, and a short-fused referee might have deprived Washington of a league championship. Washington was ahead by eight or ten points when Hayes went out. As it happened, Washington did hold on and win with Hayes out of the game. The only repercussion of the incident was that Hayes did not win the series MVP trophy, which he deserved. The trophy was won by a player who excelled in the late minutes of the decisive game after Hayes was gone.

After the game Hayes held up his championship trophy and said on national TV: "At least he (the referee) can't take this away from me."

But even if every call against Hayes had been a correct one, should he have been disqualified?

In working on the TENDEX statistical system, it has become obvious to me that even the most flagrant personal fouls do not always adversely affect the team that commits them. In the professional game a team is allowed four fouls per quarter before the other team even goes to the free-throw line. In college there are six free fouls per half, the only exception being if the fouled player is in the act of shooting.

Fouls committed in "free" situations often are good fouls, especially if they are committed to prevent easy baskets.

Why place a personal penalty on a player who is simply doing his best to keep his opponent from scoring?

It is most often the good defensive player, not the poor one, who fouls out. Example: A point guard drives past his defender and is fouled by another player when he approaches the basket. If anyone should be penalized in this situation, it should not be the player who committed the foul, but the weak defensive player who permitted the penetration in the first place.

But, really, isn't it ridiculous to disqualify any player from a professional athletic competition, mistakes or no mistakes, when he is making his best effort to compete within the rules?

The TENDEX system shows that the only type of foul that severely hurts a team, other than one that disqualifies a player, is an offensive foul. An offensive foul is a turnover, and each turnover on the average costs the offending team one point. This is because the average ball possession is worth one point, so obviously a loss of possession will normally cost a team one point.

Another factor is rule interpretation. No matter what the rulebook says, many of the NBA's referees favor small, quick players over large, cumbersome ones whenever there is a collision of bodies. If somebody has to be whistled for a foul when a collision occurs, almost invariably the penalized player is the Alton Lister or Darryl Dawkins, rather than the Tiny Archibald or Spud Webb.

Archibald made a career of driving full speed to the basket and forcing contact with big men. Then he would fall down and throw the ball at the basket, hoping for a three-point play. He knew he would get the foul call his way.

There are other "fall-down" players, and not all of them are small men. Kareem Abdul-Jabbar and Moses Malone have spent a lot of time on the court in histrionic sprawls. The officials' calls usually favor them, because of their superstar reputations, even though Kareem more often than not throws a left hook to the chops of his defender before taking a dive, and Moses generally takes his flop after stabbing his opponent in the ribs with an elbow.

A representative all-fall-down team of recent vintage would consist of Abdul-Jabbar, Malone, Michael Jordan, Dennis Johnson, and Adrian Dantley. These are not bad players. They are good players who know how to take advantage of officials who aren't inclined to make calls against them because of their exalted reputations.

The consequence, because of poor rule interpretation, is that often the players who guard these players are charged with six personal fouls and out they go, to the disadvantage of their teams and the distress of fans who want to see the best players on the court at the end of the game.

Dick Vitale advocates eliminating foul-outs and using technical fouls as an alternative to allow players to stay in the game after they have been charged with their quota of fouls. That would be a good first step. But the only fair thing would be to stop keeping track of individual fouls at all. (Does the NFL keep a log of offensive holding penalties for the purpose of ejecting the holders?)

The only fouls that should be recorded are offensive fouls. They should be classified as turnovers, which is what they are.

Individual personal foul compilations should be eliminated.

No one should foul out.

5

Minimal Minimums

*O*ne thing that is impressive about the NBA's statistical minimums is the minimal mentality that went into them.

The NBA lists eight individual statistics. To win one or more statistical titles is a major goal of the league's players each season.

A potential problem (which sometimes becomes a real problem) with these statistics is that in seven of the eight categories it is possible for a player to participate in less than half of his team's games and still win the title.

In the eighth category—rebounding—it is possible for a dominant big man to participate in three-quarters of his team's games and fail to accumulate enough rebounds to qualify for listing among the leaders.

The reason for these fatuous discrepancies is the system of "minimums" established by the league as qualifications to win individual titles.

The problem first surfaced in 1967–68 during a close race for the scoring title between Oscar Robertson and Dave Bing. At that time the scoring champion was the player who accumulated the most points, regardless of scoring average. That year, Robertson (29.2) had a higher average than Bing (27.1), but Bing was awarded the title because Robertson missed 17 games because of a persistent leg injury

and therefore scored fewer total points than Bing.

That injustice was perpetuated, for the 1987–88 *NBA Guide* stated that Bing "led the NBA in scoring with a 27.1 average in 1967–68." He did not lead in average. He led in total points. Robertson led in average.

Television commentators ridiculed the old gross-total system and so, belatedly, in 1969–70, the system was changed. The leader that season was determined by scoring average, provided he played a minimum number of games. If this change had not been made, there would have been another controversy because Jerry West, the champion with a scoring average of 31.2 points per game, actually scored fewer points than Kareem Abdul-Jabbar. Abdul-Jabbar's average was 28.8, about as far below West's mark as Bing's was below Robertson's two years previously.

The system also was changed for rebounds and assists in 1969–70 so that the players with the highest averages, rather than the highest gross totals, would win. The same games-played minimum was applied to rebounds and assists.

The problem was that the league apparently still was trying to justify the Bing scoring title,

16

for it established the minimum number of games to qualify much too high, at 70. This meant a player could play in 84 percent of his team's 82 games and fail to qualify for the three most important titles—scoring, rebounds, and assists—no matter how effectively he played. If he missed 13 games, he was disqualified. An injury no more serious than a pulled hamstring muscle or a severe ankle sprain could cause a player to miss that many games.

Minimums are now incorporated into all eight individual titles, and still they are not what they should be. Some were at one time effective, but have become archaic because of changes in the game.

For example, at the time when minimums were introduced it was not uncommon for players to average 20 or more rebounds per game. Because of lower shooting percentages, there were more rebounds to be pulled down. And there were fewer powerful big men competing for them. The Bill Russells and Wilt Chamberlains were dominating the boards.

So the minimum to qualify for the rebounding title was established exactly twice as high as the minimum for the assists title. Now, however, the assists leaders do almost as well as the rebounding leaders. In fact, during the 1984–85 season the assists champion (Isiah Thomas) averaged 13.9 per game, while the rebounds champion (Moses Malone) averaged 13.1 per game.

Yet to qualify for the assists title a player had only to accumulate 400 assists, while the rebounding qualifiers had to pull down 800 rebounds. In other words, Thomas could have won the assists title playing in just 29 games, or 35 percent of his team's schedule. Malone, on the other hand, would not even have qualified for the rebounding title without playing in at least 62 games—more than 75 percent of his team's total.

The hypothetical became reality for Akeem Olajuwon, who in 1985–86 averaged 11.5 rebounds per game, well up among the leaders, but fell short of the 800 minimum and was not even listed among the leaders. He missed only

14 games, but that was enough to disqualify him.

Similar problems are in evidence in the other categories. A typical recent season to illustrate the problems was 1986–87.

In scoring, with a minimum of 1,400 points needed to win the title, Michael Jordan could have won it by playing in just 38 games in 1986–87. Incidentally, Bernard King did win it in 1984–85 even though he played in only 55 games.

In field goal percentage, with a 300 minimum, Jordan could have won in 1986–87 (if his percentage had been high enough) by playing in 23 games. A player who participated in all 82 of his team's games could have won this title by averaging less than four field goals per game.

In free throw percentage, with a 125 minimum, a player could have won by averaging less than two free-throw attempts per game. Danny Ainge and Craig Hodges nearly did win in 1986–87, even though they took only about one-third as many free throws apiece as the champion, Larry Bird.

In steals, with a qualifying minimum of 125, 1986–87 champion Alvin Robertson could have accumulated enough steals to win the title by playing in only 39 games.

In blocked shots, with a minimum of 100, 1986–87 champion Mark Eaton could have reached the qualifying level by playing in 25 games.

In three-point field goal percentage, with a minimum of 25, both of the top two qualifiers during the 1986–87 season (Kiki Vandeweghe and Detlef Schrempf) averaged less than one attempt per game. These two players took only one-half to one-quarter as many attempts as the other players in the top ten.

Suggested changes for the NBA to make its minimums more equitable:

- SCORING—Change the minimum number of points from 1,400 to 1,750.
- REBOUNDING—Change the minimum number of rebounds from 800 to 600.

- ASSISTS—Change the minimum number of assists from 400 to 500.
- FIELD GOAL PERCENTAGE—Change the minimum number of field goals made from 300 to 400.
- FREE THROW PERCENTAGE—Change the minimum number of free throws made from 125 to 200.
- STEALS—Change the minimum number of steals from 125 to 150.
- BLOCKED SHOTS—Change the minimum number of blocked shots from 100 to 150.
- THREE-POINT FIELD GOAL PERCENTAGE—Change the minimum number of shots made from 25 to 50.

6

Not All Systems Go

As could be expected, TENDEX is not the only statistical system being used to evaluate basketball players. Some coaches have their own systems. An NBA television commentator has devised one. A few players, including Larry Bird, have their own. Schick has one that is used to determine the Pivotal Player Award.

None of the systems is perfect. TENDEX has one or two minor drawbacks. The others have more serious deficiencies.

Some of the systems, including Bird's and the one used by the TV commentator, use gross totals only. Gross systems should be ignored by the serious fan: You cannot reasonably compare the totals of players whose playing time varies from four or five minutes per game to 39 or 40. Schick's system deserves serious consideration because it is sanctioned by the NBA. The Schick formula is: Points, plus rebounds, plus assists, plus steals, plus blocked shots, minus missed field goal attempts, minus personal fouls, minus turnovers, plus team victories times ten, divided by team totals in each of the first eight categories. The result is then multiplied by 250.

Why the arbitrary numbers ten and 250 are in the formula is anyone's guess, but this system has flaws that are much worse than arbi-

trariness. In 1986–87, Michael Cage was rated the No. 3 player in the NBA, according to this system, and Buck Williams was rated No. 2 behind Charles Barkley. Williams and Cage were ranked ahead of Larry Bird, Akeem Olajuwon, Michael Jordan, Magic Johnson, Kevin McHale, and Moses Malone, all of whom rated above the .700 superstar level that season, according to TENDEX, which rated Williams at .648 and Cage at .585. It should be obvious even to a casual observer of the NBA that Bird, Olajuwon, Jordan, Johnson, McHale, and Malone (and a few others) were at that time superior players to Williams, and that there were two dozen better players than Cage.

The most severe flaw in the Schick system is that it compares a player's statistics with his teammates', thus giving a huge advantage to players on poor teams with weak teammates. Hence the high rating of Cage, a member of the weakest team in the league, the Los Angeles Clippers, and Williams, with the weak New Jersey Nets.

Another problem with this system is that it includes personal fouls as negatives. This was discussed in Chapter 4. Only offensive fouls, which are really turnovers, can always be considered "bad" fouls. Since the league does not distinguish between offensive and defensive fouls in its tabulations, it is not possible to get a fair evaluation of how many points to subtract from a player for committing offensive foul-turnovers.

A third problem with the Schick system is that it does not count missed free throws. Therefore, free throw percentage is not a factor at all, and yet all successful free throws count as points. Wilt Chamberlain and every other poor free throw shooter would have loved this system.

The idea of dividing by team totals is good in that it introduces a broad standard into the Schick system, but it is not broad enough. It is not a league-wide standard. It favors players who perform for poor teams, because obviously their statistics are going to look better by comparison with poor teammates. In a way, this is just the opposite of how a system that determines who a "Pivotal Player" is should work. All it proves is who are the best players on the worst teams, when perhaps it should be targetting the best players on the best teams.

It could be argued that the team-totals factor is offset by introducing team victories into the formula which, by the way, is a recent innovation. But this is an arbitrary statistic also. There are some excellent players performing for teams that lose a lot of games, just as there are some weak players performing for excellent teams. At best, the team-victory factor is a concession to the invalidity of the team-totals factor. Except for game pace, team statistics are irrelevant in any formula that evaluates individuals.

TENDEX is much better than the Schick system, but still is not perfect. A valid criticism of TENDEX is that it rewards the players involved in an assisted basket with a total of three points (two for the scoring player, one for the player who made the pass) whereas an unassisted basket is rewarded with only two. On the scoreboard there is obviously no difference between the two baskets.

Admitting that this is a problem, does it mean that no rating points should be awarded for assists?

This is a difficult question. It is one that needs to be faced by proponents of all of the rating systems, because all of them reward assists. My feeling is that one point should be awarded for an assist because it converts a normal one-point ball possession into an easy two points.

Although on any particular basket it may not seem justified to award three rating points to the players involved, the overall effect of having a team of players who accumulate a lot of assists is to have a good team. The top two teams in assists nearly always are the Boston Celtics and the Los Angeles Lakers.

Like the blocked shot, which has intangible value that is difficult to measure, an assist gives an emotional boost to a team and its fans. A play in which the ball changes hands one or more times on the way to a picturesque basket can be a momentum-turner; it may even spark a rally. Even though assists may not compute just right according to the basic arithmetic of basketball, they are worthy of the points that are awarded for them.

A published criticism of TENDEX is that it does not penalize the missed field goal enough. It has been suggested that if a missed free throw counts minus-one, then a missed field goal should count minus-two. By extention, I suppose this means a missed three-point field goal should count minus-three. Although the logic sounds good, the arithmetic is bad.

A missed field goal counts minus-one because it is equivalent to a turnover. It might even be contended that it should count less than the minus-one charged for a turnover because in the case of the missed shot there is an immediate opportunity to get the ball back with an offensive rebound.

If the defensive team blocks out correctly however, a missed field goal is a turnover and should count as minus-one. If an offensive rebound is retrieved, one point is given to the player who gets it. This negates the minus-one of the missed shot and puts the team back in the position where it began, with possession of the basketball.

If two points were subtracted for every missed field goal attempt, no player with a shooting average under 50 percent could be considered to be making a positive scoring contribution to his team. Here's an example. Michael Jordan, who shot 49 percent from the floor during the 1986–87 season, scored 3,041 points for the Chicago Bulls. But if missed field attempts were given a minus-two rating, Jordan's shooting from the floor would be on the negative side in the formula.

Jordan was successful on 1,086 two-point field goals in 2,211 attempts. He missed 1,125 shots. If he receives plus-two for each field goal and is charged minus-two for each missed shot, his gross rating total for two-point field goal shooting is minus-68. This means, we must assume, that Michael Jordan shouldn't shoot.

Even if it could be argued that missed field goal attempts were not related to turnovers, it wouldn't take much common sense to see that a charge of minus-two for a missed shot is totally out of line.

Other quibbles can be introduced. A player who pressures an opponent into a turnover or draws an offensive foul probably should be credited with a steal. One who totally blows a defensive play ought to be charged with a minus-one for allowing the opponent to make an easy two-pointer on a normal one-point possession. But these subtleties are difficult to tabulate consistently.

What makes TENDEX superior to other existing systems in the final analysis is that it is the only one that includes two valid stabilizing factors—minutes played and game pace.

7

Basketball's 700 Club

*J*ames Worthy and Larry Nance were collegiate contemporaries. Both played in the Atlantic Coast Conference, Worthy for North Carolina, Nance for Clemson. Their statistics were comparable, but Worthy was All-American. Nance wasn't.

Worthy was drafted No. 1 by the NBA out of college. Nance was No. 20. Worthy is a well-publicized player for the Los Angeles Lakers. Nance, who has played for Phoenix and Cleveland, is virtually ignored. And yet Nance is a superior pro, with a career TENDEX rating more than 100 points higher than Worthy's.

In the NBA, public exposure is strictly regional. If you have played for one of Boston's or Los Angeles' many champion teams, that automatically insures your reputation, even if in reality you were only a reserve.

Your name may survive if you played in Chicago or Philadelphia, but woe to the player who must toil in an obscure place such as Sacramento or San Antonio.

The purpose of this chapter is to set aside prejudices and determine which NBA players had the best seasons of all time.

It may come as a surprise to some analysts, but the Celtics and Lakers have not won championships because of a preponderance of the best talent, but rather because they had the best overall team balance and played as organized units.

There are, believe it or not, some individuals who are better at what they do in the NBA than some of the Celtics and Lakers. They just don't happen to have as many good teammates, or as good coaching, or as good public relations. Among the 55 players who have achieved .700 TENDEX ratings for at least one season during their careers, there are 25 teams represented; none of these teams has more than five players listed. (The 700 Club list is included in Chart 1, Section III.)

Boston and Philadelphia are tied with five "superstars" apiece, followed by Chicago with four. Los Angeles shares fourth place with five other teams having three players on the list: Milwaukee, Cincinnati, New York, Utah and Houston. Teams having two players listed are Portland, Detroit, St. Louis, San Francisco, Seattle, Phoenix, Baltimore, and Syracuse. Completing the list with one player each are Utah, Washington, Buffalo, Dallas, Atlanta, Denver, Fort Wayne, Minneapolis, and Kansas City.

So much for provincialism.

Individually, there is a tendency to look at the number of banners hanging from the rafters of Boston Garden and conclude that surely Bill Russell must have been a better center than Wilt Chamberlain, Bob Cousy must have been a better point guard than Oscar Robertson, and so on. The championships prove it, don't they?

The TENDEX system isn't impressed by banners and it wasn't impressed by Cousy, who didn't come close to making the 700 Club list of all-time best players. This list contains 55 names and is based solely on statistics. Admittedly, there are intangibles such as team defense and intimidation that cannot be measured statistically. There is also the fact that at the time Russell and Chamberlain were playing, blocked shots and steals were not tabulated by the NBA. If they had been, there is no question but that Russell's rating would have been much higher than his 16th place listing of .801. But so too would Chamberlain's rating have been higher. And so would Kareem Abdul-Jabbar's. He had his best season in 1971–72 when these statistics still were not being kept.

So although the ratings we are talking about certainly aren't perfect, they are probably as accurate as any statistical ratings in any major sport.

Here are the TENDEX NBA all-time, all-star first and second teams, on the basis of single best seasons:

FIRST TEAM

Wilt Chamberlain, Philadelphia, 1961–62, center............................... 1.037

Elgin Baylor, LA Lakers, 1960–61, forward .... .968

Bob Pettit, St. Louis, 1960–61, forward... .919

Oscar Robertson, Cincinnati, 1961–62, guard .... .892

Magic Johnson, LA Lakers, 1986–87, guard .... .811

SECOND TEAM

Kareem Abdul-Jabbar, Milwaukee, 1971–72, center................................... .972

Charles Barkley, Pha., 1986–87, forward... .828

Larry Bird, Boston, 1984–85, forward..... .824

Michael Jordan, Chicago, 1986–87, guard.. .808

Jerry West, LA Lakers, 1965–66, guard... .750

This is not intended to underestimate the contribution of Russell to the 11 Celtic teams that won titles with him playing center. But he did have more good teammates than his nemesis, Chamberlain, who played for only two champions; and he also had more luck. One season, when a Philadelphia team starring Chamberlain and Bill Cunningham was favored to win, an injury to Cunningham cleared the way for a Celtic victory. Another season, when a Los Angeles team starring Chamberlain and Jerry West was within one game of winning the championship series against Boston, West incurred an injury and could not play effectively in the final two games. The Celtics won again. And there was a third close miss by a Chamberlain-led Philadelphia team against a Russell-paced Boston team. In this one the Celtics won the decisive game by a single point on a steal by John Havlicek in the closing seconds after a turnover by Russell had given Philadelphia a chance to win.

Russell undoubtedly was the third best center of all time, and possibly the third best player overall, but according to TENDEX ratings Chamberlain was No. 1 and Abdul-Jabbar was No. 2.

The integrity of the TENDEX rating system is supported by the all-time list. Of the 52 players cited, only a few could be reasonably questioned as to whether they deserved to be on the list, and only one questionable player is ranked among the top 25. The exception who seems to prove the rule is Tom Boerwinkle.

Boerwinkle was a bulky center whose career for the Chicago Bulls peaked in 1970–71. His rating for that season was .865, good enough for seventh place on the all-time list, although there has been no clamor to induct him into basketball's Hall of Fame.

What happened that season was that the Chicago team's coach decided to get the ball to Boerwinkle as often as possible. This meant playing the game at a slow pace to wait for him to lumber up and down the court. It also meant benching him frequently to give him enough rest so that he would have a fresh pair of legs while he was on the court. At that time, the great centers were playing at least 40 minutes per game. Boerwinkle was limited to 29. Boerwinkle's teammate, Bob Love, averaged 43 minutes per game that season.

The focus on Boerwinkle, the slow game pace, and the bench rest he received combined to help him have an outstanding season. He averaged about 11 points, 14 rebounds, and four assists per game—excellent statistics for a man playing less than 30 minutes per game. TENDEX, remember, is based on per-minute performance. It is not a bulk statistic.

Quite frankly, the only other player who made the list, because his team decided to feature him, was Adrian Dantley. Drafted originally by Buffalo, Dantley has been traded four times during his career. The reason for this is that he is a 6'4" low-post player, and most teams have learned from experience that it is difficult to win the battle of the backboards with a player that small matching up against seven-footers.

In a brief trial with the Lakers, Dantley was beaten out for the small forward job by Jamaal Wilkes (who did not make the all-time list). With only one team has Dantley ever had a superstar rating, but with that team, Utah, he was featured as a low-post scorer and was able to achieve a rating of .710 in 1985–86.

In the cases of Boerwinkle and Dantley, where the rating system may seem inconsistent, other circumstances must be considered.

An interesting sidelight to the all-time list is a second list based on positional standards. It is normal for a center to have a rating of .550, a power forward .525, a quick forward .500, a point guard .475, and a shooting guard .450. By virtue of the position he plays, a center should have the highest rating on his team. He should have a rating 100 points better, for example, than a shooting guard. The 700 Club should be, and is, dominated by centers and power forwards.

The positional list takes this into consideration. What it does is rank the players according to the number of TENDEX points by which they exceed the standard for their positions. This is a pure method of rating the performance of a player, relative to the limitations and potential of his position.

Although some players have exceeded their positional standards by 300 or more points numerous times, only four individuals have gone 400 points or more during their careers and only 11 have gone 300 or more above. These are the elite 11 (excluding 1987–88):

1. Wilt Chamberlain, Philadelphia, 1961–62, center .... +487
2. Elgin Baylor, LA Lakers, 1960–61, forward............................. +443
3. Kareem Abdul-Jabbar, Milwaukee, 1971–72, center .... +422
4. Oscar Robertson, Cincinnati, 1961–62, guard............................. +417
5. Bob Pettit, St. Louis, 1960–61, forward............................. +394
6. Walt Bellamy, Chicago, 1961–62, center .... +379
7. Michael Jordan, Chicago, 1986–87, guard.............................. +358
8. Magic Johnson, LA Lakers, 1986–87, guard.............................. +336
9. Larry Bird, Boston, 1984–85, forward............................. +324
10. Tom Boerwinkle, Chicago, 1970–71, center .... +315
11. Charles Barkley, Philadelphia, 1986–87, forward............................. +303

There are a few obvious differences between the 700 Club list and the positional list. Elgin Baylor jumps from third place on the 700 Club list to second on the positional list, while Oscar Robertson moves up from sixth to fourth, Magic Johnson climbs from eleventh to eighth, and Michael Jordan from thirteenth to seventh. Jordan's six-place leap is the largest.

The biggest drops are Boerwinkle's three-place fall from seventh to tenth place and Charles Barkley's dip from eighth to eleventh. Walt Bellamy goes down from fourth to sixth place and Abdul-Jabbar from second to third.

No matter how many names are on an all-time best basketball rating list, there will always be somebody left off who perhaps is better than somebody on the list. Here's how close a dozen other prominent players came to joining basketball's 700 Club:

1. Larry Nance, Phoenix, 1985–86 699
2. Alex English, Denver, 1982–83 692
3. George McGinnis, Philadelphia,
   1976–77 692
4. Bobby Jones, Denver, 1976–77 683
5. Isiah Thomas, Detroit, 1984–85 681
6. Bill Laimbeer, Detroit, 1983–84 678
7. Buck Williams, New Jersey, 1982–83 676
8. Lafayette Lever, Denver, 1986–87 665
9. Walt Frazier, New York, 1971–72 665
10. Sidney Moncrief, Milwaukee,
    1982–83 665
11. Maurice Lucas, New York, 1981–82 662
12. George Gervin, San Antonio, 1983–84 . . .661

Since both the 700 Club list and the positional list include only the best seasons of each individual, in order to get a broader perspective for the players' careers it is necessary to compile two other lists (Charts 2 and 3, Section III). Chart 2 designates the all-time best 25 TENDEX ratings, including repeat leaders.

Only seven players made this chart: Chamberlain, nine times; Abdul-Jabbar, seven; Pettit, three; Robertson, two; Baylor, two; Bellamy, one; and Boerwinkle, one. This chart also discloses the fact that Chamberlain—the only player ever to reach the 1.000 mark—did it three times. In simple terminology what this means is that Chamberlain is the only player ever to be worth at least one point to his team for every minute of his court time over a full season.

Chart 3 lists the NBA leaders in TENDEX ratings for every season since minutes played were first tabulated in 1951–52. George Mikan led the league for the first three rated seasons and achieved the first .700 in 1953–54. Since then at least one player has gone over .700 every season.

An interesting difference between Chart 3 and the first two charts is that this one is not dominated by Chamberlain. The dominant player on Chart 3 is Abdul-Jabbar, who led the NBA in TENDEX rating for 11 different seasons. Chamberlain finished second with eight league-leading seasons, including an all-time best seven in a row, from 1961–62 through 1967–68.

Other repeaters on Chart 3 are Pettit with four season titles, Mikan and Larry Bird with three each, and Moses Malone with two. The other leaders, with one title apiece through 1986–87, were Baylor, Barkley, Neil Johnston, Jerry Lucas, and Bob Lanier.

It could be argued that the game has changed so much, with ever-improving defensive techniques and superior athletes, that it is not equitable to compare the ratings achieved by Chamberlain, Baylor, Pettit, Bellamy, Lucas, Robertson, and Jerry West during the 1960s with those of Abdul-Jabbar, Bird, Barkley, Jordan, Malone, and Johnson during the past decade.

I for one would be reluctant to declare with assurance that Chamberlain's slightly higher rating proved that he was a superior player to Jabbar, or that Baylor and Pettit were definitely better than Bird and Barkley, or that Robertson was clearly better than Johnson and Jordan. Indeed, with Bird, Barkley, and Jordan having their best seasons ever in 1987–88, this becomes even more of a debatable point. I think it could be said confidently, however, that these nine players—along with Bill Russell—comprise the top ten of all-time.

8

Changing of the Guards

*M*ore than half of the 51 players in the TENDEX 700 Club played the center position during their rated seasons (excluding 1987–88). Besides the 26 centers, there are 19 forwards in the club, counting both the power and small forward positions. There are only six guards, counting the point and shooting guard positions.

These statistics can be analyzed in two ways: Either there have been as many basketball superstars who played center as the combined total of the other four positions, or the preponderance of centers on this list confirms the theory that the five positions should be scaled according to norms ranging from .550 for centers to .450 for shooting guards.

Are we to believe that Jerry West, who was rated the No. 2 shooting guard of all time with a .750 rating, was an inferior player to all 13 of the centers who are listed ahead of him?

Noting that there are only six guards in the 700 Club, does this mean there have been only six superstar backcourtmen in NBA history?

Defining a point guard as one who leads his team in assists per minutes played, here is the all-time best point guard list:

1. Oscar Robertson, Cincinnati, 1961–62.. 892
2. Magic Johnson, LA Lakers, 1986–87 ... 811
3. Nate Archibald, Kansas City, 1972–73.. 712
4. Isiah Thomas, Detroit, 1984–85........ 681
5. Lafayette Lever, Denver, 1986–87 665
6. Walt Frazier, New York, 1971–72 665
7. Richie Guerin, New York, 1961–62...... 652
8. Glenn Rivers, Atlanta, 1986–87........ 648
9. Dave Bing, Detroit, 1969–70........... 644
10. Len Wilkens, Seattle, 1971–72 626
    Gus Williams, Seattle, 1981–82 626

These are the top ten shooting guards:

1. Michael Jordan, Chicago, 1986–87 808
2. Jerry West, LA Lakers, 1965–66 750
3. Walter Davis, Phoenix, 1978–79........ 714
4. S. Moncrief, Milwaukee, 1982–83 665
5. G. Gervin, San Antonio, 1979–80 661
6. J. Havlicek, Boston, 1969–70 660
7. Ray Williams, New York, 1979–80 660
8. Sam Jones, Boston, 1965–66........... 655
9. Paul Westphal, Phoenix, 1977–78 655
10. David Thompson, Denver, 1977–78...... 633

A few of the guards on these two lists played both the point and shooting positions.

West and Jordan are two who, for as much as they handled the ball during their best seasons, could certainly have been classified as point guards. For the sake of compromise, let's say that Jordan and West could have been placed on either list. If we count their ratings equally on the two lists, the average rating for the top ten point guards is .714, while the average for the shooting guards is .669.

When we list the guards according to position, instead of selecting the top two overall, Michael Jordan replaces Magic Johnson on the all-time NBA first team. Oscar Robertson beats out Johnson for point guard honors, and Jordan makes the team as the best shooting guard.

Here are the best ten power forwards:

1. Elgin Baylor, LA Lakers, 1960–61 968
2. Bob Pettit, St. Louis, 1960–61 919
3. Charles Barkley, Philadelphia, 1986–87 . . .828
4. Bailey Howell, Detroit, 1960–61 804
5. Jerry Lucas, Cincinnati, 1964–65 790
6. Maurice Stokes, Cincinnati, 1957–58 747
7. Kevin McHale, Boston, 1986–87 742
8. Spencer Haywood, Seattle, 1972–73 734
9. Gus Johnson, Baltimore, 1970–71 728
10. Dolph Schayes, Syracuse, 1957–58 718

The top ten small forwards:

1. Larry Bird, Boston, 1983–84 824
2. Julius Erving, Philadelphia, 1979–80 788
3. Billy Cunningham, Philadelphia,
   1969–70 750
4. Rick Barry, San Francisco, 1966–67 747
5. Cliff Hagan, St. Louis, 1959–60 746
6. Bernard King, New York, 1984–85 735
7. Marques Johnson, Milwaukee, 1978–79 . . .721
8. Terry Cummings, Milwaukee, 1984–85 717
9. Adrian Dantley, Utah, 1985–86 710
10. Larry Nance, Phoenix, 1985–86 699

With the forwards separated into power and small classifications, Larry Bird takes the place of Bob Pettit on the all-time best NBA team. And Julius Erving, who was only tied for 20th place on the 700 Club chart, makes the second team ahead of Charles Barkley.

Overall, the list of small forwards averages .744, while the power forwards average .807. Here are the top ten centers:

1. Wilt Chamberlain, Philadelphia,
   1961–62 . . . . 1.037
2. Kareem Abdul-Jabbar, Milwaukee,
   1971–72 972
3. Walt Bellamy, Chicago, 1961–62 929
4. Tom Boerwinkle, Chicago, 1970–71 865
5. Bob Lanier, Detroit, 1973–74 820
6. Moses Malone, Houston, 1981–82 810
7. Bob McAdoo, Buffalo, 1974–75 806
8. Bill Russell, Boston, 1961–62 801
9. Bill Walton, Portland, 1976–77 799
10. Akeem Olajuwon, Houston, 1986–87 . . .789

The average for these centers is .861, giving us a gradient that looks like this for the leaders at each position: Centers, .861; power forwards, .807; small forwards, .744; point guards, .714; and shooting guards, .669.

It does not take a world-class mathematician to see that this scale is directly proportional to the TENDEX guideline of positional norms (.550 for centers, .525 for power forwards, .500 for small forwards, .475 for point guards, .450 for shooting guards). There is a little wider gap than 25 percentage points between positions, but the scale is almost identical because the numbers are higher. The average for the leaders at each position is almost exactly 1.5 times as great as the positional norm, which proves the theory that a player's position can affect his rating, that is, guards should not be expected to be rated as high as forwards, or forwards as high as centers.

Here is how the top ten lists compare with the positional norms. (Formula: Average for the top ten at a position divided by the TENDEX norm for that position):

- CENTERS 1.57
- POWER FORWARDS 1.54
- SMALL FORWARDS 1.49
- POINT GUARDS 1.50
- SHOOTING GUARDS 1.49

Although .700 is a good overall standard for superstardom, there were ten centers who had ratings between .700 and .750 who perhaps were not as great players relative to their positions as the ten guards who rated between .650 and .700. A guard who achieves a rating of .650 or better probably should be considered a superstar, at least for the rated season, and a good case could be made for shooting guards with ratings as low as .600. Clyde Drexler (.622) and Pete Maravich (.602) are in the fringe area.

Chapters 7 and 8 are full of top ten lists, but perhaps the most significant of these lists is the one with which this chapter concludes. It is a list of the all-time top ten NBA players based on a comparison between their TENDEX ratings and the norms for their positions. For example, when Wilt Chamberlain's rating of 1.037 is divided by a center's positional norm of .550, the resultant ratio is 1.885. Wilt is No. 1, but notice how closely Oscar Robertson follows him on this remarkable chart:

1. Wilt Chamberlain, Philadelphia, 1961–62 .... 1.885
2. Oscar Robertson, Cincinnati, 1961–62... 1.878
3. Elgin Baylor, LA Lakers, 1960–61 ...... 1.844
4. Michael Jordan, Chicago, 1986–87...... 1.795
5. Kareem Abdul-Jabbar, Milwaukee, 1971–72 .... 1.767
6. Bob Pettit, St. Louis, 1960–61 .... 1.750
7. Magic Johnson, LA Lakers, 1986–87 .. 1.707
8. Walt Bellamy, Chicago, 1961–62 ...... 1.689
9. Jerry West, LA Lakers, 1965–66 ...... 1.667
10. Larry Bird, Boston, 1984–85.......... 1.648

Expanding this list to include the top 50 players of all time, on the basis of positional standard, yields Chart 4, which is listed in Section III. The breakdown of names on this chart is much better balanced than the 700 Club chart. The positional chart contains 13 centers, exactly half as many as the 700 Club chart. The positional chart contains 17 guards, ten more than the 700 Club chart.

Overall, the positional chart has excellent representation for all kinds of players. In addition to the 13 centers, it contains nine power forwards, 11 quick forwards, six point guards, and 11 shooting guards. If Jordan and West were switched to the point guard list, as they could be, the balance would be even better with eight point guards and nine shooting guards.

The positional list is at least as significant as the 700 Club list. The 700 Club players are superior impact players, but centers have a tremendous advantage in this respect because of their size and function on the court. The chart that compares TENDEX ratings with positional norms is better representative of the all-time greatest players, with consideration for physical limitations. It gives the smaller man a chance.

Sidney Moncrief, an outstanding hard-working guard, did not make the list of 55 players on the 700 Club chart. But he ranks No. 24 on the positional chart, and a well-deserved rating it is.

Neither Ray Williams nor Gus Williams, probably the best brother tandem ever to play in the NBA, was able to make the 700 Club chart, but both earned places on the positional chart. Gus was a great guard for a full decade and Ray had a season that should not be forgotten in 1979–80 with 20.9 points, 6.2 assists, 5.0 rebounds, and 2.0 steals per game.

Any player who was good enough to earn a spot on either the 700 Club chart or the positional norm chart is deserving to have his name capitalized in NBA archives.

9

The Shootists

*T*he word shootist is derived from the final motion picture role played by John Wayne. He portrayed an old gunfighter in *The Shootist*.

There are two ways of determining the best shootists in pro basketball. The best way is to figure the average of points scored for all shots taken, counting attempted free throws, two-point field goals and three-point field goals. The other way is to total all shots made in the three categories and divide by all shots taken to yield an overall shooting percentage.

At first glance the two methods may seem to be almost identical, but actually the second way is not as good as the first because it favors players who shoot a lot of free throws but do not try many three-point field goals. The first method requires good shooting from all ranges.

Larry Bird typifies the difference. He consistently ranks first or second in the NBA when the points-per-shots method is used, but is generally not among the top ten when the overall shooting percentage method is employed. Bird is one of only four players in NBA history who averaged less than 50 percent field goal percentage (counting two- and three-pointers) and still managed to exceed

one point for every shot taken for a full season. All four were excellent three-point shooters:

	Season	FG%	FT%	Rating
Ainge, Boston	1984–85	.486	.897	1.044
Scott, LA Lakers	1986–87	.489	.892	1.009
Bird, Boston	1985–86	.496	.896	1.008
Cooper, LA Lakers	1983–84	.497	.838	1.007

Dan Ainge's .486 field goal shooting percentage was the lowest ever by a player averaging better than one point per shot. Ainge was the only one of the four players who did not exceed .500 in two-point field goal percentage. His percentages in 1984–85 were .498 on two-point shots, .897 on free throws and an excellent .443 on three-pointers (85-for-192).

The shooting is so good in the NBA today that the league average has climbed close to .500 for two-point field goals. This makes it easy to forget that not a single player shot .500 or better until Wilt Chamberlain did it in 1960–61—the NBA's 15th season.

Jerry Lucas of Cincinnati was the first player to exceed the one-point-per-shot (1.000) standard. He did it for the Royals in 1968–69 with a field goal percentage of .551, a free throw percentage of .755 and a rating of 1.017.

Kareem Abdul-Jabbar holds the record with 14 seasons in which his points-per-shots ratio reached 1.000.

The first player to go over the 1.100 mark was Kevin McHale with 1.104 in 1986–87. That same season, McHale also became the first player to average .600 or better from the field and .800 or better from the free throw line.

The ten all-time best shootists, from 1946–47 through 1986–87, on the basis of points-per-shots for a single season (minimum 2,000 minutes played) are the following:

	Season	FG%	FT%	Rating
1. Kevin McHale, Boston	1986–87	.604	.838	1.104
2. Matt Guokas, Kansas City	1972–73	.570	.822	1.096
3. Kareem Abdul-Jabbar, LA Lakers	1979–80	.604	.765	1.094
4. Artis Gilmore, Chicago	1981–82	.652	.768	1.092
5. Maurice Cheeks, Philadelphia	1984–85	.570	.879	1.090
6. James Donaldson, LA Clippers	1984–85	.637	.749	1.088
7. Brad Davis, Dallas	1982–83	.572	.845	1.079
8. James Worthy, LA Lakers	1984–85	.572	.776	1.076
9. Larry Nance, Phoenix	1984–85	.587	.709	1.071
10. Swen Nater, San Diego	1978–79	.569	.800	1.068

Overall, a total of 78 players reached the 1.000 mark 168 times in NBA history. Chart 5 in Section III gives a full listing of the 78, with their best ratings.

All of the top ten achieved their high ratings during the past 15 seasons. Six of the ten were within the past five seasons. Since the league is 42 years old, this is statistical support for the contention that NBA players are becoming better all the time.

That there is a difference between the two types of shootist statistics is shown by the fact that only three of the players who made the top ten in the points-per-shots ratings also made the top ten in overall shooting percentage (shots made in all categories divided by shots taken). Here are the top ten in overall shooting percentage:

	Season	FG%	FT%	Rating
1. Artis Gilmore, Chicago	1981–82	.652	.768	.698
2. Cedric Maxwell, Boston	1979–80	.584	.802	.685
3. Adrian Dantley, Utah	1983–84	.558	.859	.677
4. James Donaldson, LA Clippers	1984–85	.637	.749	.677
5. Kevin McHale, Boston	1986–87	.604	.838	.670
6. Bobby Jones, Denver	1977–78	.578	.751	.669
7. Ricky Pierce, Milwaukee	1986–87	.534	.880	.657
8. Magic Johnson, LA Lakers	1984–85	.561	.843	.657
9. Bill Cartwright, New York	1983–84	.561	.805	.654
10. Charles Barkley, Philadelphia	1986–87	.594	.761	.651

It is interesting that at no time in NBA history did a player sink at least 70 percent of his combined field goal and free throw attempts for a full season. The only player ever to have achieved a .700 field goal percentage was Wilt Chamberlain with .727 in his final season, 1972–73.

Chamberlain managed his high percentage by being very selective in his shots. He shot the ball only 586 times in 3,542 minutes of playing time that season, compared with his own record total of 3,159 shots in 3,882 minutes in 1961–62. But Chamberlain made a career of shooting better from the field (.540) than from the free throw line (.511). It was because of his poor free throw shooting that he did not rank among the top ten shootists in either category.

Here are the best two-point field goal shooters of all time (minimum 500 attempts):

	Season	2FG%
1. Wilt Chamberlain, LA Lakers	1972–73	.727
2. Artis Gilmore, Chicago	1978–79	.670
3. Charles Barkley, Philadelphia	1986–87	.643
4. James Donaldson, LA Clippers	1984–85	.637
5. Steve Johnson, San Antonio	1985–86	.632
6. Cedric Maxwell, Boston	1978–79	.609
7. Darryl Dawkins, Philadelphia	1977–78	.607
8. Kevin McHale, Boston	1986–87	.606
9. Kareem Abdul-Jabbar, Milwaukee	1976–77	.604
10. Mike McGee, LA Lakers	1983–84	.604

Three-point field goals were introduced into the NBA during the 1979–80 season. Here are the top three-point field goal shooters (minimum 100 attempts):

	Season	3FG%
1. Craig Hodges, Milwaukee	1985–86	.451
2. Danny Ainge, Boston	1986–87	.443
3. Byron Scott, LA Lakers	1986–87	.436
4. Larry Bird, Boston	1984–85	.427
5. Chris Ford, Boston	1979–80	.427
6. Trent Tucker, New York	1986–87	.422
7. World B. Free, Cleveland	1985–86	.420
8. Kevin McKenna, New Jersey	1986–87	.419
9. Brian Winters, Milwaukee	1981–82	.411
10. Brad Davis, Dallas	1984–85	.409

The following are the best free throw shooters of all time from 1946–47 through 1986–87 (minimum 200 attempts):

	Season	FT%
1. Murphy, Houston	1980–81	.958
2. Ricky Sobers, Chicago	1980–81	.935
3. Bill Sharman, Boston	1958–59	.932
4. Rick Barry, Golden State	1977–78	.924
5. Larry Bird, Boston	1986–87	.910
6. Bobby Wanzer, Rochester	1951–52	.904
7. Dolph Schayes, Syracuse	1956–57	.904
8. Adrian Smith, Cincinnati	1966–67	.903
9. Flynn Robinson, Milwaukee	1969–70	.898
10. Fred Brown, Seattle	1977–78	.898

Comprehensive lists for all five of the top tens that appear in this chapter are presented in Charts 5–9 of Section III.

10

PAR for the Court

"*P*ar for the course" is a familiar phrase to golfers, but an equally good sports phrase could be "PAR for the court."

A basketball court, that is.

PAR in basketball lingo is the combination of points (P), assists (A), and rebounds (R)— the three most important categories of player performance. It is a gauge of a player's offensive versatility.

Only once in pro basketball history did a player average ten or more points, assists, and rebounds per game for an entire season. It was done by Oscar Robertson in 1961–62 in what certainly was the best season an NBA guard ever had and may have been the best any player ever had.

That season, Robertson averaged 30.8 points, 11.4 assists, and 12.5 rebounds per game for an 80-game schedule. To give an idea of the magnitude of Robertson's achievement, during the 1980s the number of triple-double (10P-10A-10R) games for all players in the league usually has not totaled 50 for an entire season. Most players do not have a triple-double game in their entire careers.

With point, assist, and rebound averages exceeding 11, Robertson had a PAR-11 season in 1961–62. No other player has ever had a PAR-11 season or a PAR-10 season, and only one, Magic Johnson, has had a PAR-9.

Following Robertson and Johnson are two players who had PAR-8 seasons and three PAR-7's.

The greatest PAR players:

1. Oscar Robertson, Cincinnati, 1961–62.. PAR-11
2. Magic Johnson, LA Lakers, 1981–82 ... PAR-9
3. Wilt Chamberlain, LA Lakers, 1967–68.. PAR-8
4. Lafayette Lever, Denver, 1986–87 ...... PAR-8
5. Larry Bird, Boston, 1986–87 .... PAR-7
6. John Havlicek, Boston, 1970–71 .... PAR-7
7. Norm Van Lier, Cincinnati, 1970–71 ... PAR-7

In its own way, Chamberlain's PAR-8 season was almost as remarkable as Robertson's PAR-11. The unique thing about Chamberlain's season was that he led the league in both rebounds (23.8 per game) and assists (8.6 per game). This was the only time in NBA history that a player led in both of these categories in the same season.

Of the 47 players who registered seasons of PAR-5 or better, Chamberlain's gross total of points, assists, and rebounds was the highest. Wilt's sum for the three PAR categories (24.3 + 8.6 + 23.8) totaled 56.7. Robertson's (30.8 + 11.4 + 12.5) was 54.7. No one else on this list totaled 50 or more, although there is a second list, which disregards the PAR-5 minimum, that contains a few other players whose totals were 50 or higher. These players had a great imbalance between the three categories.

In 1961–62, for example, Chamberlain could have made the 50-plus list without a single assist or rebound. His scoring average that season was 50.4. Actually, that season Chamberlain's total for the three PAR categories was an all-time high 78.5, counting his assists average of 2.4 per game and his rebounding average of 25.7. His low assists average kept him off the PAR list.

Here is a list of the top seven players, counting points, assists, and rebounds, with no minimum for any of the three categories:

1. Wilt Chamberlain, Philadelphia, 1961–62 .. 78.5
2. Elgin Baylor, LA Lakers, 1961–62 .... 61.5
3. Kareem Abdul-Jabbar, Milwaukee, 1971–72 .... 56.0
4. Oscar Robertson, Cincinnati, 1961–62 .... 54.7
5. Bob Pettit, St. Louis, 1961–62 .... 53.5
6. Walt Bellamy, Chicago, 1961–62 .... 53.3
7. Bob McAdoo, Buffalo, 1974–75 .... 50.8

Interestingly, five of the seven on this list were from the magical 1961–62 season—the year the NBA entered its modern era of superstar players.

Baylor and Abdul-Jabbar actually came close to reaching the PAR-5 level. Both men averaged 4.6 assists in their big seasons, assists being the weakest of the three categories for both. The other three players on this list fell far short of being PAR-5 players. Pettit had a low of 3.7 assists, while Bellamy's assist total was 2.7 and McAdoo's was 2.2. Robertson was the only backcourtman on the list.

Before listing the all-time leaders in the individual categories of points, assists and rebounds, it is necessary to determine which of several standards is best to use as a basis for the listings. The gross-total standard has been discounted because totals will naturally differ for players who, because of illness and injury, do not play a full 82-game schedule.

In our PAR listings, for the sake of simplicity in compiling the statistics, we have used the per-game method. The NBA uses this method and when you must rate thousands of players in three categories over the full 42-year history of the league, it is impractical to recompute them all on the basis of another standard.

But now that we are in the process of breaking down the PAR statistics into their three component parts, we must decide which of three possible methods would be most representative of excellence—the per-game method, the team-comparison method, or the per-minute method.

Let's use Chamberlain's 1961–62 season (50.4 points per game) as an example. Using the team-comparison method, his gross point total of 4,029 was 40.2 percent of Philadelphia's scoring for the full season. Using the per-minute method, his scoring average was 1.038 points per minute. Chamberlain was the only player in NBA history to average more than one point per minute for an entire season.

The way it works out, Chamberlain ranks No. 1 on every all-time scoring list. But there are differences on the leader lists depending on which standard is used.

Of course, the points-per-game standard is the most commonly used, but it has two major disadvantages. Depending on the game pace of a player's team, he will have more or fewer opportunities to score. It is much more difficult to maintain a high scoring average for a team that scores 100 points per game than for one that scores 125 points per game, and this wide a range often does exist between the NBA's best and worst offensive teams.

The second disadvantage of the points-per-game criterion is that it does not take into account discrepancies in minutes played. This is to be discussed in depth in connection with the team-comparison standard, but it is just as applicable to the points-per-game standard.

Team-comparison and points-per-minute ratings are based on the two universal standards of the TENDEX system—game pace and minutes played. The determination that must be made is which of these two rating methods is superior.

The team-comparison method is good. It rates players according to the percentage of their contribution to their team's overall scoring. Because Philadelphia's fast game-pace resulted in an average of 125.4 points per game during 1961–62, Chamberlain's rating for that season does not seem to be quite as dominant on the team-comparison list as it does on the per-game scoring average list. Here is a list of the all-time top ten scorers in the team-comparison category. (Formula: Player's total points divided by team's total points equals player's percentage rating):

1. Wilt Chamberlain, Philadelphia, 1961–62 .... 40.2
2. Michael Jordan, Chicago, 1986–87 ...... 37.8
3. George Mikan, Minneapolis, 1950–51 .... 34.3
4. Joe Fulks, Philadelphia, 1946–47 .... 33.8
5. Bob McAdoo, Buffalo, 1974–75 .... 32.0
6. Neil Johnston, Philadelphia, 1953–54 .... 31.2
7. Nate Archibald, Kansas City, 1972–73 ... 30.8
8. Kareem Abdul-Jabbar, Milwaukee, 1971–72 .... 30.0
9. Adrian Dantley, Utah, 1980–81 .... 29.5
10. Elgin Baylor, LA Lakers, 1962–63 .... 29.4

One thing that is immediately evident in scanning this list is that it enables players from the early years of the NBA (Mikan, Fulks, Johnston) to qualify. In those days, all of the teams in the league were averaging less than 90 points per game, some as low as 70 per game. A 20-point scoring average for a team that averages 70 points per game has much more impact than a 20-point average for a team that scores 100 or more points.

But there is one serious negative about this method. Our standard minimum to qualify among the leaders in any category is 2,000 minutes per game. This is slightly more than half of the total for a team for a full season. It limits the listings to regulars and reserves who play as much or more than regulars. It omits players who don't play enough to be major contributors.

However, with a 2,000-minute minimum and an unlimited maximum, often the comparisons will not be equitable. Chamberlain played 3,882 minutes in 1961–62. Is it fair to

expect a player who plays only 2,000 minutes to contribute as high a percentage of his team's total points as one who plays nearly 3,900 minutes? The potential is here for a difference in rating of nearly 100 percent between two players who actually are very similar in scoring production on the basis of their playing time, although obviously the one who plays more will be of more overall value to his team.

The minutes-played standard eliminates this inequity and therefore is best for our purposes. Here are the all-time top ten scorers on the basis of points-per-minute:

1. W. Chamberlain, Philadelphia, 1961–62 . 1.038
2. M. Jordan, Chicago, 1986–87 .... .927
3. G. Gervin, San Antonio, 1981–82 ...... .906
4. B. King, New York, 1984–85 .... .877
5. R. Barry, San Francisco, 1966–67 ...... .874
6. E. Baylor, LA Lakers, 1961–62 .... .862
7. K. Tripucka, Detroit, 1981–82 .... .853
8. K. Vandeweghe, Denver, 1983–84 ...... .839
9. A. Dantley, Utah, 1985–86 .... .826
10. P. Westphal, Phoenix, 1977–78 .... .812

Even though this list disregards game pace, I feel much more comfortable with it than with the others that permit direct comparisons between players who have vast differences between their minutes-played totals. The per-minute standard produces a fair list of the best pure scorers in NBA history. These players were not all Hall of Famers, but they were great scorers. Having seen some of the early players in the league in person, with their awkward set shots and their low shooting percentages, I feel more comfortable with a list that includes the likes of George Gervin, Rick Barry, and Kelly Tripucka than one that includes George Mikan, Joe Fulks, and Neil Johnston.

Using the same per-minute standard for the same reason, Isiah Thomas heads the list of all-time assists leaders with an average of .364 per minute in 1984–85. Here are the top ten in assists:

1. Isiah Thomas, Detroit, 1984–85......... .364
2. Kevin Porter, Detroit, 1978–79 .... .359

3. Magic Johnson, LA Lakers, 1985–86 352
4. Johnny Moore, San Antonio, 1981–82 332
5. Glenn Rivers, Atlanta, 1986–87 318
6. Ennis Whatley, Chicago, 1983–84 307
7. Norm Nixon, San Diego, 1983–84 299
8. John Bagley, Cleveland, 1985–86 297
9. Guy Rodgers, Chicago, 1966–67 296
10. Eric Floyd, Golden State, 1986–87 277

The increase in assists totals in recent seasons has coincided with the increase in shooting percentages. This is because an assist cannot be awarded for a good pass when the shot is missed. With a higher percentage of shots being made, there will be more assists awarded. Therefore, we have eight of the top ten on this list achieving their ratings during the 1980s. This makes Guy Rodgers's .296 in 1966–67 stand out as a great rating.

With rebounds, the opposite principle takes effect. Since a higher percentage of shots are being made during recent seasons, there are fewer rebounds to be had. And so the top ten rebounders do not include anyone from the 1980s:

1. Bill Russell, Boston, 1957–58 592
2. Wilt Chamberlain, Philadelphia, 1959–60. . .581
3. Bob Pettit, St. Louis, 1960–61 509
4. Nate Thurmond, San Francisco, 1967–68. . .505
5. Walter Dukes, Detroit, 1960–61 503
6. Wes Unseld, Baltimore, 1968–69 502
7. Tom Boerwinkle, Chicago, 1970–71 478
8. Jerry Lucas, Cincinnati, 1965–66 474
9. Gus Johnson, Baltimore, 1970–71 474
10. Maurice Stokes, Rochester, 1955–56 471

As a matter of fact, there has been only one NBA player who has averaged as many as two rebounds for every five minutes of court time (.400) during the 1980s. Moses Malone had a .409 rating in 1982–83.

Charts containing more complete player listings than those in the text of this chapter are found in Section III (Charts 10–14).

11

The BEST Players

Manute Bol is not a superstar. His name hasn't been listed on a single one of the first 14 TENDEX charts in this book—charts that were compiled to determine the best players in the history of professional basketball.

And yet Manute Bol is the BEST player in NBA history. Not the best player, but the BEST player.

Let me explain.

Like the letters in PAR, those in BEST represent elements of a statistical formula. B stands for blocked shots, S for steals, T for turnovers. Taken as a unit, B-S-T spells ball control. The formula is:

$$B + S - T = BEST$$

An individual player whose BEST rating is on the plus side is a good ball-control player. A team that has two or three good ball-control players will be able to compensate for deficiencies in other areas of play, such as below-average shooting. The reason for this is that ball control results in more shooting opportunities.

Let's say that the Boston Celtics play a tough game with the Atlanta Hawks in which most of the statistics are about equal; but the Celtics outshoot the Hawks from the field, 50

percent to 45 percent. The only chance the Hawks have to win this game is to take more shots than the Celtics, and a good way to get more shots is to gain an edge in the ball-control statistics.

In the hypothetical Boston–Atlanta game, suppose that the Hawks commit 12 fewer turnovers than the Celtics and this enables the Hawks to take 12 more field goal attempts than the Celtics. The Celtics sink 44 of 88 shots for their 50 percent, while the Hawks make 45 of 100 for their 45 percent.

All other things being equal, the Hawks win the game by two points.

Individual BEST ratings can be computed only since 1977–78, when turnovers were introduced in NBA statistics. Blocked shots and steals were first tabulated in 1973–74. It is likely that if these three statistics had been kept since the NBA began play in 1946–47, Bill Russell would have headed the BEST list. With its limitation to the past decade, the leader is Bol.

In 1985–86, Bol blocked 360 shots, made 28 steals, and committed only 65 turnovers. Bol's turnover count was low because he handled the ball seldom on offense. Great ball-handlers such as Magic Johnson and Isiah Thomas may commit five times as many turnovers in a season as Bol did that year, but they will also do many more positive things on offense than the Bullets' one-dimensional center, whose lifetime scoring average is less than four points per game. Limiting ourselves for the moment to the ball-control statistics, however, Bol's rating for that season computes:

$$B + S - T = BEST$$
$$397 + 28 - 65 = +360$$

Here are the ten BEST players:

1. Manute Bol, Washington, 1985–86 ...... +360
2. Wayne Rollins, Atlanta, 1983–84 .... +297
3. Mark Eaton, Utah, 1984–85 .... +286
4. Akeem Olajuwon, Houston, 1985–86 ... +170
5. Terry Tyler, Detroit, 1978–79 .... +164
6. Wayne Cooper, Denver, 1985–86 .... +152
7. George Johnson, New Jersey, 1978–79 .. +143
8. Larry Nance, Phoenix, 1982–83 .... +126
9. Benoit Benjamin, LA Clippers, 1985–86 .. +125
10. T.R. Dunn, Denver, 1985–86 .... +120

The list is dominated by shot-blocking defensive specialists who don't play much offense. The only players on the list who do not fit into this mold are guard T.R. Dunn of Denver, forward Larry Nance of Phoenix, and center Akeem Olajuwon of Houston. Dunn, the only guard on the list, made it because of strong defense that translated into a predominance of steals, instead of blocked shots, with few turnovers.

The exceptions are Nance and Olajuwon. These two are extraordinary players, who simply have no major weaknesses in their game. Both are excellent defenders who accumulate many steals and blocked shots, and yet both are excellent offensive players who lead their teams in scoring and rebounding. Despite the fact that they are featured offensive players, they manage to hold their turnovers to a minimum.

Olajuwon has been generally recognized for the past three seasons as the dominant center in the NBA, probably the only superstar seven-footer in the league. Nance, the third highest TENDEX-rated cornerman in the NBA (behind Larry Bird and Charles Barkley) during the past four seasons, nearly always is overlooked for All-Star Game and post-season honors. Nance is the most underrated player in professional basketball.

The next top ten list recognizes the Olajuwon-Nance type of player. This list contains players who in a single season accumulated at least 100 blocked shots and 100 steals, while having a positive BEST rating. It is a list of outstanding athletes who have also refined their ball-handling skills.

Ironically, Nance does not make this list because he totaled only 99 steals in his BEST season. With one more steal, he would have jumped all the way to third place on this list. But chances are the Cleveland forward is getting used to being left out. Here is the list:

	B	S	BEST
1. Akeem Olajuwon, Houston, 1985–86	231	134	+170
2. Terry Tyler, Detroit, 1978–79	201	104	+164
3. Garfield Heard, Phoenix, 1977–78	101	129	+110
4. Michael Jordan, Chicago, 1986–87	125	236	+89
5. Julius Erving, Philadelphia, 1981–82	141	161	+88
6. Robert Parish, Golden State, 1978–79	217	100	+84
7. Kareem Abdul-Jabbar, LA Lakers, 1977–78	185	103	+80
8. Bobby Jones, Philadelphia, 1979–80	118	102	+74
9. Sam Lacey, Kansas City, 1977–78	108	120	+42
10. Dan Roundfield, Atlanta, 1979–80	139	101	+7

Although Erving's top season in this category put him only in fifth place, he dominates the all-time list, which includes players who have accomplished this feat more than once (Chart 16, Section III). Out of the 25 names on the list, Erving's appears six times.

A BEST-related statistic that is popular with basketball analysts compares turnovers with steals. Because of the fact that many turnovers are not forced by good defense, it is common for NBA teams to accumulate twice as many turnovers as steals. It stands to reason then that the players who are able to steal the ball more often than they turn it over are excellent ball-control players. The top ten list follows:

	S	TO	BEST
1. T.R. Dunn, Denver, 1985–86	155	51	+104
2. Don Buse, Indiana, 1981–82	164	95	+69
3. Alvin Robertson, San Antonio, 1985–86	301	256	+45
4. Dudley Bradley, Indiana, 1979–80	211	166	+45
5. Ricky Green, Utah, 1983–84	215	172	+43
6. Lafayette Lever, Denver, 1986–87	201	167	+34
7. Derek Harper, Dallas, 1986–87	167	138	+29
8. Maurice Cheeks, Philadelphia, 1981–82	209	184	+25
9. Lester Conner, Golden State, 1984–85	161	138	+23
10. Gus Williams, Seattle, 1979–80	200	181	+19

Dunn dominates this list when it is expanded (Chart 17, Section III). He takes the first three places. Don Buse ranks fourth, fifth, and sixth.

A related statistic, which is seldom mentioned although it is probably just as important as the steals–turnovers ratio, is the blocked shots–turnovers ratio. Here are the top ten players on the list of those who manage to garner more blocked shots than turnovers:

	B	TO	BEST
1. Manute Bol, Washington, 1985–86	397	65	+332
2. Mark Eaton, Utah, 1983–84	351	98	+253
3. Wayne Rollins, Atlanta, 1982–83	343	95	+248
4. Wayne Cooper, Denver, 1985–86	227	117	+110
5. George Johnson, New Jersey, 1978–79	253	178	+75
6. Benoit Benjamin, LA Clippers, 1985–86	206	145	+61
7. Terry Tyler, Detroit, 1978–79	201	141	+60
8. Tom Poquette, Utah, 1979–80	162	103	+59
9. Kurt Nimphius, Dallas, 1983–84	144	98	+46
10. Herb Williams, Indiana, 1981–82	178	137	+41

Bol has reached the qualifying minimum of 2,000 minutes only once in his career, and so he has been eligible to make the expanded list in this category only that one time (Chart 18, Section III). Mark Eaton and Tree Rollins are the dominant players with four appearances each in the top ten in Chart 18. Terry Tyler makes five appearances on this 43-player chart.

The following are the outstanding shot blockers since blocks were first tabulated in 1973–74. This list is based on blocks per minutes played (minimum 2,000 minutes):

	BPM
1. Manute Bol, Washington, 1985–86	.190
2. Mark Eaton, Utah, 1983–84	.164
3. Wayne Rollins, Atlanta, 1982–83	.139
4. Elmore Smith, LA Lakers, 1973–74	.134
5. George Johnson, New Jersey, 1978–79	.123
6. Wayne Cooper, Denver, 1985–86	.107
7. Kareem Abdul-Jabbar, LA Lakers, 1974–75	.100
8. Bobby Jones, Philadelphia, 1976–77	.099
9. Benoit Benjamin, LA Clippers, 1985–86	.099
10. Akeem Olajuwon, Houston, 1985–86	.094

The NBA's first steals champion, appropriately, was Larry Steele of Portland in 1973–74 (.082 steals per minute). Here are the steals-per-minute leaders of all time (minimum 2,000 minutes):

	SPM
1. A. Robertson, San Antonio, 1985–86	.105
2. D. Bradley, Indiana, 1979–80	.104
3. Buse, Indiana, 1976–77	.095
4. Watts, Seattle, 1975–76	.094
5. Quinn Buckner, Milwaukee, 1976–77	.092
6. Ed Jordan, New Jersey, 1978–79	.089
7. Micheal Ray Richardson, New York, 1982–83	.088
8. Johnny Moore, San Antonio, 1984–85	.085
9. Maurice Cheeks, Philadelphia, 1981–82	.084
10. Larry Steele, Portland, 1973–74	.082

The turnover leaders, on the basis of least per minute, since 1977–78 (minimum 2,000 minutes):

		TPM
1.	Manute Bol, Washington, 1985–86	.031
2.	Don Buse, Phoenix, 1979–80	.036
3.	T.R. Dunn, Denver, 1983–84	.036
4.	Bingo Smith, San Diego, 1979–80	.038
5.	Wayne Rollins, Atlanta, 1982–83	.038
6.	Terry Tyler, Detroit, 1984–85	.038
7.	John Paxson, Chicago, 1986–87	.039
8.	Dave Robisch, Denver, 1980–81	.039
9.	Greg Ballard, Washington, 1981–82	.040
10.	Robert Reid, Houston, 1986–87	.040

Charts 19–21 in Section III expand these final three lists from ten to 25 names, with no repeaters.

12

Overrated
and Underrated

*L*arry Nance is underrated because he plays for a low-visibility team. Some of the Boston Celtics and Los Angeles Lakers are overrated for the opposite reason. But there are other factors that can contribute to the lopsided public image of a player.

If a player enters the NBA as a non-lottery draft choice with little fanfare, he may become a standout long before he is acknowledged as one, especially if, like Nance, he has the disadvantage of playing for a team that seldom has its games televised nationally.

If, on the other hand, a player develops a superstar reputation, he may still be recognized as such long after in fact he has become an average player on the way down. An example is Kareem Abdul-Jabbar, who still is playing in All-Star Games two or three years after his playing ability has declined to below star level.

Another case is the player who finds it difficult to emerge from a shadow cast by a superstar, even after he has become a star on his own. An example is Byron Scott, the Lakers' second best player, who is still only No. 4 or 5 on the team in terms of public image.

And then there is the freak syndrome. Some players, because of physical abnormalities (too fat, too thin, too tall, too short) are marked for attention, even if they don't seek it. The 7'6" Manute Bol and 5'3" Tyrone Bogues are ordinary players who receive extraordinary attention because of the size of their bodies.

Every NBA team has at least one player who is either overrated or underrated. Here is a team-by-team sampling:

Atlanta

The Hawks push the ball inside to a rugged front line featuring Dominique Wilkins, but at times their excellent backcourt does not receive the recognition it deserves. The two Atlanta guards who are most underrated are Glenn (Doc) Rivers and John Battle.

Rivers was an excellent point guard as early as four years ago, with a TENDEX rating of .555. He became a star, making the all-time point guard list in the No. 8 position (.648) in 1986–87. He maintained a similar rating last season, and yet there were critics who questioned his 1988 All-Star Game selection. The only thing wrong with it was that it came two or three years late.

Battle is an unheralded reserve who averaged nearly two points for every three minutes on the court last season, second to Wilkins on the Hawks. To put Battle's offensive contribution into perspective, it must be understood that he and Wilkins were the only Hawks to average more than one point for every two minutes played. Battle's TENDEX rating was over .500 most of last season, well above the average for regular shooting guards, including Randy Wittman, Atlanta's starter.

Boston

It is almost impossible for any member of the Boston Celtics to be underrated, although there are a lot of basketball addicts who believe that Larry Bird is even better than his reputation and rating, because his style of play uplifts his teammates. Could Kevin McHale attain a superstar rating without the feeds for easy baskets he gets from Bird?

On the overrated side, it is much easier to pick out a Celtic. At age 34, Dennis Johnson's best years are behind him, far behind. In five well-hyped seasons with the Celtics, he has yet to achieve a rating as high as the .475 norm for an average point guard. He is the player designated by Celtic opponents to "give the open shot" because, open or not, he misses 56 percent of the time.

Chicago

Unlike Bird, Michael Jordan does not do much for his teammates besides dwarf them to insignificance. But there is one other Bull worthy of recognition for what he does on his own, power forward Charles Oakley.

Oakley is a powerful big man who has been among the league leaders in rebounding every season since he was a rookie three years ago. He led the league in rebounding last season. His TENDEX ratings have been consistently around .600 every season. Oakley was traded to New York shortly after this was written.

Cleveland

Another way to spell underrated is L-a-r-r-y N-a-n-c-e.

Also, during the 1986–87 season there was much ado about the Cavaliers' three highly-touted rookies (Brad Daugherty, John Williams, and Ron Harper), all of whom had good seasons. But the Cavs actually had four rookies and the fourth, Mark Price, an unheralded second-round draft choice, could turn out to be the best of them all.

After an injury-marred rookie season, Price was as good as any of the four in 1987–88, with a rating that held above .550 for most of the season.

Dallas

The Mavericks have two overrated players, Detlef Schrempf and Steve Alford. These two possess limited skills but somehow gained publicity far in excess of their abilities as collegians.

On the underrated side is Roy Tarpley, the NBA's best sixth man, who would have won the rebounding title if he had played as many minutes as the other contenders for the title. Tarpley's rating was more than 100 points better than Sam Perkins's last season, but Perkins started and played more minutes.

Denver

Blair Rasmussen was the 15th player selected in the 1985 draft, but the Nuggets, who selected him, made it clear they considered this seven-footer a project who would take three or four years to develop.

Three seasons later, in 1987–88, he began to show signs of fulfilling that potential. Alternating as a starter and reserve, he maintained a TENDEX rating close to .600.

Detroit

The Pistons have two underrated players— Joe Dumars and Dennis Rodman. Dumars is a versatile guard, tough on defense, whose commonplace TENDEX rating belies his value to Detroit as a complementary guard for sensational point man Isiah Thomas.

Rodman, a reserve forward, is a great athlete. When the Pistons replace Adrian Dantley with Rodman, they lose absolutely nothing. Rodman has superstar potential if he can learn to shoot free throws. His TENDEX figure was .559 in his rookie season two years ago, and he improved it last year. With normal free throw shooting, he could add another 50 points to it.

Golden State

It is fashionable around NBA circles to label the slumping Ralph Sampson as overrated. This is especially true in Boston and Los Angeles where there are still some sour grapes because he rejected opportunities to leave college early in order to play for the Celtics (after his freshman year) or Lakers (after his junior year).

But there is no question that Sampson's performance has slipped dramatically from his rookie season when he attained immediate superstardom with a .717 rating. Moved out of position to forward, he dropped until reaching a low of about .500 last season. But there is still hope for him. If he can recover from a knee injury that was not allowed time to heal while he was at Houston, he could again become a dominant center.

Houston

Like many Georgetown University players, Eric (Sleepy) Floyd was slow to reach his pro potential, and now that he has reached it is slow to receive the recognition he merits.

After three below-average NBA seasons, he has had three excellent ones, with a best rating of .609 in 1986–87, almost good enough to make the all-time top ten for his position. But only once has he been selected to play in an All-Star Game.

Indiana

Vern Fleming is Indiana's Eric Floyd, just a notch below the level of the all-time great

guards for the past two seasons. He has yet to make an All-Star team in four NBA seasons, even though the overall guard strength is much weaker in the Eastern Conference than it is in the Western Conference, where Floyd plays.

Los Angeles Clippers

Another player who is targeted, often unjustly, by some of the more sarcastic NBA writers and commentators is Benoit Benjamin. He makes our underrated list.

Although Benjamin is an excellent shotblocker, he is not a great center, but neither is he a lousy one, despite often being labeled as one. He is certainly no worse than average as a player.

Los Angeles Lakers

Three of the Lakers' starting five belong in the underrated or overrated categories. Abdul-Jabbar, one of the all-time great players, is three years past his best days although he is still generally regarded as a prime player.

The other overrated player is forward James Worthy, who has played well, but not quite up to the alleged superstar potential he was said to have when he was drafted No. 1 out of North Carolina in 1982. He has always rated behind Terry Cummings and Dominique Wilkins, who were selected No. 2 and No. 3, respectively.

Both Abdul-Jabbar and Worthy are weak rebounders considering their size.

On the underrated side is Byron Scott, complementary guard to Magic Johnson and the Lakers' second-best player after Johnson.

Milwaukee

Randy Breuer, once considered a career backup center, not only became a starter in 1987–88, but was actually a pretty good one with a rating that stayed consistently near the .550 norm.

New Jersey

Far from being the savior of the Nets, as he was acclaimed when they drafted him in

1986, Dwayne (Pearl) Washington went from pearl-of-great-price to plastic in his first two NBA seasons. Washington was chosen by Miami in the 1988 expansion draft.

New York

The Knicks' counterpart of Pearl Washington is Kenny Walker, chosen in the same draft. Walker did show some improvement in his shooting range last season, but still was unable to play a significant role, even though the Knicks' cornermen were very weak. Do you think the Knicks would like to have Bernard King back?

Philadelphia

Ben Coleman came to the 76ers last season as a secondary player in a major trade with New Jersey involving three more-notable players. He was the least experienced of the four but could turn out to be the best of them in the long run.

Phoenix

Like Coleman, Mark West was involved in a multi-player deal last season, in which Larry Nance went from Phoenix to Cleveland. West went to Phoenix, became a starter, and played well.

Portland

Two years ago, when Kiki Vandeweghe finished fifth in the NBA with a scoring average of 26.9, I suggested in a column that the Trail Blazers should turn over the starting small forward job to Jerome Kersey.

Last season, when Vandeweghe was injured, Kersey took his place and never relinquished it. The trouble with Vandeweghe, who makes our All-Overrated team, is that he can do nothing but score.

Kersey, who makes the All-Underrated team, can do everything, including score.

Sacramento

If Larry Nance were not the most underrated player in the NBA, the honor would go to Otis Thorpe. Highly regarded in the NBA's inner circles, but practically unknown to the casual fan, Thorpe consistently maintains a rating of .600 in obscurity for the Kings.

San Antonio

One of the NBA's amazing stories of 1987–88 was the development of Frank Brickowski. The 6'10" Brickowski came to the Los Angeles Lakers in 1986 after playing three seasons abroad and two with the Seattle SuperSonics.

But the Lakers, who desperately needed a center to back up Abdul-Jabbar, traded him, plus Peter Gudmundssen, plus a first-round draft choice, plus a second-round draft choice, plus cash, for 33-year-old Mychal Thompson.

Brickowski, 29, had as good a season at center last year as Abdul-Jabbar and a better one than Thompson.

Seattle

Nate McMillan is the SuperSonics' underrated player. Although McMillan does not score much, he does everything else well. He is a good playmaker, good rebounder for a guard and an excellent defensive player. He gives Magic Johnson more one-on-one defensive problems than any point guard in the league.

Despite his general lack of recognition, he was the No. 8 rated point guard in the league in 1987–88 with a TENDEX rating of .558.

Utah

Utah's overrated player is Darrell Griffith. It isn't that we are picking on a guy who is past his prime at age 30. It is rather that Griffith has not in seven NBA seasons lived up to the potential he showed in leading Louisville to an NCAA championship in 1980.

He has scored well throughout his pro career but has not shot particularly well for percentage and has done precious little else. He has had to struggle to achieve a .450 rating from year to year, which is just average for shooting guards.

The Jazz also have an underrated player, John Stockton, who has become one of the best point guards in the NBA during the past two years. He is recognized as a good guard, but is much better than the recognition he receives.

Washington

With overrated players Tyrone Bogues and Manute Bol gone (Bogues drafted by Charlotte and Bol traded to Golden State), the Bullets have no outstanding examples of overrated or underrated players.

For 1987–88 ratings of all players mentioned in this chapter, see Charts 22A and 22B, Section III.

13

Up and Coming

*E*very time a professional sports league votes for expansion the story is reported the same way—public criticism of the league for "watering down" its talent.

Positive factors such as the financial prosperity that permits expansion, reduction of the percentage of weak teams in the playoffs, and addition of new jobs and markets are usually ignored.

In the case of the NBA, which expands from 23 to 25 teams in 1988 and to 27 in 1989, expansion is a healthy thing. Yes, the talent will be thin for a few years, but basketball is a sport in which there is great competition between many fine athletes for too few jobs.

No superstars have entered the league since the trio of Michael Jordan, Akeem Olajuwon, and Charles Barkley four years ago, but during the past three seasons a large number of fine players have come in. Some of these up-and-coming players are stars, or even superstars, of the future:

Atlanta

John Battle, drafted by the Hawks in the fourth round in 1985, has improved steadily through his first three NBA seasons and de-serves a chance to start at the shooting guard position this year.

Battle has increased his minutes each season while improving his TENDEX rating along the way. His rating stayed consistently around .500 (50 points above the positional norm and well ahead of regular Randy Wittman) until he was injured last season.

Boston

It's difficult to select an up-and-coming player on a team on which the youngest starter is 29 and the reserves don't play enough to perspire.

But there is hope in Boston that, given time, youthful Brad Lohaus and Mark Acres will develop into competent big men.

Both are physical players who need to improve their quickness and mobility.

Chicago

The Bulls got two excellent young players—forward-center Horace Grant and guard-forward Scottie Pippen—in the 1987 draft.

Since Pippen's best position probably is shooting guard (played by Michael Jordan) and Grant's is power forward (played by Charles Oakley), these two players did not get much chance to show what they could do as rookies last season.

If the Bulls don't plan to use them as regulars, there are about 15 other teams in the league that would welcome them to the starting lineup.

Cleveland

Barring any miraculous trades by the Boston Celtics, the Cavaliers could be the team of the future in the Eastern Conference of the NBA.

The Cavs have four excellent young players who were selected in the 1986 and 1987 drafts—guards Ron Harper and Mark Price, forward John Williams, and center Brad Daugherty.

Harper has superstar potential and the others are all good NBA players right now, even though their average age is only 24.

Dallas

The Mavericks have only one good young player, but Roy Tarpley may be the best of all the up-and-comers.

The 6'11" Tarpley, who had not reached his 24th birthday when the 1988–89 season began, can play center and both forward positions and is already one of the best rebounders in the NBA.

He had the best rating of all the rookies in 1986–87 and the best of the second-year players last season.

The first season he starts and plays full time, he will be regarded as an authentic star.

Denver

Like the Celtics, the Nuggets are not loaded with young talent, but they do have one good young player—point guard Michael Adams.

Adams, drafted in 1985, started for the first time last season and played well as the complementary guard to All-Star Lafayette Lever.

Detroit

John Salley and Dennis Rodman are excellent young frontcourtmen with outstanding athletic talent. Both were chosen in the 1986 draft and both have played as reserves for the Pistons for two years, but they are as good as starters Adrian Dantley and Rick Mahorn.

Salley is probably close to reaching his potential, but Rodman, a helter-skelter player at times, has much room for improvement, especially at the free throw line. If he can develop mental toughness, he'll be an all-star some day.

Golden State

The Warriors are a team with a multitude of problems, but at least the backcourt seems set for a while, with shooting guard Chris Mullin, drafted in 1985, and point man Winston Garland, a 1987 selection.

Garland was only the 40th player taken in the 1987 draft, but won the starting point guard job by mid-season and was as good as any rookie in the league other than Mark Jackson of the Knicks.

Houston

Considered the team of the future as recently as 1984, when Akeem Olajuwon was a rookie and Ralph Sampson and Rodney McCray were in their second seasons, the Rockets now appear to be slipping quietly into the past.

The only player with three or fewer years on the roster last season was little-used reserve Buck Johnson, a 1986 draftee.

Indiana

Reggie Miller (Class of '87) can shoot, but must learn to do some other things if he is to become a good NBA player.

He has the essential skills to start at the shooting guard position, but must work at defense and fundamentals other than shooting.

Los Angeles Clippers

Don't pay any attention to Reggie Williams' awful 1987–88 rookie season.

Players who graduate from John Thompson's tight-fisted system at Georgetown always take at least three years to develop as good pros. Sleepy Floyd became a standout in his fourth season, Patrick Ewing in his third.

Give Williams another two years and then watch out.

Los Angeles Lakers

A.C. Green (Class of '85) is the least known of the Laker starters, but plays an important role.

He is the team's only powerful rebounder and is the best defensive player of the starting five (reserve Michael Cooper is the best defender on the roster).

A fine athlete with exceptional speed and shooting range, Green has improved each year and should continue to improve in years ahead as he becomes less timid in handling and shooting the ball.

Milwaukee

The Bucks are aging, but Jerry Reynolds (Class of '85) may be a star of the future.

A quick guard despite his 6'8" height, Reynolds must avoid injuries in order for his game to improve offensively. He is a good defensive player.

New Jersey

Dennis Hopson is in the same situation as Reggie Williams. Ignore his rookie season.

Hopson was expected to step in as a rookie in 1987–88 and score bushels of points for a disorganized team.

The Nets must first find a coach who will allow them to develop an identity, and then Hopson will fit in just fine. He is a multitalented shooting guard.

New York

Would the Knicks have drafted Mark Jackson if it weren't for a clamorous pro-Jackson crowd at the 1987 draft in New York?

No one will ever know for sure, but a more pertinent question is: What were the 17 teams that drafted ahead of New York thinking about when they overlooked this Walt Frazier clone?

Jackson doesn't shoot as well as Frazier, but he does some basic point guard things better than his Hall of Fame predecessor.

Philadelphia

The 76ers have something in common with the Celtics, Nuggets, Lakers, and Bucks. They are an old team. Trouble is, unlike the other four, Philadelphia is not a good team.

Except for Charles Barkley and Mo Cheeks, the 76ers are in desperate need of help, but their best young player, David Wingate (1986), can't even break into the starting lineup.

Phoenix

Another aging team, but the Suns do at least have two promising young players, forward Armon Gilliam and guard Kevin Johnson.

Gilliam and Johnson both were lottery selections in the 1987 draft and both earned starting jobs with the Suns by the end of the 1987–88 season.

Portland

Jerome Kersey (1984) and Terry Porter (1985) both have shown steady improvement since their rookie seasons and both became NBA stars last season.

Kersey is as good a cornerman as there is in the league's Pacific Division. Porter needs to improve his man-to-man defense to prevent opposing point guards from penetrating, but offensively he is just below the top echelon of point guards in the NBA.

Sacramento

Kenny Smith began the 1987–88 season with the Kings looking like a contender for Rookie of the Year honors. An injury set him back.

Smith has great point guard skills, but must prove he can survive the physical grind of the NBA. Even in college his durability was questionable.

San Antonio

With the exception of the Cavaliers, the Spurs have acquired more good young players during the past three years than any other NBA team.

With forward Walter Berry (trade) and guard Johnny Dawkins (draft) joining the Spurs in 1986, and forward–center Greg Anderson playing well after being drafted only No. 23 last season, the Spurs—who already had all-star guard Alvin Robertson—were one player away from championship contention; and they already had signed that player, David Robinson, in 1987. Robinson will join the team in 1989 following two years of naval service.

Seattle

Derrick McKey left college a year early to enter the hardship draft in 1987, and at times during his rookie season his inexperience showed.

But this is a player who has athletic ability comparable to all-star teammate Xavier McDaniel. The SuperSonics are fixed in the corners for years to come with McDaniel and McKey, soon to become known as the Big Macs.

Utah

In four NBA seasons, John Stockton has improved from an unheralded reserve to become a member of the TENDEX 700 Club.

Stockton breezed to the league's assists title last season and also ranked among the top five in field goal percentage and steals. He was the first player ever to rank that high in those three categories in the same season.

Washington

Yes, the Bullets do have one up-and-coming young player. John Williams (1986) is only 22 years old and already has two good NBA seasons behind him. Before another two seasons are completed, he will be a star.

Chart 23, Section III, gives 1987–88 TENDEX ratings of players mentioned in this chapter.

14

Down and Going

*F*or every up-and-coming NBA player, there is one who is best described as down-and-going. These are the old players and the ones whose careers are being prematurely shortened because of serious injuries.

The current list of down-and-goers includes one certain Hall of Famer, Kareem Abdul-Jabbar, and three others who may some day be enshrined: Bill Walton, Artis Gilmore, and Sidney Moncrief.

The list also includes two players—Wayne (Tree) Rollins and Alvan Adams—whose careers may not have been Hall of Fame caliber, but who had seasons that registered their names in the TENDEX 700 Club.

The full list follows.

Atlanta

Rollins, 33, is a defensive specialist who in 11 seasons with the Hawks never has averaged more than nine points per game. However, his rebounding and shot-blocking enabled him to achieve a TENDEX rating of .744 in 1979–80.

Personal foul trouble has limited his court time through the years, but he was one of the league's better centers before losing his starting job this past season to Jon Koncak.

Boston

The acquisition of Gilmore this past season made the aging Celtics just a little older. Although Gilmore, 39, never has received much acclaim, his career NBA–ABA averages of better than 20 points and 13 rebounds per game are Hall of Fame statistics. Only a few points away from joining the exclusive 25,000-point club, he has been relegated to very sparse playing time.

As a collegian Walton, 36, was the equal of Abdul-Jabbar at UCLA, but a series of injuries abbreviated his playing time in ten NBA seasons. It is perhaps surprising that he managed to play that many pro seasons, but his immense skills kept teams such as the Celtics hoping for comebacks, and he did make a fine comeback—winning Sixth Man of the Year honors in 1985–86—before practically disappearing during the past two seasons.

Dennis Johnson, 34, has slipped perceptibly the past two seasons and could find his starting job in jeopardy this season.

Chicago

When your most notable down-and-going player is Dave Corzine, it means you probably have a good young team, as in fact the Bulls do.

Corzine's best season was 1982–83 when he averaged 14.0 points and 8.7 rebounds as the Bulls' center.

Cleveland

The Cavaliers are even younger than the Bulls. Their veteran is forward Phil Hubbard, 31, who still occasionally starts but is a weak link when he does.

Dallas

It wasn't James Donaldson's fault that he was unjustly selected for the All-Star Game last year instead of the year before, when he deserved it.

Donaldson, 31, hit the skids last season after an excellent 1986–87 campaign in which he averaged 10.8 points, 11.9 rebounds, .586 field goal shooting, and .812 free throw shooting for the Mavericks.

Denver

Like Gilmore, Calvin Natt has not received the recognition he has deserved.

Natt, 31, has had an excellent pro career, but has not been able to come back after incurring an Achilles tendon injury in the first game of the 1986–87 season.

An outstanding defensive player, Natt also was a threat on offense. His best TENDEX rating was .655 in 1984–85 with Denver.

Detroit

A player who had a few good years, but has not lived up to his superstar potential, is Darryl Dawkins.

Now 31, Dawkins is just about at the end of the line unless his career is resurrected with an expansion team. Drafted in the first round by Philadelphia directly out of high school, Dawkins has played 13 seasons in the NBA with a best TENDEX rating of .637 in 1978–79.

Golden State

Power forward Larry Smith, 30, has been one of the best rebounders in the NBA since entering the league in 1980–81.

He has averaged about 11 rebounds a game for his first seven seasons and played good defense, but he has been unable to diversify his offensive contribution.

He spent most of the 1987–88 season on the injury list or on the bench.

Houston

The Rockets are stacking up old players like cord wood.

With Cedric Maxwell, 32, obtained from the Celtics; World B. Free, 34, from Cleveland; and Purvis Short, 31, from Golden State, the Rockets have three players on the way out who at one time were standouts.

Indiana

Herb Williams, 30, still starts at times for the Pacers but has been gradually supplanted for the power forward job by Wayman Tisdale.

Williams has had a fine career, with a peak season of 1985–86 in which he averaged 19.9 points, 9.1 rebounds, and had a TENDEX rating of .619.

Los Angeles Clippers

The impression that is given by glancing at the Clippers' roster is that they are a young team with the future ahead of them.

But the backcourt creaks like the door of a haunted house. Larry Drew, Mike Woodson, Norm Nixon, Quentin Dailey, and Darnell Valentine all are candidates for the expansion draft, retirement, or cutting. Two or three of these players probably won't be with the team when the 1988–89 season opens.

Los Angeles Lakers

Kareem Abdul-Jabbar, 41, continues to gut it out at center for the Lakers because they have no other center and need him in order to continue as contenders.

But let's not kid ourselves: Abdul-Jabbar's last 700 Club season was 1984–85 and since then his vital signs have deteriorated. Last year, for the first time, his TENDEX rating was below average for an NBA center.

Milwaukee

Drug abuse probably has shortened the NBA career of guard John Lucas, 35, while injuries have taken their toll on Sidney Moncrief, 31.

Moncrief, a great defensive player, also has been superb on offense with a best TENDEX rating of .665 in 1982–83, No. 4 on the all-time list of shooting guards. Here is one unofficial vote for Moncrief for the Hall of Fame.

New Jersey

At this point in Otis Birdsong's career, it is difficult to remember when he averaged 24.6 points as he did for Kansas City in 1980–81.

Although not a Hall of Fame candidate, Birdsong, 32, has been a solid NBA player for 11 seasons, averaging nearly 19 points per game for his career. He'll be missed.

New York

There may still be some basketball life left in Bill Cartwright, 31, although it won't be with the Knicks as listed here, because he has been traded to Chicago and will open the 1988–89 season with the Bulls.

Injuries have limited the playing time of Cartwright during recent years, so that he probably could not be expected to be the workhorse big man of an expansion team.

Philadelphia

One of the negative stories of the 1980s was the premature demise of the career of Andrew Toney, 31, who was an outstanding offensive player, especially in close games, for five seasons with the 76ers.

Foot injuries caused his benching for most of the past three seasons. The 76ers' fall from a championship-caliber team to an ordinary one coincided more closely with the slide of Toney than with the retirement of Julius Erving.

Phoenix

Alvan Adams, a 700 Club member, is another player who probably has not received the credit he deserves for an excellent 13-year career. Adams, 34, was still a versatile reserve last season for the Suns, more efficient than sometime starter Eddie Johnson.

Portland

At 27, Sam Bowie is the youngest player on our down-and-going list. Broken bones have shattered his career, which once was so promising that he was drafted ahead of Michael Jordan and Charles Barkley in 1984–85.

Another Blazer who may be at the end of the trail is Maurice Lucas, 36, once an excellent power forward with a best TENDEX rating of .662 in 1981–82.

Sacramento

Almost as sad as the Toney story is that of Derek Smith, who was venturing on stardom after a fine 1984–85 season (22.1 points per game, .577 TENDEX rating), and after a few games of the 1985–86 season looked like a contender for the scoring title. But then he incurred a serious knee injury and, in his eagerness to play, returned before his rehabilitation was complete. He hasn't been the same player since and, at 27, seems on his way out.

Terry Tyler, 32, is a ten-year man in the NBA, but played so little last season that it might have been his last, unless he is picked up by an expansion team.

San Antonio

Mike Mitchell, 32, is a career 20-point scorer during ten seasons in the NBA. He too might hang on for another year or two in an expansion situation, or he might decide to retire with his scoring average intact. Not many players average 20 points during a full decade in the NBA.

Seattle

Alton Lister, 30, has been a pretty good NBA center for seven seasons. For a guy of whom it was predicted that he would never be more than a reserve, Lister has played well most of the time, especially on defense. But last year he slumped badly and lost his starting job for the SuperSonics.

Utah

Darrell Griffith, 30, and Kelly Tripucka, 29, are players with a fine history as high scorers in the NBA.

Griffith had a career-best 22.6 scoring average in 1984–85, while Tripucka's top mark was 26.5 in 1982–83.

Neither player was a significant factor for the Jazz last season and probably don't figure prominently in plans for this season with any-

one other than, perhaps, one of the two expansion teams.

Washington

Bernard King made a gritty comeback from a knee injury last season, but at age 31 it is doubtful that he can again become the superstar he was before injuring the knee in 1985.

It may be too early to count out this courageous player, but he could be on the down side of a great career.

Chart 24, Section III, gives 1987–88 ratings for all players mentioned in this chapter.

15

Money Men

*T*he court of Charles VII of France was dominated by an economic genius who came to be known as the Money Man. At playoff time in the NBA, basketball court geniuses could well be called money men.

These are the players who excel when the stakes are highest—when the league championship is on the line.

From season to season, a player's performance may fluctuate in the playoffs. He may do well one season, poorly the next, so it may be unfair to label a player as a money man (or the opposite) on the basis of a single season.

Even so, it is interesting to do an analysis of which players have had the greatest playoff records in comparison with their regular season performances, and which have done the worst in the post-season.

In studying playoff trends I have noticed that usually the statistic that shows the most change is scoring. Rebounds, assists, and other statistics generally seem to follow the same pattern in playoffs as in the regular season.

I decided, therefore, to use point fluctuations as the basis for determining the greatest money men in NBA history. Players who did not participate in at least ten playoff games during a particular season do not qualify.

If they did, the greatest money man by far, according to this criterion, would have been Philadelphia guard Mo Cheeks. In nine playoff games in 1979, Cheeks increased his scoring average from a regular-season mark of 8.4 to 18.8—an improvement of 123.8 percent.

Cheeks exemplified another principle that became prominent in this study, namely, that certain players often played above their normal level during playoffs, while certain others played poorly on a repeated basis.

Even though Cheeks's sensational playoff series of 1979 could not be counted because he didn't play in enough games, he came back in 1985–86 to prove it was no accident by averaging 20.8 points in 12 playoff games after averaging 15.4 points for the regular season. The increase was 35.1 percent and placed Cheeks No. 2 on the all-time best list.

The No. 1 NBA money man was Gus Williams of Seattle, who in 1978–79 averaged 19.2 points per game during the regular season and increased that by more than seven points to 26.6 in the playoffs, a 38.5 percent gain.

Of the 17 players who increased their scoring averages by at least ten percent in playoffs, nine were guards who had reputations of wanting the ball in clutch situations. Although

NBA basketball is a big man's game, this proves the value of outstanding backcourtmen in important games.

Another thing that is notable about these 17 players is that every one of them was considered to be a star player. There are no average players on this list. (See Chart 26, Section III.)

These are the all-time best money men based on a comparison of regular-season scoring to playoff scoring:

FIRST TEAM

Gus Williams, Seattle, guard,
1978–79 .... +38.5%
Maurice Cheeks, Philadelphia, guard,
1985–86 .... +35.1%
Bernard King, New York, forward,
1983–84 .... +32.3%
Kareem Abdul-Jabbar, Milwaukee, center,
1976–77 .... +31.3%
Tom Heinsohn, Boston, forward,
1962–63 .... +30.7%

SECOND TEAM

Andrew Toney, Philadelphia, guard,
1981–82 .... +32.1%
Dennis Johnson, Seattle, guard,
1978–79 .... +31.4%
Rick Barry, Golden State, forward,
1976–77 .... +30.3%
Akeem Olajuwon, Houston, center,
1986–87 .... +24.8%
James Worthy, LA Lakers, forward,
1986–87 .... +21.6%

The list of players who just missed earning places on these teams is impressive. The near-missers include Jerry West, Hal Greer, Walt Frazier, John Havlicek, Bill Russell, Isiah Thomas, and Elvin Hayes.

It is interesting that the four guards on the two all-time best teams consisted of two sets of backcourt teammates, Cheeks–Toney and Williams–Johnson. Williams and Johnson both had their top ratings in the same season, so it is no coincidence that this happened to be the only season in NBA history in which the SuperSonics won the championship.

Fans of Bill Russell insist that in important games the Celtic center played above his normal level, while Wilt Chamberlain did not quite play up to his regular-season norm. This point of view seems to be supported by statistical evidence. Although Russell was not primarily a scorer, he made the list of playoff overachievers in 1961–62 by averaging 22.4 points in the playoffs, compared with 18.9 during the regular season. Significantly, he also improved his rebounds (from 23.6 to 26.4) and assists (from 4.5 to 5.0) at about the same 18.5 percent ratio.

Chamberlain, on the other hand, made the list of playoff underachievers that same season by taking a 30.6 percent dip in scoring. The converse of this is that even with the radical scoring decline, Chamberlain still averaged 35.0 points per game in the playoffs and increased his rebounds from 25.7 to 26.6 per game. So in bulk totals he actually topped Russell in both categories.

Here is a list of eight players who experienced severe playoff scoring slumps:

Larry Foust, St. Louis, center,
1959–60 .... −46.7%
George McGinnis, Philadelphia, forward,
1976–77 .... −33.6%
Jerry Lucas, Cincinnati, forward,
1963–64 .... −31.1%
Wilt Chamberlain, Philadelphia, center,
1961–62 .... −30.6%
Gus Johnson, Baltimore, forward,
1970–71 .... −28.6%
Mark Aguirre, Dallas, forward,
1983–84 .... −25.4%
Bailey Howell, Boston, forward,
1968–69 .... −23.9%
Walt Bellamy, Baltimore, center,
1964–65 .... −15.7%

The common denominator for these players is that all of them were frontcourtmen with high scoring potential. Although in some cases it is possible that they simply succumbed to pressure, in most instances it is more likely that they were stifled by double-teaming defenses.

With so much money and prestige on the line, teams tend to play much more aggressive defense at playoff time, especially when they are concentrating on stopping a single player who might be able to generate enough offense to dominate a game.

It is much easier to stifle a low-post player than a guard, who has room to operate in the open court. This undoubtedly was a factor in the low ratings of some of these excellent big men.

The way to determine if a player himself was to blame, instead of the defenses of opponents, is to check the field goal percentage. If he shot about the same percentage that he did during the regular season, but had a lower scoring average, the defense should be credited. If he got about the same number of shots as usual, but made a lower percentage of them than normal, chances are the pressure got to him.

An example of a player who apparently felt the pressure was Aguirre, whose scoring average fell from 29.5 during the regular 1983–84 season to 22.0 during the playoffs, and who experienced a comparable dropoff in field goal percentage from .524 to .478.

Conversely, in 1986–87 Olajuwon built his superior playoff scoring totals by improving his field goal percentage from .508 to .615. To prove this was not mere good fortune, he also increased his shot-blocking in the playoffs from 3.4 to 4.3 per game.

Although in most cases a player's statistics other than scoring will follow the same pattern during the playoffs as the regular season, occasionally an inspired player will improve himself in other areas as Olajuwon did in blocked shots. The most difficult category for a player to improve when he is doing a lot of scoring is assists. Find a player who increases his assists at the same time that he is increasing his scoring and you have a winning player, because obviously if he is shooting the ball more he has less opportunity to make good passes.

Four players who dramatically improved their assists, at the same time that they were boosting their scoring, were Andrew Toney, Walt Frazier, Hal Greer, and James Worthy. Toney improved his assists by 32.4 percent (from 3.7 to 4.9 per game) in 1982 and he also raised his scoring dramatically. Greer improved 39.5 percent in the assists category in his big 1967 playoff (from 3.8 to 5.3), while Frazier raised his assists 15.2 percent (from 7.9 to 9.2) in 1969. Unlike the other three players, Worthy was a forward instead of a guard, but his 1987 improvement of 25 percent in assists (from 2.8 to 3.5) was noteworthy.

And then there were a few players, in addition to Olajuwon, who defied routine patterns by improving themselves across the board in the playoffs. Thomas improved in steals (36.9 percent) and rebounds (15.4 percent) in 1987. Russell made gains of 11.9 percent in rebounds and 11.1 percent in assists in 1962. Abdul-Jabbar soared in rebounds by 33.8 percent in 1977 and also made slight gains in field goal percentage and blocked shots. Johnson's positive areas in 1979 included blocked shots (25 percent up), steals (33 percent), assists (17 percent), and rebounds (23 percent). King improved his mettle by hiking his assists (43 percent) and rebounds (21.6 percent) in 1984.

If you had to choose an all-time top ten in all-around playoff performance, you couldn't go far wrong with these:

Bill Russell, Boston, center 1961–62
Hal Greer, Philadelphia, guard 1966–67
Walt Frazier, New York, guard 1968–69
Kareem Abdul-Jabbar, Milwaukee,
    center 1976–77
Dennis Johnson, Seattle, guard 1978–79
Andrew Toney, Philadelphia, guard 1981–82
Bernard King, New York, forward 1983–84
Akeem Olajuwon, Houston, center 1986–87
Isiah Thomas, Detroit, guard 1986–87
James Worthy, LA Lakers, forward 1986–87

16

Iron Men

*I*t has been mentioned that Tom Boerwinkle's 1970–71 season was not quite as good as his .865 TENDEX rating made it appear to be.

Wilt Chamberlain, who was 34 years old in 1970–71, had a TENDEX rating of only .731 that season, one of the lowest of his career. And yet, in spite of the apparent 134 percentage-point advantage for Boerwinkle over Chamberlain, Wilt was still the better center.

Here's why.

Boerwinkle played 2,370 minutes that season, precisely 40 percent of his team's total. Chamberlain played 3,630 minutes, about 92 percent of his team's total.

This means that other big men must have played 40 percent of the time for the Bulls, while the Lakers needed reserve help for Chamberlain only 8 percent of the time.

Let's assume that the reserves for both teams were just average NBA players, with a .500 TENDEX rating. If you figure in .500 for the missing minutes, the overall figure for the Los Angeles center position for the entire season was .714, while the Chicago centers rated .719, still slightly ahead.

However, this was before blocked shots, turnovers, and steals were officially tabulated in the NBA. Anyone who saw Chamberlain must remember what a defensive intimidator he was and how many shots he blocked. He concentrated on defensive play when his offensive skills eroded late in his career. Boerwinkle, on the other hand, was a weak defender who committed more than his share of turnovers.

There is little question but that the overall TENDEX rating for the Laker centers that season featuring Chamberlain should have been about .750, while the Bulls' centers with Boerwinkle should have been below .700, if complete statistics had been kept.

The significant difference was minutes played. Because Chamberlain was able to spend so much time on the court, keeping less-skilled players on the bench, he made up the apparent deficit in his TENDEX rating compared with that of Boerwinkle, who had to be benched frequently for rest.

There have been players throughout NBA history whose lack of durability contributed to inflated TENDEX ratings, as was the case with Boerwinkle in 1970–71. One such player today is Patrick Ewing, who averaged only 30 minutes per game in 1987–88 when he joined the TENDEX 700 Club.

One difference between good players such as Boerwinkle and Ewing, and great ones such as Chamberlain and Akeem Olajuwon, is durability. The great players always seem to put in more court time than the good ones. Great players may become tired, causing their ratings to decline slightly, but they stay in the game and their mere presence on the court helps their teams.

The best benchmark of durability is the 3,000-minute season. Show me a list of players who consistently play 3,000 or more minutes, season after season, and I'll show you a list of Hall of Fame players. Great players play a lot of minutes because they are willing to put forth the effort to do so and because coaches, recognizing their greatness, try to keep them on the court as much as possible.

The following chart gives the all-time leaders in seasons playing 3,000 or more minutes (3,000-minute seasons divided by total seasons played equals rating):

	Total Seasons	3,000 Min.	Rating
Wilt Chamberlain	14	13	.929
Elvin Hayes............	16	12	.750
Bill Russell	13	9	.692
Oscar Robertson	14	9	.643
Walt Bellamy	14	8	.571
Kareem Abdul-Jabbar ..	19	9	.474
Hal Greer	15	7	.467
John Havlicek..........	16	7	.438

Chamberlain failed to play 3,000 minutes only once in his career. In 1969–70 an injury sidelined him for all but 12 games of the season. For his career Wilt averaged 45.8 minutes of playing time per game, a remarkable accomplishment.

Although Abdul-Jabbar had nine 3,000-minute seasons, while Bellamy had eight, Bellamy is rated ahead on the basis of having accomplished his feat in 14 NBA seasons for a percentage of .571. Abdul-Jabbar's percentage of 3,000-minute seasons is lower (.474) because he has played more seasons (19). Abdul-Jabbar did it in nine of his first 11 NBA seasons, but has not done it in his last eight. As he has aged, he has needed more rest.

The appearance of John Havlicek's name on this list might be considered surprising because Havlicek was known as the Celtics' sixth man, meaning that he came off the bench for much of his career. But he was not a reserve in the sense of playing fewer minutes than the starters. He often led the Celtics in minutes played.

A longer list, showing all players in NBA history who had three or more 3,000-minute seasons, appears in Chart 27, Section III. A corollary to that is Chart 28, which lists the players who did it three or more seasons in a row. These two charts are similar. Leaders in the latter chart are Chamberlain with ten 3,000-minute seasons in succession, Russell, 8; Robertson, 7; Hayes, 7; Havlicek, 7; Bellamy, 6; Greer, 6; Walt Frazier, 6; and Jo Jo White, 6.

Both charts feature players from the 1960s and 1970s. In the 1950s the schedule was shorter, making it more difficult to play 3,000 minutes because players had to average more minutes per game to do so. In the 1980s the intensity of the NBA game has peaked to such an extent that players are becoming tired more quickly. Coaches are being forced to use reserves for longer periods of time.

In the history of the NBA only two players—Chamberlain and Hayes—have led the league more than twice in minutes played. Chamberlain did it eight times, Hayes four. Chart 29 gives a full list of league leaders, beginning with the 1951–52 season when minutes played was first tabulated.

Total games played are not as important as minutes played. It is possible for a player to play a few minutes in every one of his team's games for a total of less than 1,000 minutes for a season, while a star player might miss a few games because of injury or illness and wind up with a 3,000-minute season. Nonetheless, it is a measure of a player's durability for him to be able to put together a long streak of consecutive games played.

Here is a list of the players who participated in every one of their teams' games for the most consecutive seasons (2,000 minutes minimum per season):

	Number of Seasons
Randy Smith, 1972–73—1981–82	10
John Kerr, 1955–56—1963–64	9
Dolph Schayes, 1952–53—1960–61	9
Vern Mikkelsen, 1951–52—1958–59	8
Jack Twyman, 1955–56—1962–63	8
Jim Chones, 1975–76—1980–81	6
Bill Laimbeer, 1982–83—1987–88	6
Jo Jo White, 1972–73—1976–77	5
Jack Sikma, 1977–78—1981–82	5
Reggie Theus, 1978–79—1982–83	5
Michael Cooper, 1982–83—1986–87	5

Kerr actually holds the record for most consecutive seasons (11) without missing a game, but he is listed here with nine because in 1954–55 and 1964–65—the first and last seasons in his streak—he did not attain the 2,000-minute minimum.

Chamberlain's name is notable for its omission from the games-played list, but this is misleading. Chamberlain had streaks of four and three straight seasons without missing a game. Another player with a double streak was Artis Gilmore, who twice went through three seasons in a row without missing a game.

The only player whose name appears near the top of both the games-played list and the minutes-played list is Jo Jo White, a guard who probably did not receive as much credit as he deserved for his durability. White played most of his career for Boston, as did many of the other players listed in Chart 30. The ability to keep their regular players in the lineup has been a significant factor in the Celtics' winning 16 NBA championships.

17

Sixth Men

*T*he Boston Celtics were the first NBA team to make efficient use of their bench, although it is questionable whether it was really because of the innovative genius of Coach Red Auerbach or because the Celtics were the first team in league history to have more than five good players on their roster.

While opposing teams with limited player talent struggled to keep up with the Celtics, Boston had enough depth to be able to trot a Frank Ramsey or a John Havlicek off the bench to spur rallies at critical moments.

During the 1980s, the situation has recycled. The Celtics have not had an effective sixth man since Havlicek retired ten years ago. Most of the other teams in the league have developed good benches, with strong sixth men—many of them shooting guards in the mold of Ramsey and Havlicek.

Fourteen of the 25 sixth men mentioned in this chapter are shooting guards:

Atlanta

It is difficult to select the Hawks' sixth man because Coach Mike Fratello's strategy seems to be to surround stars Dominique Wilkins and Glenn (Doc) Rivers with whichever three other players seem to be hot on a particular night.

The choice here is John Battle, the Hawks' second best scorer. Battle, 26, was the only player on the team in 1987–88 other than Wilkins to average more than one point for every two minutes of court time.

Boston

The Celtics' bench is so weak that the team's best sixth man probably is Jim Paxson, who was acquired in a minor trade midway through the 1987–88 season.

The 31-year-old guard spelled the Celtics' Dennis Johnson and Dan Ainge, and sometimes played as well as either of them. Ainge probably should be the sixth man.

Chicago

The Bulls' best sixth man last season probably won't retain that role much longer, because Scottie Pippen should earn a starting berth this season.

Pippen probably would have started as a rookie in 1987–88, except that his best position is shooting guard, and the Bulls happen to have a guy named Jordan at that position.

Pippen is athletically talented and versatile. He could start at either point guard or quick forward.

Cleveland

The Cavaliers' fine reserve guard, Craig Ehlo, gets significant playing time behind starter Ron Harper. Ehlo is a strong complementary player who can rebound and play good defense.

Dallas

The best sixth man in the NBA is the Mavericks' Roy Tarpley.

A 6'11" center–forward, Tarpley had a higher TENDEX rating for most of the 1987–88 season than all but two starting centers in the league.

Tarpley is an awesome rebounder, a good shooter and shot-blocker and a fine open-court player.

Denver

It's hard to pick between frontcourt players Jay Vincent and Blair Rasmussen, but the choice is Rasmussen because, at 26, he is three years younger.

Rasmussen is a mobile seven-footer who is comfortable at power forward or center. He can score, rebound, and block shots.

Detroit

Shooting guard Vinnie Johnson has been replaced as the Pistons' top reserve by quick forward Dennis Rodman.

Quick is an inadequate adjective to apply to Rodman, who is as good as any player in the league at finishing a fast break.

Also an excellent rebounder, Rodman rated second to Tarpley as a sixth man for the 1987–88 season.

Golden State

From a team that has no set lineup it is difficult to choose a sixth man, but shooting guard Terry Teagle probably fits the job description better than any other Warrior.

Teagle led the Warriors last season in points per minutes played, making him an ideal guy to provide instant offense off the bench.

Houston

With Teagle as the reserve shooting guard, the Warriors were able to trade Purvis Short to the Rockets in 1987–88, and Short became Houston's most effective substitute.

Short can play either shooting guard or quick forward, but makes a more efficient guard because he is better as a long-range shooter than an inside scorer–rebounder.

Indiana

Reggie Miller is another sixth man who probably isn't going to stay on the bench.

As a rookie in 1987–88, Miller played about as many minutes per game as regular shooting guard John Long. Miller has great potential as an NBA scorer, and there seems to be little reason to continue the pretense of having Long as the regular much longer.

Los Angeles Clippers

With an abundance of "has been" backcourtmen, perhaps the Clippers will unload a couple of them this year and put Reggie Williams where he belongs, at shooting guard.

Williams' rookie 1987–88 season was a washout and he probably will need a year of work as a sixth man as preparation for a starting role in 1989–90.

Los Angeles Lakers

Michael Cooper was a third-round draft choice of the Lakers in 1978. If Boston had used one of its higher picks for Cooper, it is likely that the Celtics would have won six or seven NBA titles during the 1980s, while the Lakers would have had difficulty winning any.

One of the most underrated players in the the NBA, Cooper can substitute for Magic

Johnson, Byron Scott, or James Worthy. If the Lakers lose any offense with one of these players on the bench, they make up for it on defense with Cooper. He is the best one-on-one defensive player in the NBA and a pretty good offensive player, too.

Cooper is one of the three best sixth men in the NBA.

Milwaukee

After struggling through the first half of the 1987–88 season just above .500, the Bucks went on a winning streak immediately after Ricky Pierce ended his salary holdout and joined the team at mid-season.

Of all the NBA's sixth men, Pierce is the most dangerous scorer, the closest thing to a Havlicek of the 1980s. He won the league's Sixth Man award in 1986–87.

New Jersey

Dennis Hopson of the Nets is the seventh consecutive shooting guard to be chosen as his team's top sixth man.

Like Reggie Williams, Hopson had a terrible 1987–88 rookie season, but he is talented and needs only good coaching and a cohesive team around him to develop in 1988–89 as a good sixth man or even possibly as a starter.

New York

Since center Bill Cartwright has been traded to Chicago, it is difficult to tell who will be the best sixth man on the thin Knicks team.

Perhaps shooting guard Trent Tucker, one of the NBA's best three-point field goal shooters, will take over this role.

Philadelphia

The 76ers can't even put a well-balanced starting five on the court, so it's not easy to pick their sixth man.

Here's a vote for Ben Coleman, a good young power forward who had the bad luck of beginning the 1987–88 as a reserve behind New Jersey's Buck Williams and the worse

luck of finishing the season as a backup to the 76ers' Charles Barkley.

Phoenix

The Suns' best sixth man is shooting guard John Hornacek, if he happens not to be a member of the coin-flip starting lineup.

Portland

When Kiki Vandeweghe became injured early in the 1987–88 season, he lost his starting quick forward job to Jerome Kersey.

Even if Vandeweghe is 100 percent healthy this season, he won't win his job back. As great a scorer as he is, he's ideal for the sixth-man role but not good enough to be an effective full-time player.

Sacramento

When John Battle beat out Mike McGee as Atlanta's No. 2 shooting guard last season, McGee became expendable and was traded to the Kings.

McGee provides bench scoring for Sacramento almost as well as Battle does for the Hawks.

San Antonio

The Spurs have six good players and most of the time in the 1987–88 season the one who didn't start was rookie Greg Anderson.

Anderson could win a regular job this season, but if he doesn't he'll be one of the NBA's better sixth men.

The 6'10" power forward can score, rebound, and block shots.

Seattle

Precisely the same things that were said about Greg Anderson can be said about the SuperSonics' Derrick McKey, with one addition: McKey can also run the floor like a gazelle.

It will be difficult for the Sonics to bench Xavier McDaniel or Michael Cage, so the guess is that McKey will be a sixth man for one more season.

Utah

Sometimes a player who isn't quite good enough to match up against the best players at the opening tipoff does better as a substitute because he gets to play a lot of minutes against other substitutes.

Thurl Bailey seems to be one of those players. The 6'11" Bailey didn't excel as a starter early in his career, but had his best season in 1987–88 coming off the bench.

Washington

John Williams of the Bullets is in the same category as McKey, Rodman, and Tarpley.

He is a frontcourt player who was a sixth man until late in the 1987–88 season before being given a chance to start.

In all probability, Williams will become an all-star someday. It should be remembered that he left LSU to enter the hardship draft after his sophomore year, so he is the same age as most of the 1988–89 rookies.

Williams is a gifted all-around player. He is very strong and yet has quick hands and good passing instincts.

TENDEX ratings for all players mentioned in this chapter are found in Chart 31, Section III.

18

Wheeler-Dealers

*T*he best wheeler-dealers in the NBA are the Boston Celtics. If it's a spokeless hub you are looking for, try the Phoenix Suns. Or the Cleveland Cavaliers. Or the Utah Jazz.

The Celtics built championship teams primarily on the strength of four of the best trades in league history, while the Suns, Cavaliers, and Jazz preserved their mediocrity by combining to make six of the worst deals, two apiece.

Wilt Chamberlain, Kareem Abdul-Jabbar, and Bill Russell, the three best big men in NBA history, all were involved in major trades; but perhaps the greatest deal of all was made by the Celtics in 1980. Boston obtained two TENDEX 700 Club players and gave up practically nothing in exchange.

In that deal, Golden State traded Robert Parish and a No. 1 draft choice to the Celtics for two No. 1 picks. For their draft choice, Boston took Kevin McHale. For their selections, the Warriors took Joe Barry Carroll and Rickey Brown. Brown is long gone from the league and Carroll has been no better than an average NBA center for the past eight seasons.

Parish and McHale have been outstanding players for Boston, helping the Celtics win three league titles. Both men are possible future Hall of Famers.

On the basis of titles alone, the Celtics' 1956 trade for Bill Russell might be termed the best of all time. Boston obtained the draft rights to Russell from St. Louis for Ed Macauley and the rights to Cliff Hagan.

There were two differences between the Russell deal and the Parish–McHale deal that favored the latter, even though Russell led the Celtics to 11 NBA championships. One was that the Celtics got two great players instead of one in the 1980 deal. The other was that they gave up two good players for Russell with whose help St. Louis went on to win a championship in 1957–58. Hagan actually became an excellent player, a 700 Club member. But, of course, he was no Russell.

The Chamberlain and Abdul-Jabbar deals also were among the best of all time for the teams (Philadelphia and Los Angeles) that obtained the two dominating seven-footers.

Philadelphia got Chamberlain, probably the greatest of all NBA players, from San Francisco in 1965 for Paul Neumann, Connie Dierking, and Lee Shaffer. If that had been the end of the story, this might have been the greatest trade in NBA history. But in 1968

63

the 76ers inexplicably traded Chamberlain to the Lakers for Archie Clark, Jerry Chambers, and Darrall Imhoff.

There was also an extenuating circumstance attached to the Lakers' acquisition of Abdul-Jabbar in 1975. Otherwise, this might have been the best trade of all, because Los Angeles did not give up any exceptional players in the deal. For Abdul-Jabbar they traded Elmore Smith, Brian Winters, Dave Meyers, and Junior Bridgeman to Milwaukee.

But the Bucks had little choice. Abdul-Jabbar, who had never been surrounded by ordinary teammates, could not tolerate staying on with the Bucks after Oscar Robertson retired and insisted on being traded to the Lakers. He gave Milwaukee a "trade-me-or-I-quit" ultimatum. The Bucks got the best deal they could for him and the Lakers were the fortunate beneficiaries.

The following, in chronological order, were probably the ten best deals of all time:

- 1951: Boston obtained Hall of Famer Bill Sharman and Bob Brannum from Fort Wayne for rights to Charlie Share.
- 1956: Boston got Bill Russell from St. Louis for Ed Macauley and rights to Cliff Hagan.
- 1965: Philadelphia acquired Wilt Chamberlain from San Francisco for Paul Neumann, Connie Dierking, Lee Shaffer, and cash.
- 1970: Los Angeles Lakers obtained Gail Goodrich from Phoenix for Mel Counts.
- 1971: New York Knicks got Earl Monroe from Baltimore for Dave Stallworth, Mike Riordan, and cash.
- 1972: Baltimore acquired Elvin Hayes from Houston for Jack Marin and future considerations.
- 1975: Los Angeles Lakers obtained Kareem Abdul-Jabbar from Milwaukee for Elmore Smith, Brian Winters, Dave Meyers, and Junior Bridgeman.
- 1980: Boston got Robert Parish and a No. 1 draft choice (Kevin McHale) from

Golden State for two No. 1 picks (Joe Barry Carroll and Rickey Brown).
- 1984: Milwaukee acquired Terry Cummings, Ricky Pierce, and Craig Hodges from the Los Angeles Clippers for Marques Johnson, Junior Bridgeman, Harvey Catchings, and cash.
- 1984: Denver obtained Lafayette Lever, Calvin Natt, Wayne Cooper, a No. 1 draft choice, and a No. 2 draft choice from Portland for Kiki Vandeweghe.

The two 1984 deals require commentary. At first glance the deal in which Milwaukee received Cummings and Pierce does not appear to be that exceptional. Like Cummings, Marques Johnson was a 700 Club member and Junior Bridgeman was as good a player as Pierce. The key word is "was." Both Bridgeman and Johnson were approaching the end of their careers when the deal was made.

It could be argued that the Vandeweghe deal was actually the most one-sided in history. The deal in which the Celtics got Parish and McHale was a combination trade–draft. The first of the Warriors' two first-round draft choices that season was, in reality, higher than the Celtics' top choice, but the Warriors compounded the error of the trade by drafting Carroll instead of McHale.

The Vandeweghe deal was pure gold for Denver. The Nuggets got four good players for Vandeweghe, who was benched in his fourth season for Portland and probably should have gone to the pines the year before that.

In addition to all-star Lever, Denver received a solid center, Cooper, and a forward, Natt, who was a better all-around player than Vandeweghe at the time the deal was made. Natt had two excellent seasons for Denver before his career became jeopardized because of injuries. Additionally, one of the two draft choices turned out to be Blair Rasmussen, who is developing into a fine big man for the Nuggets.

Here are ten other trades that just missed being included on our first list:

- 1964: Baltimore obtained all-star Bailey Howell, plus Bob Ferry, Don Ohl, Wally Jones, and Les Hunter from Detroit for Terry Dischinger, Don Kojis, and Rod Thorn.
- 1970: Milwaukee got Oscar Robertson from Cincinnati for Flynn Robinson and Charlie Paulk.
- 1980: Denver acquired Alex English from Indiana for George McGinnis.
- 1982: Atlanta received a No. 1 draft choice (Dominique Wilkins) from Utah for John Drew and Freeman Williams.
- 1982: Detroit obtained Bill Laimbeer and Kenny Carr from Cleveland for Paul Mokeski, Phil Hubbard, and two second-round draft choices.
- 1983: Boston pilfered Dennis Johnson from Phoenix for Rick Robey.
- 1985: Chicago picked up rebounder Charles Oakley from Cleveland for Keith Lee and Ennis Whatley.
- 1986: Detroit got Adrian Dantley from Utah for fading reserves Kelly Tripucka and Kent Benson.
- 1986: Washington acquired Moses Malone, Terry Catledge, and two first-round draft choices from Philadelphia for Jeff Ruland and Cliff Robinson.
- 1986: Seattle picked up all-star guard Dale Ellis from Dallas for substitute Al Wood.

Cincinnati could perhaps have been excused for trading Robertson, who was 31 years old at the time. But the Bucks got what they wanted—a league title in 1971 keyed by Robertson and Abdul-Jabbar.

Indiana also could have been pardoned for trading English for McGinnis, because McGinnis had a superstar reputation and English had not yet established his star credentials.

The Moses Malone deal was inexcusable from Philadelphia's point of view and eventually may take its place next to the Parish–McHale and Lever–Natt–Cooper–Rasmussen deals as the most lopsided of all time. Ruland

was an exceptional player, better and younger than Malone at the time of the deal. But the 76ers knew Ruland had serious knee trouble and either they didn't give the knee time enough to heal or they didn't do a good job of examining the knee, because Ruland played only five games for them before being forced into retirement. Malone was an all-star for Washington, Catledge was a starting forward, and the 1988 draft choice was among the top ten.

There were also two trades made during the 1987–88 season that could make these lists some day, because they involved dominating big men. Cleveland got Larry Nance, the best-rated forward in the Western Conference, from Phoenix, and Golden State acquired Ralph Sampson from Houston. There were other good players involved in these deals, but none with the superstar potential of Nance and Sampson.

This chapter would not be complete without mentioning three of the strangest deals in professional basketball history, involving players who later became NBA stalwarts.

In 1970, in the American Basketball Association, Rick Barry, in the prime of his Hall of Fame career, was traded by Virginia to New York for cash and a first-round draft choice.

In 1975, also in the ABA, Dan Issel was traded twice for mediocre players. In the first deal Issel went from Kentucky to Baltimore for Tom Owens and cash. A month later he was dealt by Baltimore to Denver for Dave Robisch and cash.

The ABA folded at the end of the 1975–76 season, which in retrospect may have been the reason for the Issel trades: The Kentucky and Baltimore teams were trying to square their accounts before folding.

However, Denver was one of four ABA teams which did not fold. The Nuggets were admitted to the NBA the next season with essentially the same players they had on their ABA roster and, led by Issel and David Thompson, shocked the NBA by registering the second-best record in the league in their first season.

19

Caught in the Draft

*T*he worst that can happen to a normal person who gets caught in a draft is to catch a head cold; but if an NBA general manager gets caught unprepared for the annual player draft, he's likely to find himself out in the cold looking for another job.

Two teams that never even seem to get so much as a chill at draft time are the Boston Celtics and Milwaukee Bucks.

Beginning with Bob Cousy, selected in a lottery by the Celtics in 1950 after the Chicago Stags folded, Boston's draft fortunes have been nothing but excellent. Franchise-builders Bill Russell (1956), John Havlicek (1962), Dave Cowens (1970), Larry Bird (1978), and Kevin McHale (1980) all were Celtic first-round draft choices.

Milwaukee has been in the NBA for only 20 years, but the Bucks' draftees include Kareem Abdul-Jabbar (1969), Julius Erving (1972), Marques Johnson (1977), and Sidney Moncrief (1979).

For one season, it is doubtful if any team will ever match the Celtics' draft of 1956. In addition to Russell, Boston drafted K.C. Jones and Tom Heinsohn that season. Those three players earned a total of 27 league championship rings as players and six more as head coaches.

Here is a list of the top drafting teams' choices in their best seasons:

1. Boston 1956: Bill Russell, Tom Heinsohn, K.C. Jones.
2. Cleveland 1986: Brad Daugherty, Ron Harper, Mark Price.
3. Milwaukee 1969: Kareem Abdul-Jabbar, Bob Dandridge.
4. San Antonio 1987: David Robinson, Greg Anderson.
5. Detroit 1981: Isiah Thomas, Kelly Tripucka.
6. Houston 1983: Ralph Sampson, Rodney McCray.
7. Dallas 1981: Mark Aguirre, Rolando Blackman.
8. Golden State 1965: Rick Barry, Fred Hetzel.
9. L.A. Lakers 1977: Kenny Carr, Brad Davis, Norm Nixon.
10. Dallas 1983: Dale Ellis, Derek Harper.

San Antonio's high 1987 draft rating is based on what Robinson is expected to do in the future, while Houston's 1983 rating ignores what Sampson did in 1987–88 before being traded to Golden State.

It is arguable that Dallas' 1983 draft (Ellis, Harper) was actually better than the Mavericks' 1981 draft (Aguirre, Blackman), but the Mavs didn't know it and traded Ellis without giving him a chance to play regularly.

Detroit in 1970 and Atlanta in 1975 almost made the top ten. The Pistons' first two choices in 1970 were Bob Lanier and Dan Issel, while the Hawks selected David Thompson and Marvin Webster five years later. Trouble was, Detroit couldn't sign Issel and Atlanta couldn't sign Thompson. Both players began their professional careers in the American Basketball Association.

The strangest draft was Portland's in 1984. In a year in which Akeem Olajuwon, Charles Barkley, and Michael Jordan all were available, Portland had the No. 2 choice overall and somehow managed not to select any of the three. After Houston picked Olajuwon, with Jordan and Barkley still on the board, Portland took Sam Bowie. Bowie was so susceptible to injuries that he missed two entire seasons as a collegian and averaged only ten points per game as a fifth-year senior at Kentucky. In his first four NBA seasons, Bowie missed more games than he played.

But to the Trail Blazers' credit, they managed to salvage their 1984 draft by taking Jerome Kersey as the No. 46 player overall. Kersey is no Jordan or Barkley, but he is as good as any cornerman in the NBA's Pacific Division. Portland was fortunate he was still available after 45 other players were chosen.

The pool of players drafted in 1984 was the best of all time. Besides superstars Olajuwon, Jordan, and Barkley, there were seven other all-star quality players in that draft: Kersey, Vern Fleming, Michael Cage, John Stockton, Alvin Robertson, Otis Thorpe, and Kevin Willis.

Another strong draft was 1982's. Even though the Los Angeles Lakers made a mistake choosing James Worthy ahead of Terry Cummings or Dominique Wilkins as No. 1 overall, this was a deep draft with Wilkins, Cummings, Worthy, Eric (Sleepy) Floyd, Lafayette Lever, Ricky Pierce, and Paul Pressey. A trade for

Cummings enabled Milwaukee to end up with three of these seven players.

Probably the third best draft year was 1970. This one included Pete Maravich, Bob Lanier, Dave Cowens, Dan Issel, Nate (Tiny) Archibald, and Calvin Murphy.

Other draft highlights by teams:

ATLANTA—The Hawks' best draftee was one they didn't even choose. In 1982, Utah drafted Dominique Wilkins, but he was traded to Atlanta for Freeman Williams and John Drew before playing a game for the Jazz.

BOSTON—Some basketball experts believe drug overdose victim Len Bias, the Celtics' 1986 first-round draft choice, was potentially as good a player as any Boston ever drafted with the exceptions of Russell and Bird and that, with Bird, McHale, and Bias, the Celts would have launched another dynasty.

CHICAGO—How Michael Jordan lasted as long as the third pick in 1984 is a mystery that may never be solved. Draft analysts expected Houston to pick him No. 1. He was certainly the Bulls' greatest draft choice.

CLEVELAND—The Cavaliers actually had four rookies in 1986, because John Williams, drafted in 1985, did not play until 1986. Daugherty, Williams, Price, and Harper all are regulars for the Cavs, who essentially rebuilt their entire team in one year.

DALLAS—Although the Mavericks have had some great drafts during the 1980s, they also had one clunker. In 1985, with three first-round selections, they bombed with Detlef Schrempf, Bill Wennington, and Uwe Blab.

DENVER—The only gold Nuggets in 23 years of Denver draft history were Spencer Haywood, Tom Boerwinkle, and Walt Frazier, all of whom wound up playing for other teams. Denver opted to retain such stalwarts as Cliff Meely, Bob Presley, John Belcher, Mike Bantom, James Williams, Anthony Roberts, Rod Griffin, James Ray, Rob Williams, Howard Carter, and Carl Nix. Good names for a trivia quiz.

DETROIT—The day may come when the Pistons' 1986 draftees, Dennis Rodman and John Salley, will be compared with the 1981 duo (Thomas and Tripucka). Pistons won't have to hold their breath waiting for acclamation for the 1979 first-round triumvirate of Greg Kelser, Roy Hamilton, and Phil Hubbard.

GOLDEN STATE—Although the Warriors had some glorious draft moments, they haven't done well during the past ten years. Three times they have traded their first choices, and the rest of the time they might as well have made trades for the nonentities they picked.

HOUSTON—The Rockets unloaded their No. 1 choices in 1977, 1978, 1980, and 1981 before finally getting smart and taking Ralph Sampson and Rodney McCray in 1983 and Akeem Olajuwon in 1984.

INDIANA—The Pacers are middle-of-the-roaders. They always seem to select somebody pretty good in the draft, but never anyone good enough to make them a title contender.

LOS ANGELES CLIPPERS—The Clippers always seem to get clipped. Occasionally they will draft fine players (Adrian Dantley, Terry Cummings, Byron Scott) only to trade them.

LOS ANGELES LAKERS—Like everyone else, the Lakers have had their share of ups (Jerry West, 1960; Magic Johnson, 1979) and downs (Travis Grant, 1972; Earl Jones, 1984).

MILWAUKEE—As well as the Bucks have done in the draft, they have made some mystifying choices, too. In 1972, when they drafted Julius Erving, they picked Russell Lee ahead of him. In 1977, they chose Kent Benson before Marques Johnson.

NEW JERSEY—How could the Nets acquire so many first-round draft choices and do so poorly with them? They had nine first-rounders between 1979 and 1982 but only Buck Williams (1981) became a star for them.

NEW YORK—Everybody wanted Patrick Ewing in 1985. The Knicks won the lottery and got him. Nobody wanted Mark Jackson in 1987, but the Knicks reluctantly deferred to a screaming mob of St. John's alumni and took him. Now the question is: If these two players were to be traded, would there be more offers for Jackson than Ewing?

PHILADELPHIA—Here's a poser: How could the same team that chose Charles Barkley in 1984 also have picked such nonentities as Chris Welp, Leon Wood, Tom Sewell,

Leo Rautins, Mark McNamara, Franklin Edwards, and Monti Davis, all during the 1980's.

PHOENIX—Drafting No. 20 in 1981, the Suns got a pearl in Larry Nance. Choosing much higher than that most of the time since then, they have netted a bunch of oysters.

PORTLAND—If it weren't for the Bowie debacle, you couldn't help being impressed by other recent Trail Blazer draftees Walter Berry, Terry Porter, Clyde Drexler, and Lafayette Lever, even though Berry and Lever were traded.

SACRAMENTO—The Kings seem to do better when they have one first-round draft choice than when they burden themselves with the responsibility for two. In drafts when they had single first-rounders, they obtained Kenny Smith, Otis Thorpe, Otis Birdsong, and Scott Wedman. In double-first-round years, they flopped with Bill Robinzine–Bob Bigelow, Steve Johnson–Kevin Loder and LaSalle Thompson–Brook Steppe.

SAN ANTONIO—The minute David Robinson sets foot in the NBA the Spurs will be champion contenders, because they already have good young draftees Johnny Dawkins, Greg Anderson, and Alvin Robertson at other positions.

SEATTLE—The SuperSonics' 1987 pair of first-rounders, Scottie Pippen (now with Chicago) and Derrick McKey, may someday make a listing of the all-time best combinations drafted by one team in the same year.

UTAH—The 1984 and 1985 first-round selections were not among the top ten players drafted, but there aren't more than one or two players in the NBA better at their positions today than point guard John Stockton (1984) and power forward Karl Malone (1985).

WASHINGTON—In 1971, when the Bullets were still based in Baltimore, they took Phil Chenier as a hardship choice. Since then the annual draft has been a hardship for the Bullets. They have managed to pick 18 players without getting a single one who made a genuine impact on the team, although John Williams (1986) could change that this year. It almost goes without saying that Williams was another hardship case who left college early.

20

TENDEX Draft Basketball

*T*he most popular sports games of the 1980s aren't the ones that come with dice and cardboard. They are simulated draft games, and the only thing you need to play them are the players.

About 25 years ago, when I moved to Fort Lauderdale, I began corresponding with a friend I had known since high school, a Syracuse physician, Art Van Voolen. We were both sports fans, so we decided to play sports draft games by mail. We began with basketball and later added baseball and finally football.

One of Art's first-year choices in basketball was Kareem Abdul-Jabbar, who was then known as Lew Alcindor. He was only a freshman in high school at that time. Art and I play an ongoing game, retaining the same players year after year, adding some and cutting some and making trades each season. He still has Abdul-Jabbar on his roster.

Through the years we have developed a set of rules that could be used by anyone wanting to start their own game, for fun or money, for one season or for a lifetime.

Let's use as an example a one-season draft basketball game that can be played by any number of players from two to 12. Ideally, there should be no more than a dozen game players. The good basketball players available for selection will run out if there are more than 12 players in the game.

Let's say that our sample game involves four players, for fun, not money. But let it be understood that there are many possible rule variations, one of them being an option to put money into the draft-game treasury. Let's call our game "TENDEX Draft Basketball."

THE RULEBOOK

Before any drafting can be done, basic playing rules must be established. The players should meet in advance of the draft to write these rules. Although there is much room for flexibility, here is a suggested set of rules for a draft game for the 1988–89 season.

The order of draft in the first round is to be chosen by lottery similar to the actual NBA draft lottery. Each player is to draw a number and each is to draft in the first round in the order of who draws the numbers 1-2-3-4. After the first round, the draft order is reversed for each subsequent round. The player who drafts first in the first round is to draft last in the second round, first in the third round, and so on. The player who drafts second in the first round is to draft third in the second round, second in the third round, and so on.

Drafting is to continue through ten rounds. We shall mention other rules as they apply during the course of this chapter, but in reality all rules must be written in advance so that game players will have a statistical basis for deciding which NBA players will have the most to offer to their teams.

The game players are Jim, Eddie, Alan, and Kim. In the lottery Kim draws No. 1, Eddie No. 2, Jim No. 3, and Alan No. 4. Players are given five minutes to make their first-round choices, two minutes for their picks in all succeeding rounds.

In the first round, Kim selects Larry Bird, Eddie chooses Michael Jordan, Jim takes Akeem Olajuwon, and Alan picks Charles Barkley. Reversing the order in the second round, choices are Magic Johnson by Alan, Clyde Drexler by Jim, Patrick Ewing by Eddie, and Kevin McHale by Kim.

In our rules we have decided that each player, on his or her ten-man roster, must have two centers, four forwards, and four guards. Another rule we have included is that each team must have at least one rookie. Without detailing every round of the draft, let's say that the four rosters wind up looking like this:

KIM: Larry Bird, Kevin McHale, Larry Nance, Glenn Rivers, Alvin Robertson, Bill Laimbeer, Isiah Thomas, Xavier McDaniel, Brad Daugherty, David Rivers.

EDDIE: Michael Jordan, Patrick Ewing, John Stockton, Danny Manning, Terry Porter, Jack Sikma, Otis Thorpe, Terry Cummings, Byron Scott, Alex English.

JIM: Akeem Olajuwon, Clyde Drexler, Dominique Wilkins, Moses Malone, Eric Floyd, Hersey Hawkins, Ron Harper, Jerome Kersey, Charles Oakley, Michael Cage.

ALAN: Charles Barkley, Magic Johnson, Karl Malone, Lafayette Lever, Roy Tarpley, Mark Aguirre, Gary Grant, Ralph Sampson, Derek Harper, Robert Parish.

Notice that each player has fulfilled the rookie requirement. The rookies are Danny Manning, selected in the fourth round, Hersey

Hawkins (sixth), Gary Grant (seventh), and David Rivers (tenth).

SCORING FORMULA

Using the entire TENDEX formula would make computations too difficult for the average game player, who would have no idea how to compute his team's game pace. Indeed, there could be no valid game-pace computation for a team that exists on paper only. What we need is a statistical formula that is simple and well-balanced and yet comprehensive enough to cover all major aspects of play. An amended version of TENDEX serves this purpose.

In our formula, we obviously do not want to give as much weight to statistics such as blocked shots and steals as we do to scoring and rebounding. A good system for a draft game uses five categories, with scoring and shooting accuracy accounting for 20 percent each; rebounding, 20 percent; assists, 20 percent; and a combination of the BEST ball-control statistics (blocked shots, steals, and turnovers) the other 20 percent.

The five categories are total points, total assists, total rebounds, the Shootist formula (points per total shots taken, [see Chapter 9]), and the BEST formula (blocked shots plus steals minus turnovers, [see Chapter 11]).

At the end of each month of the season, every player in the game is responsible for listing all of his or her players' contributions in all five areas in a chart that, for Kim, might look like this after the first month:

	P	A	R	Shots	BEST
Larry Bird	300	80	120	300	−20
Kevin McHale......	300	40	120	275	+20
Larry Nance	280	50	120	275	+25
Glenn Rivers.......	175	150	55	210	−25
Alvin Robertson....	200	80	80	225	+15
Bill Laimbeer	175	25	150	200	−25
Isiah Thomas.......	225	150	50	275	−30
Xavier McDaniel ...	275	25	110	300	−25
Brad Daugherty.....	200	60	100	210	−15
David Rivers.......	100	100	50	125	−20
TOTALS	2,230	760	955	2,395	−100

In order to compute the correct statistic for the fourth category (points per total shots) the total points (2,230) are divided by shots (2,395). The percentage is .931. So Kim's statistical line reads 2,230 points, 760 assists, 955 rebounds, .931 shooting, and −100 ball control. In the ball-control category, the lowest negative total wins. It is unlikely that any team will be positive in this category.

Kim's team's statistical line is compared with the stats of the other three players and points are awarded: Three for the first-place team in each category, two for the second-place team, one for third, and zero for fourth. The team with the highest overall point total, counting all five categories, wins the month and is awarded three permanent points. The second-place team receives two points, third receives one, and fourth zero.

For the month of November suppose Kim's team finishes first in points scored, second in assists, second in rebounds, third in shooting efficiency, and third in ball-control. With three permanent points for first in a particular category, two for second, and one for third, she receives nine points for the month (three for points, two for assists, two for rebounds, one for shooting, and one for ball control). Let's say that Jim and Alan each wind up the month with eight points and Eddie with five. The permanent point awards for the first month are Kim, 3 (for first place); and Jim and Alan 1½ each (tied for second and third places). Eddie gets no points for finishing in last place.

This procedure is followed for each of the first five months of the season. But in order for the game to retain interest until the end, with all teams having a chance to win, the final month's statistics should be given five times as much weight as each of the previous five. In other words, the final stats should count 50 percent of the total, thereby giving even the third- and fourth-place teams a chance to catch up. Late-season trades, players recovering from injuries and strong finishes by players acquired in the mid-season draft are factors that could enable a low-ranking team to win the final month, with its 15-point award. The second-place team earns ten points and the third-place team earns five.

Now the points earned from all six tabulations are added and the team champion for the season is decided.

PLAYER MOVES

There are two ways a game player may attempt to strengthen a team after the initial draft—through trades and a draft held during the All-Star Game break. Players may make trades at any time as long as they retain the required number of players at each position. Draft choices may be included in the trades.

At mid-season, as near to the NBA All-Star Game as possible, the game players meet for a second draft. This time the selection order is determined by giving the last-place team in the permanent point standings the first draft choice, the next-to-last team the second choice, and so on. This draft consists of two rounds and the selection order is the same in both rounds. This gives the weaker teams a chance of catching up by making earlier choices than the stronger teams. If Eddie is last in permanent points at All-Star Game time, he gets the first choice in both rounds of this draft.

Now each player has a 12-man roster, so that trades are much more feasible. For the second half of the season (the three months after the mid-season draft), each player selects ten of his 12 players to be counted in the monthly tabulations. This helps the team that may have lost a player due to injury early in the season. For example, in a draft basketball game last season Player D chose Ron Harper in the first round. Harper was injured in the second game of the season. However, because this game provided for a two-round mid-season draft, Player D still had a chance to win because after the mid-season draft he did not have to count Harper on his roster. It was as if he were putting Harper on the disabled list and adding someone else to the roster to take his place.

Also, because Harper's injury had dragged Player D down statistically during the early months, he had high mid-season draft choices which also helped him improve his team. A player who was available in the second round of the mid-season draft was Winston Garland, who turned out to be one of the most productive rookies of the 1987–88 season.

Because of features that sustain interest throughout an entire season, TENDEX Draft Basketball is an intriguing sports game.

21

One-Hundred Young Players

*W*hen it comes time to hand out college basketball awards, the logic of the selections can be mystifying. Last year there was a lot of hype for Indiana's Steve Alford as Player of the Year and until late in the season he was favored to beat out Navy's David Robinson.

Alford is a good shooter, but is an otherwise ordinary guard who has two chances of becoming an NBA star—the proverbial slim and none. Robinson is merely the best college player since 1984, when Michael Jordan, Akeem Olajuwon, and Charles Barkley graduated.

The second best player since 1984 is Danny Manning and he had the same kind of opposition in 1988 from Hersey Hawkins supporters that Robinson had the year before from Alford fans.

There is a difference: Hawkins is an excellent player, who undoubtedly will have a long and prosperous NBA career.

Manning, however, could be another Larry Bird. His equal probably will not be seen again in the college sport until 1992, when Alonzo Mourning is due to graduate from Georgetown.

Is there something negative about Robinson and Manning that causes some basketball experts to consider voting for lesser players over these dominant big men?

Part of the answer to this question is implied by the wording of the question itself. With the introduction a few years ago of the easy three-point field goal, and the continuing prevalence of zone defenses, college basketball has become a perimeter game. Guards are doing more shooting and scoring than big men, and therefore backcourtmen are the players who are noticed on many teams.

It is to be hoped that application of the TENDEX principles in this chapter will help put the true abilities of college basketball players into perspective.

In addition to the fact that college basketball is dominated by open-court players and long-range shooters—that is, mostly backcourtmen—there are two other factors that make the rating of collegians difficult.

First is a much more wide-ranging game pace than exists in the NBA. Some college teams, including Bradley, regularly score over 90 or 100 points. Others, such as Notre Dame, like to keep the score in the 60s if possible.

Hawkins's 1987–88 average of 36.0 points per game was indeed remarkable. But when put into the perspective of game-pace, it appears to be much less exceptional.

In comparison with his team's total, Hawkins's 36-point average wasn't substantially higher than the 22.4 average of Notre Dame's David Rivers. Hawkins scored 38.7 percent of his team's points, while Rivers scored 30.7 percent of his team's points. There is a difference, but it isn't much, especially when it is considered that Rivers, in his role of point guard, did more passing and less shooting than Hawkins did.

This is not an argument to prove that David Rivers is a better basketball player than Hersey Hawkins. As a matter of fact, Hawkins's 1988 TENDEX rating was 134 percentage points higher than that of Rivers.

There is a second problem to contend with, in addition to the game-pace problem, and this is one that has no counterpart at all in the NBA: Some of the best players in college basketball play against weak opposition. Is there some way to adjust for the ease with which statistics can be padded against weak opponents in comparison with strong ones?

There are basically five levels of play in the NCAA in terms of strength of schedule:

- Level one includes the Big Eight, Big Ten, Big East, Atlantic Coast, and Southeastern conferences.
- Level two includes the Pacific Ten, Metro, Southwestern, and Western Athletic conferences plus major independents DePaul and Notre Dame.
- Level three includes the Pacific Coast Athletic Association, Sun Belt, Atlantic Ten, and Missouri Valley conferences and most of the other independent teams.
- Level four includes the Ohio Valley, Mid-American, Colonial, Metro Atlantic, American South, Southern, Midwestern Collegiate, and West Coast Athletic conferences.
- Level five includes everybody else.

But what does this mean in terms of individual statistical comparisons? To answer this question, let's use as an example Rik Smits, the only one of the top 30 rated players from the Class of 1988 to play for a team rated at the fifth and lowest level.

Smits played for Marist in the ECAC Metro Conference. Against opponents that included the likes of Southampton, Siena, Fairfield, and Robert Morris, the 7'3" Smits compiled an impressive set of statistics, including about 25 points, 9 rebounds, and 4 blocked shots per game. His TENDEX rating, including game-pace, was .945—best of the 1988 graduating seniors.

Does this mean Rik Smits was the best player in the Class of '88?

Smits is an excellent big man. He is potentially the best NBA player of the centers who graduated this year. But on the rating list, compiled later in this chapter, he is placed behind Manning, Hawkins, and forward Charles Smith of Pittsburgh.

The question remains: What if anything can be done about inflated TENDEX ratings for lower level players, such as Smits? After statistical experimentation, the question was answered. It was determined that players could be expected to do about 5 percent better against level-two competition than against level-one competition. The same players will probably add another 5 percent of statistical padding against level-three opponents, and so on.

In order to balance the scales, it is necessary to subtract 5 percent from the TENDEX rating of a player who competes at level two, 10 percent from the rating of a level-three player, 15 percent from a level-four player, and 20 percent from a level-five player.

We now have an adjusted rating of .756 for Smits. Hawkins, a level-three player, figures out at .713. But this does not necessarily mean that Smits is a better player than Hawkins, for even in the backcourt-oriented college competition, a center should compile a TENDEX rating higher than a shooting guard's rating because of rebounding, shot-blocking, and shooting advantages. Smits, who took many close-range shots, had a field goal mark of 62.3 percent.

In most cases, our list of the top 30 follows pretty closely the order of the TENDEX ratings, but there are exceptions based on intangibles, personal observations, and the proven success of certain players at the international level of competition. This list includes only graduating seniors. Hardship players who decided to leave school early are listed later in this chapter with their respective classes. Here are the top 30 NBA prospects from the Class of '88:

1. DANNY MANNING, 6-10, Kansas—The most versatile big man to enter the NBA since Larry Bird, Manning in some ways is very much like the Celtic superstar. He is an excellent shooter from short and long range, rebounds well, passes well, and excels in the open court. His TENDEX rating of .830 is the best of the players in this class.

2. HERSEY HAWKINS, 6-3, Bradley—Hawkins is a clone for Sidney Moncrief, one of the best shooting guards in NBA history. Like Moncrief, Hawkins plays a total game, including tenacious defense.

3. CHARLES SMITH, 6-10, Pittsburgh—In his ability to run, rebound, block shots, and score from inside and outside, Smith is similar to Kevin Willis and Roy Tarpley. He is probably a little better than Atlanta's Willis but not quite as good as Dallas's Tarpley.

4. RIK SMITS, 7-3, Marist—Smits is much quicker and more athletic than Milwaukee Bucks' center Randy Breuer, another 7'3" player. Because of inexperience and weak collegiate opposition, however, Smits is probably three years away from NBA excellence.

5. CHRIS MORRIS, 6-8, Auburn—Morris is a talented athlete, good shooter, and good rebounder who runs the court well. He still needs more maturity, but has as much all-court ability as former Auburn star Chuck Person, now with the Indiana Pacers.

6. MITCH RICHMOND, 6-5, Kansas State—Richmond sneaked up the draft list during his senior season in college. He can rebound and handle the ball. Impressive ability to lob artillery in from all angles makes him a double for Detroit's Vinnie Johnson, although he is probably a better all-around player than Johnson.

7. MARK BRYANT, 6-9, Seton Hall—An awesome physical specimen, resembling Karl Malone of the Utah Jazz, Bryant is more imposing than Armon Gilliam, the No. 2 NBA draft choice of 1987. Bryant has quick feet for his bulk, and a good shooting touch, and can run the floor.

8. TIM PERRY, 6-9, Temple—Limited to low-post duties during his collegiate career, Perry improved his standing with NBA scouts when given the opportunity to run the floor as a forward during the Orlando All-Star Classic. He ran, and ran, and ran, until the scouts thought they were seeing the second coming of James Worthy.

9. GARY GRANT, 6-3, Michigan—Grant's NBA counterpart is Alvin Robertson, whose strongest asset is defense. One of the best defensive players in the country at the collegiate level, Grant is also a good scorer and playmaker.

10. RONY SEIKALY, 6-10, Syracuse—A mystery man, inconsistent throughout his college career, Seikaly has offensive ability not far short of 1986 No. 1 NBA draftee Brad Daugherty.

11. WILL PERDUE, 6-11, Vanderbilt—The hard-working Perdue may already have made himself just about as good a player as he has the potential to be. He has strength and quickness, like Mike Gminski; he could be a first-year NBA starter for a weak team, but don't expect superstardom from him.

12. DERRICK CHIEVOUS, 6-7, Missouri—If the Band-Aid Man can patch up one or two weaknesses in his game, he can go from being a guy with a limited future, like Kenny Walker, to one with star potential, like Dale Ellis. Lean and mean, he needs to pass the ball better and more often and to improve his shooting between 15 and 20 feet.

13. WILLIE ANDERSON, 6-7, Georgia—An intriguing prospect, he has the size and

essential ability to blossom as a pro like another former Georgia player, Vern Fleming, who is now an Indiana Pacer.

14. JEFF GRAYER, 6-5, Iowa State—Grayer may get caught between being too small to play forward and too slow to play guard in the NBA, or he may turn out to be another Adrian Dantley. He has the skills.

15. ERIC LECKNER, 6-11, Wyoming—Leckner played throughout college in the shadow of teammate Fennis Dembo, but he may be a better NBA prospect than Dembo. An unselfish player, with inside strength and an outside shooting touch comparable to Bill Laimbeer, he has a chance to become as good as any center in this class.

16. DAVID RIVERS, 6-0, Notre Dame—The only negative about Rivers is that at his height it sometimes is difficult for him to get good shots over taller opponents. But if he is willing to shoot less and pass more, he could be as good as last season's top rookie, Mark Jackson. He has the requisite cockiness to play the point guard position in the NBA.

17. HARVEY GRANT, 6-9, Oklahoma—Despite a 21-point scoring average, a big part of Grant's game is defense. He is strong enough to clear the defensive backboard, quick enough to play against guards at the point. The jump-shooting Grant is similar to former NBA scoring champ Bob McAdoo, but doesn't have as many offensive moves as McAdoo.

18. DEAN GARRETT, 6-10, Indiana—Garrett is a little timid at times, and does not go after the ball aggressively or take it to the basket with power. But he is a defensive intimidator with good athletic skills. The pros will be patient with him. He's a lot like John Salley of Detroit.

19. RICKY BERRY, 6-9, San Jose State—Berry is an ideal player for an NBA team that needs instant offense. Virtually unstoppable as a scorer, the rail-thin Berry resembles former NBA scoring champion George Gervin. His defense is questionable.

20. SHELTON JONES, 6-9, St. John's—Jones came on strong at the end of his senior year. He has full-court ability with potential to improve. Could be another Dennis Rodman.

21. FENNIS DEMBO, 6-5, Wyoming—Dembo has been one of the most visible players in college basketball for three years because of his flamboyant personality. He has some of Mark Aguirre's flashiness, but also has some of Aguirre's self-centeredness and lethargy. His talent is so great, however, that he must be considered a good prospect.

22. DAN MAJERLE, 6-6, Central Michigan—A player who really did not gain attention until post-season play, Majerle is a talented guard–forward, about the same size as Chris Mullin and with comparable ability.

23. KEVIN EDWARDS, 6-3, DePaul—Junior point guard Rod Strickland was a more spectacular player than Edwards last season for DePaul, but the senior was excellent in his own right. He is a good scorer, rebounder, and passer and a fine athlete who can steal the ball and block shots.

24. BRIAN SHAW, 6-6, California-Santa Barbara—Shaw is a multiskilled player, but lacks the most basic skill of all, that of shooting the basketball. If he can learn to shoot, he could become a copy of the Lakers' Michael Cooper.

25. EVERETTE STEPHENS, 6-2, Purdue—Not as visible as neighboring Indiana U's Keith Smart during their Big Ten careers, Stephens in some ways is a better player. An excellent defender and good ball-handler, Stephens lacks the supreme confidence that characterizes good pro point guards.

26. KEITH SMART, 6-2, Indiana—Smart resembles Glenn (Doc) Rivers, who showed flashes of potential in college but did not develop until entering the NBA. A good scorer, the speedy but erratic Smart will be expected to sharpen his playmaking skills as a pro.

27. VERNON MAXWELL, 6-5, Florida—Maxwell was ticketed for the first round of the draft until a series of personal problems pushed him to the bottom half of the second round. But from the standpoint of pure talent, he is as good as Mitch Richmond, the first backcourtman drafted.

28. ANTHONY TAYLOR, 6-4, Oregon—Taylor is a slashing driver, like Philadelphia 76ers reserve David Wingate. But, like Wingate, his other skills are limited.

29. DERRICK LEWIS, 6-7, Maryland—Lewis had to subordinate his talents to mesh with a young Terrapin team in 1988 after being encouraged to be a dominator the year before. A power player who can score and block shots, he'll need to develop corner moves. Could be this year's Greg Anderson.

30. JARVIS BASNIGHT, 6-8, Nevada-Las Vegas—It's a shame that Basnight didn't get as much chance to play in spring all-star games as Perry did, because he is a similar player. He was stifled as a low-post player in college, and was at his best in the open court. TENDEX likes him (.599), even though NBA scouts don't.

There are ten other players who deserve mention as good potential pros from the Class of '88: Forward Anthony Mason, 6-7, of Tennessee State; forward Randolph Keys, 6-8, of Southern Mississippi; center Andrew Lang, 6-11, of Arkansas; center Greg Butler, 6-10, of Stanford; center Barry Sumpter, 6-11, of Austin Peay; forward Jose Vargas, 6-10, of LSU; forward Todd Mitchell, 6-7, of Purdue; center Rolando Ferreira, 7-1, of Houston; guard Vinny Del Negro, 6-5, of North Carolina State; and guard Tom Garrick, 6-2, of Rhode Island.

Overall, the Class of '88 is outstanding, the best since the Class of '84 and maybe one of the best ever. Time will determine that, of course. The top 30 players in the Class of '88 are listed in order of TENDEX ratings in Chart 32, Section III.

An interesting thing about the Class of '88 is the predominance of players who can play the quick forward position. Exactly 18 of the 30 players (60 percent) can and probably will at some time in their NBA careers play this position.

In Section II the 1988 draftees, including undergraduate hardship cases, are listed with the NBA teams that selected them.

The classes of 1989, 1990, and 1991 each also show a predominance of players at one position. The Class of '89 is dominated by power forwards, with ten of the 20 listed players able to play that position. Here are the top 20 players in that star-studded class:

1. SEAN ELLIOTT, 6-7, Arizona
2. JEROME LANE, 6-6, Pittsburgh*
3. PERVIS ELLISON, 6-10, Louisville
4. STACEY KING, 6-10, Oklahoma
5. ROD STRICKLAND, 6-3, DePaul*
6. MICHAEL SMITH, 6-9, Brigham Young
7. DANNY FERRY, 6-10, Duke
8. GLENN RICE, 6-7, Michigan
9. DYRON NIX, 6-7, Tennessee
10. SHERMAN DOUGLAS, 6-0, Syracuse
11. TOM HAMMONDS, 6-9, Georgia Tech
12. TODD LICHTI, 6-4, Stanford
13. CHARLES SHACKLEFORD, 6-10, North Carolina State*
14. MOOKIE BLAYLOCK, 6-1, Oklahoma
15. JEROME (POOH) RICHARDSON, 6-1, UCLA
16. B.J. ARMSTRONG, 6-2, Iowa
17. DOUG WEST, 6-6, Villanova
18. KENNY BATTLE, 6-6, Illinois
19. ANTHONY COOK, 6-9, Arizona
20. JEFF LEBO, 6-3, North Carolina

*Hardship draft choice

The Class of '90 is dominated by big men, with five pure centers and five others in the 6'9" and 6'10" range who are comfortable playing the low-post position. Nine of the top 12 prospects in this class are at least 6'9" and a tenth, 6'7" Lionel (Train) Simmons, plays as if he were 6'10". The top 20:

1. J.R. REID, 6-9, North Carolina
2. DERRICK COLEMAN, 6-9, Syracuse
3. SCOTT WILLIAMS, 6-10, North Carolina
4. LIONEL SIMMONS, 6-7, LaSalle
5. GARY PAYTON, 6-2, Oregon State
6. REX CHAPMAN, 6-4, Kentucky*
7. ELDEN CAMPBELL, 6-10, Clemson
8. TITO HORFORD, 7-0, Miami*
9. TOM GREIS, 7-2, Villanova
10. KEITH ROBINSON, 6-9, Notre Dame
11. TERRY MILLS, 6-10, Michigan
12. DWAYNE SCHINTZIUS, 7-3, Florida
13. RON HUERY, 6-6, Arkansas
14. SAM IVY, 6-7, Wake Forest

15. RUMEAL ROBINSON, 6-2, Michigan
16. NICK ANDERSON, 6-6, Illinois
17. BO KIMBLE, 6-4, Loyola Marymount
18. STEPHEN THOMPSON, 6-4, Syracuse
19. TREVOR WILSON, 6-8, UCLA
20. CHRIS MUNK, 6-9, USC

*Hardship draft choice

If the classes of 1988, 1989, and 1990 are dominated by frontcourtmen, the Class of '91 at least partially counterbalances them. Of the top 20 players in the Class of '91, 12 are backcourtmen, including eight shooting guards. The top three prospects in this class are shooting guards. Here are the top 20:

1. MARK MACON, 6-5, Temple
2. DENNIS SCOTT, 6-7, Georgia Tech
3. JAY EDWARDS, 6-5, Indiana
4. BRIAN WILLIAMS, 6-10, Maryland
5. DOUG SMITH, 6-10, Missouri
6. LARRY JOHNSON, 6-6, SMU
7. RODNEY MONROE, 6-3, North Carolina State
8. RICHARD DUMAS, 6-7, Oklahoma State
9. LaBRADFORD SMITH, 6-5, Louisville
10. ELLIOTT PERRY, 6-0, Memphis State
11. STACEY AUGMON, 6-7, UNLV
12. ERIC MANUEL, 6-6, Kentucky
13. GERALD MADKINS, 6-4, UCLA
14. LeRON ELLIS, 6-11, Kentucky
15. DWAYNE DAVIS, 6-9, Florida
16. LUKE LONGLEY, 7-0, New Mexico
17. SEAN MILLER, 6-1, Pittsburgh
18. LIVINGSTON CHATMAN, 6-7, Florida
19. KING RICE, 6-0, North Carolina
20. LYNDON JONES, 6-3, Indiana

The only position not well stocked in the four college classes is point guard. This position, however, was well taken care of by the Class of '87, which made up the 1987–88 season's NBA rookie crop. Excluding David Robinson, the 7'1" center who won't be allowed to play until 1989, the top three rook-ies of 1987–88 were point guards. In fact, only four rookies earned season-long starting jobs, including the three point men. This was perhaps the weakest year for rookies during the 1980s. Here are the top ten members of the Class of '87, with their collegiate and professional teams listed:

1. DAVID ROBINSON, 7-1, Navy/San Antonio
2. MARK JACKSON, 6-3, St. John's/New York Knicks
3. KEVIN JOHNSON, 6-2, California/Phoenix
4. GREG ANDERSON, 6-10, Houston/San Antonio
5. DERRICK McKEY, 6-9, Alabama/Seattle
6. HORACE GRANT, 6-10, Clemson/Chicago
7. SCOTT PIPPEN, 6-8, Central Arkansas/Chicago
8. ARMON GILLIAM, 6-9, Nevada-Las Vegas/Phoenix
9. WINSTON GARLAND, 6-2, Southwest Mo. St./Golden State
10. KENNY SMITH, 6-3, North Carolina/Sacramento

Looking at the 100 players mentioned in this chapter from the perspective of ultimate NBA potential, it appears that there are at least ten who have a chance to become 700 Club members. Headed by Robinson, who has .800 or even .900 potential, these are the ten with the best chances of attaining the superstar level:

1. DAVID ROBINSON
2. DANNY MANNING
3. SEAN ELLIOTT
4. J.R. REID
5. MARK MACON
6. CHARLES SMITH
7. CHRIS MORRIS
8. HERSEY HAWKINS
9. PERVIS ELLISON
10. STACEY KING

22

Remembering
Pistol Pete

*T*here are a few memorable days in
every person's life. Births, marriages, deaths,
special events. Most people recall where they
were on the day President Kennedy was as-
sassinated.

I remember that sad day, and I also remember the happy day when basketball was
born in the Deep South.

I was attending a retreat at a cabin in the
Everglades on a Saturday in January (I think
it was January) of 1968. During an afternoon
break, we turned on a television set and
watched a basketball game between the University of Kentucky and Louisiana State University.

At that time Kentucky had the only good
basketball team in the Southeastern Conference. The sport was all but ignored by the
other nine teams in the conference, most of
which played in gyms that would have embar-
rassed some of the better high school teams
in the Northeast.

Football was the king of sports in the South.

On that day it began to change. A gangly,
long-haired, floppy-socked youngster named
Pete Maravich came as close as an individual
ever has come to defeating a superior oppo-

nent by himself. Maravich scored more than
50 points that day, but it was his Houdini act
with the basketball—between the legs, behind the back, around the neck, and all at top
speed—that was unforgettable.

The innovations Maravich brought to the
college game during the next three seasons,
and then to the NBA for ten seasons, became
legendary and he was elected to the Basketball Hall of Fame a year before his death in
January 1988.

But this didn't begin to tell the story of Pete
Maravich.

Bob Davies, another Hall of Famer and the
first man to attempt magical things with a
basketball, believes Maravich has had no peer
in basketball wizardry.

"Pete was the ultimate in ball-handling,
the absolute ultimate," Davies said. "He did
things with a basketball that I don't think
anyone else will ever be able to equal."

Davies played basketball against Press
Maravich, Pete's dad and mentor. He recalls
visiting the elder Maravich when he was
coaching at Clemson University.

Over coffee, Press Maravich casually told
Davies that his son had been out playing

basketball since dawn and probably would not return home until dusk.

Davies said: "No one ever loved basketball more than Pete Maravich, and no one ever worked at it more than Pete. It was something he loved and put a lot of intensity into."

Maravich's biggest problem was that the generation of basketball players that preceded him, with the exception of Davies and, a little later, Bob Cousy, had been mostly two-handed set shooters who passed the ball from the chest. These were the game's coaches while Maravich was playing, and they deplored his style of play. One of them was Butch Van Breda Kolff, who coached the New Orleans NBA team for which Maravich played.

Van Breda Kolff was constantly nagging Maravich to eliminate some of the florid edges from his game.

"I knew Butch and I remember suggesting that he should let Pete alone, but Butch didn't want to hear that," Davies said. "Pete was inhibited. He wasn't allowed to do the things he wanted to do, but he was the pioneer for the spectacular players of today."

A second negative in Maravich's basketball experience was his chemistry with teammates. Through three years of college and nine prime years in the NBA, he never had a teammate capable of consistently keeping pace with him.

As often as not his best passes would surprise less-skilled teammates and bounce off their chests or whiz past their ears for turnovers. Even though he broke nearly all of the NCAA scoring records, the finest part of Maravich's game wasn't shooting; it was play making.

He would have been at his best scoring 18 points a game and handing out 15 assists, but was always obligated to shoot more than he wanted to and never averaged more than seven assists per game.

Despite the drawbacks, Maravich maintained a lifetime TENDEX rating of .565 and twice exceeded .600, narrowly missing the all-time top ten list for his position. How good could he have been if he had had talented teammates and visionary coaches?

In the end, though, he had an impact on the sport of basketball that was immeasurable by TENDEX or any other statistical system. The great teams in the South today, and the large arenas in which they play, are a legacy to Maravich, who showed them not only that it could be done, but how to do it.

Here's to Pete Maravich, for what was, and what is, and what could have been.

SECTION II

THE 1987–88 AND
1988–89 SEASONS

Introduction

*T*his one was for Jerry West.

If there can be make-up calls by referees to compensate for earlier mistakes, then maybe the 1988 playoff finals could be considered a "make-up" call for Jerry West, to compensate for an undeserved playoff loss 19 years earlier.

During the championship playoff series of 1969, the Los Angeles Lakers, led by West and Wilt Chamberlain, took a 3–2 lead over the Boston Celtics and seemed to be gaining momentum. But then West injured a leg and the Celtics won the final two games with him hobbling. It was an NBA title the Lakers undoubtedly would have won if West had not been injured.

In 1988 the Lakers appeared to be losing ground in the playoff finals to a strong young Detroit Piston team, but late in the sixth game Piston star Isiah Thomas injured an ankle, and the Lakers managed to win the final two games, both by close scores, for the title.

They won the final game on the strength of the best single-game performance in the pro career of James Worthy, named series MVP. But Worthy was a Laker last season only because Jerry West, as Lakers' general manager, vetoed a deal that would have sent him to Dallas the previous season.

West had been criticized for vetoing the deal, and with some justification. If completed, the trade would have brought Mark Aguirre (comparable in ability to Worthy) plus Roy Tarpley (a potential superstar to succeed Kareem Abdul-Jabbar as center) to the Lakers.

Analyzing from a long-range perspective, West probably did make a mistake, but on a Tuesday night last June, when Isiah Thomas couldn't get started and James Worthy couldn't be stopped, Jerry West must have felt vindicated.

Section II previews 1988–89 prospects for the champion Lakers, runner-up Pistons, and 21 other teams that comprised the NBA last season. Also presented are an overview of the best individual performances of the 1987–88 season and a chapter on the new Charlotte and Miami franchises.

Because of this book's publishing deadline, there may be some players listed with former teams instead of teams they have signed with for 1988–89. Some free agents remained unsigned at press time.

But even with a few players in the wrong places, it is doubtful that the strength of the top teams could be substantially changed by late summer personnel moves. The league's salary cap limits loading up on star players, so most of the team ratings in this section are valid, changes or no changes. Individual player ratings, of course, are not affected at all by trades.

1

The Best
of 1987-88

*T*he question most often asked with reference to the TENDEX statistical rating system is: Who is the best basketball player in the NBA?

I have to admit I don't have a positive answer to the question. The TENDEX system has limitations. It is unable to measure intangibles.

From the evidence of statistics, team as well as individual, I'd have to say Larry Bird.

Bird led the TENDEX ratings for three seasons, from 1983-84 through 1985-86. Charles Barkley led in 1986-87. Michael Jordan led in 1987-88. Personally, I think Bird was the best player, even the past two seasons when he didn't head the rating list. In 1987-88, Jordan led with a rating of .887. Then came Barkley at .829 and Bird at .824.

Since TENDEX is a comprehensive system based on all measurable phases of play, it would seem that Jordan was clearly the best player in the game last season. On what basis can a case be made for Bird?

Let's start with the fact that Jordan and Barkley are individual talents, capable of dominating a game. Bird is less skilled athletically than the other two, but he is a consummate team player. He makes his teammates better. There is evidence to indicate that Jordan and Barkley hinder the play of some of their teammates.

Jordan requires the ball. The Bulls are told by Coach Doug Collins to put the ball into Jordan's hands and then crash the boards in case there is a rebound. Offensively, they tend to stand around and watch him, which perhaps is why, in spite of his league-leading 35-point individual scoring average, the Bulls ranked 19th in team scoring last season.

Chicago has a point guard problem. Since Jordan became a member of the Bulls in 1984-85, they have not had an effective point guard. They had one in 1983-84, rookie Ennis Whatley, who averaged 8.3 assists per game and fell only 28 short of matching Oscar Robertson's existing rookie record for assists.

In 1984-85, with Jordan controlling the ball, Whatley disappeared. His confidence crushed, he has not been a significant player since that season.

With Jordan, who is not a pure point guard, possessing the ball much of the time, the Bulls have been forced to make do with complementary guards such as John Paxson and Sam Vincent, who are not really point men, but are content to stand to one side and watch Jordan perform.

Perform he does! There is little doubt but that Michael Jordan is the best pure talent in basketball today, probably the most talented athlete in all of professional sports.

Barkley does not need the ball quite as much as Jordan, but in his own way he disturbs the chemistry of his team. Before Barkley became a member of the Philadelphia 76ers, center Moses Malone was a superstar. After Barkley arrived, it became evident that he was as enthusiastic about knocking his own teammates out of his way as opponents.

Barkley began dominating the low-post area in his second season, 1985–86. That same season Malone's TENDEX rating dropped by 85 points from .721 to .636. It was assumed that the 31-year-old Malone was entering the twilight of his career and he was traded to the Washington Bullets.

However, the next season with Washington, Malone rebounded with a TENDEX rating of .731, effectively killing the washed-up theory about himself.

That wasn't all. Both Roy Hinson and Tim McCormick, who teamed with Barkley last season before being traded to New Jersey, had ratings of nearly 100 TENDEX points higher after the trade than they had while playing in the same frontcourt with Barkley.

The opposite is true of the Boston Celtics' frontcourt. Kevin McHale and Robert Parish have been teammates of Larry Bird throughout the 1980s. McHale has never played for another team, so there is no way to make a before-and-after comparison for him. But Parish's scoring improved by two points per game and his field goal percentage soared by more than 50 percentage points when he joined the Celts after spending four seasons with Golden State.

Bird doesn't occupy the ball. He gets rid of it quickly with touch passes, keeping all of his teammates alert. If Parish or McHale gets open near the basket, they know Bird will get the ball to them in position for easy baskets.

TENDEX is a per-minute rating system. If there were some way to rate players according to production on the basis of the number of seconds they possess the ball during a game, instead of the number of minutes they spend on the court, Bird would surpass Jordan and Barkley.

Parish, McHale, and Danny Ainge led the NBA in the Shootist statistic at their respective positions last season. This happened partly because of Bird. Bird in some ways is a point guard playing in the corner. He is as quick with the pass off the dribble as any point man in the league.

Parish and McHale ranked one–two in the NBA in overall field goal percentage last season, another tribute to Bird, who hand-feeds them for several easy baskets every game. Take away those hoops and they probably lose 50 points from their field goal percentage and 50 TENDEX rating points apiece.

The greatest testimonial for Bird is the Boston record with him as a member of the team. In 1978–79, the season before Bird joined the Celtics, they had one of their worst seasons ever with a record of 29–53. In his rookie season, 1979–80, they improved by a league-record 32 games to 61–21. Bird was the only impact player they added that season. They have consistently won 60 or more games, season after season, since then.

With Jordan the Bulls have improved, but much more modestly. They went from 27–55 in 1983–84 to 38–44 in his rookie season of 1984–85—an improvement of 11 games. Jordan missed nearly the entire 1985–86 season because of an injury and the Bulls slid eight games to 30–52. When he came back the season after that, they improved ten games to 40–42. Taking the average of those three changes, Jordan's presence in the lineup seems to be worth ten games to his team. His impact on a team's won–loss record is only about 30 percent as great as Bird's.

Barkley's effect on a team is questionable. In his first great year, 1985–86, the 76ers' record was four games worse than the year before. Since then the 76ers have lost Julius

Erving and Andrew Toney, two of their top players at that time, so further comparisons may be unfair. But the fact is that they have decreased in winning percentage every season, while Barkley has become more dominant and other players have become disgruntled.

Individually, Michael Jordan is the most dominant player in the NBA, with Charles Barkley second. But if I am trying to build a contending team, I start with Larry Bird.

Based on TENDEX, with intangibles taken into consideration, here are the first three NBA All-League teams for 1987–88:

FIRST TEAM
- AKEEM OLAJUWON, Houston, center... .782
- LARRY BIRD, Boston, forward......... .824
- KARL MALONE, Utah, forward .... .693
- MICHAEL JORDAN, Chicago, guard ... .887
- JOHN STOCKTON, Utah, guard....... .749

SECOND TEAM
- PATRICK EWING, New York, center ... .760
- CHARLES BARKLEY, Phila., forward .. .829
- DOMINIQUE WILKINS, Atl., forward.. .646
- MAGIC JOHNSON, LA Lakers, guard .. .721
- CLYDE DREXLER, Portland, guard.... .700

THIRD TEAM
- MOSES MALONE, Washington, center.. .677
- ROY TARPLEY, Dallas, forward........ .701
- LARRY NANCE, Phoe.-Cle., forward ... .677
- LAFAYETTE LEVER, Denver, guard ... .642
- GLENN RIVERS, Atlanta, guard....... .652

Other than Barkley, who yields a first-team position to Malone because of team chemistry, the only player who is listed out of order, according to TENDEX ratings, is Wilkins. He makes the second team because his importance to the Atlanta offense is comparable to Jordan's importance to Chicago's. Wilkins ranked No. 7 in the league in average minutes per game, while higher-rated players Tarpley, Nance, and Kevin McHale had less playing time because of injuries or coaching decisions. Wilkins had about 20 percent more playing time than these other three cornermen.

The first-team selection of Stockton over Magic Johnson is based strictly on 1987–88

performance. It's hard to overlook a guy who had the kind of season Stockton did, setting an NBA record for assists and ranking third in the league in both steals and two-point field goal percentage. Johnson had injury problems and when he did play was not as effective as the previous season, when his rating was .811 and he won Player of the Year honors.

Here are the top ten rated players from the 1987–88 season, regardless of position (minimum 2,000 minutes):

1. Michael Jordan, Chicago .... .887
2. Charles Barkley, Philadelphia .... .829
3. Larry Bird, Boston.................... .824
4. Akeem Olajuwon, Houston .... .782
5. Patrick Ewing, New York.............. .760
6. John Stockton, Utah.................. .749
7. Magic Johnson, LA Lakers .... .721
8. Roy Tarpley, Dallas................... .701
9. Clyde Drexler, Portland .... .700
10. Karl Malone, Utah .... .693

Full lists of leaders by positions are found in Chart 33 of Section III.

It is evident from the top ten list that the 1987–88 season was a good one for the 700 Club, with nine players achieving ratings of .700 or better. Four players joined the club by achieving .700 ratings for the first time— Ewing, Stockton, Tarpley, and Drexler.

In Rookie of the Year competition, there is a big difference between the voting of the NBA's coaches and the TENDEX ratings. New York's Mark Jackson was an easy winner in both, but Armon Gilliam and Kenny Smith, who tied for second in the coaches' voting, ranked only No. 8 and No. 11, respectively, in the ratings. Kevin Johnson, No. 9 in the coaches' voting, finished second in the TENDEX ratings. The top ten rookies according to TENDEX:

1. Mark Jackson, New York............. .545
2. Kevin Johnson, Cleveland-Phoenix .... .517
3. Derrick McKey, Seattle .... .492
4. Greg Anderson, San Antonio .... .490
5. Horace Grant, Chicago............... .478

6. Winston Garland, Golden State .... .453
7. Scottie Pippen, Chicago .... .451
8. Armon Gilliam, Phoenix .... .445
9. Tyrone Bogues, Washington .... .431
10. Reggie Miller, Indiana .... .419

The Boston Celtics dominated the Shootist statistics, utilizing the formula of points per total shots taken. A combination of ball-handling skills and individual shooting talent resulted in the Celtics finishing first on four of the five positional lists.

Robert Parish led the centers with a rating of 1.071. Kevin McHale paced the power forwards with a 1.075 rating. Bird led the small forwards with 1.071. Danny Ainge was the overall leader and headed the shooting guards with a rating of 1.093.

The only non-Celtic to win a position was John Stockton of Utah, the point guard leader with a rating of 1.080.

The top ten Shootists:

1. Danny Ainge, Boston 1.093
2. John Stockton, Utah................ 1.080
3. Kevin McHale, Boston 1.075
4. Larry Bird, Boston................. 1.071
5. Robert Parish, Boston.............. 1.071
6. Byron Scott, LA Lakers 1.053
7. Mark Price, Cleveland.............. 1.043
8. Chris Mullin, Golden State 1.014
9. Charles Barkley, Philadelphia 1.013
10. Dale Ellis, Seattle.................. 1.013

In the second Shootist category (percentage of all shots made), the leader was McHale, who sank .666 of all his field goal and free throw attempts. The second category is not as significant as the first because it is dominated by players who spend a lot of time at the free throw line. The pure shooters who attempt many three-pointers are virtually excluded from the second category.

The top ten two-point field goal percentage leaders (minimum 500 attempted) were:

1. Charles Barkley, Philadelphia .... .630
2. Kevin McHale, Boston .... .604
3. John Stockton, Utah................ .594
4. Robert Parish, Boston................ .590

5. Dennis Rodman, Detroit .... .568
6. Walter Berry, San Antonio............ .563
7. Buck Williams, New Jersey .... .560
8. Cliff Levingston, Atlanta .... .557
9. Patrick Ewing, New York............. .556
10. Byron Scott, LA Lakers .... .554

This list is different from the NBA's official field goal percentage leaders because, for some inexplicable reason, the NBA lists separate categories for two- and three-point field goal percentages while still incorporating the three-pointers into the regular field goal percentage listings. The listings for two- and three-pointers should be kept separate. As it is now, the three-pointers are included in both categories.

These are the three-point field goal percentage leaders (minimum 100 attempted):

1. Craig Hodges, Phoenix............... .491
2. Mark Price, Cleveland................ .486
3. Gerald Henderson, Philadelphia....... .423
4. Danny Ainge, Boston .... .415
5. Larry Bird, Boston................... .414
6. Trent Tucker, New York.............. .413
7. Dale Ellis, Seattle................... .413
8. Leon Wood, Atlanta .... .409
9. Michael Adams, Denver.............. .367
10. Dudley Bradley, New Jersey .... .363

It was a record-breaking season for three-point field goals. Both Hodges and Price exceeded the former record for highest percentage. Ainge, Adams, Ellis, and Bird all broke the mark for most total three-pointers in a season. Ainge's total of 144 three-pointers was 52 more than the previous record held by Darrell Griffith. Reggie Miller of Indiana made 61 three-pointers to top Bird's rookie record of 58.

The reason for the proliferation of three-pointers was that NBA coaches began discovering what a powerful weapon the three-point shot is. A player who averages .333 on three-pointers is equivalent to a .500 shooter on two-pointers. Hodges' .491 mark on three-pointers is equivalent to a two-point field goal percentage of .742.

Here are the free throw percentage leaders for 1987–88 (minimum of 200 attempts):

1. Jack Sikma, Milwaukee .... .922
2. Larry Bird, Boston. .... .916
3. Mike Gminski, New Jersey-Philadelphia... .906
4. Johnny Dawkins, San Antonio .... .896
5. Walter Davis, Phoenix .... .887
6. Chris Mullin, Golden State .... .885
7. Jeff Malone, Washington .... .882
8. Mark Price, Cleveland. .... .877
9. Bill Laimbeer, Detroit .... .874
10. Rolando Blackman, Dallas .... .873

With Sikma, Bird, and Gminski all exceeding .900, it was the first time in NBA history that three players had topped that mark in the same season. John Long of Indiana (.907) also went over .900, but fell 17 attempts short of the qualifying level.

Selecting the league's best sixth man was easy. Roy Tarpley of Dallas, with the best per-minute rebounding percentage of the 1980s, was the runaway leader with a TENDEX rating of .701. The rest of the starting five consisted of center Bill Cartwright of New York, .627; forward Dennis Rodman of Detroit, .618; guard Otis Smith of Denver–Golden State, .553; and guard Kevin Johnson of Cleveland–Phoenix, .517. Johnson actually trailed Sam Vincent of Chicago by one percentage point but was cited because he played over 400 more minutes than Vincent.

The sixth man ratings are not identical to the listing of reserves (Chart 51, Section III) because the listing of reserves is limited to players playing less than 2,000 minutes. The basis for our sixth-man ratings is that players must not have started as many as half of their teams' games, regardless of how many minutes they played. By this standard, Tarpley, Rodman, Cliff Levingston of Atlanta (.530), and John Williams of Washington (.497) all played more than 2,000 minutes but qualified for the sixth-man ratings.

In the PAR category, the only PAR-7 player was Lafayette Lever of Denver. He averaged better than 7 points, 7 assists, and 7 rebounds per game. His actual averages were

18.9 points, 7.8 assists, and 8.1 rebounds. Magic Johnson, Larry Bird, and Alvin Robertson all attained PAR-6 ratings, while Clyde Drexler, Michael Jordan, and Paul Pressey were PAR-5 players.

In the most important category related to PAR (points plus assists plus rebounds divided by minutes played) the leader was Bird. The top ten in this listing:

1. Larry Bird, Boston. 1.162
2. Michael Jordan, Chicago 1.148
3. Charles Barkley, Philadelphia 1.096
4. Karl Malone, Utah 1.079
5. Dominique Wilkins, Atlanta 1.042
6. Clyde Drexler, Portland 1.041
7. Akeem Olajuwon, Houston 1.034
8. Magic Johnson, LA Lakers 1.032
9. Mark Aguirre, Dallas 1.012
10. Alex English, Denver .... .977

In the BEST ball-control ratings, the top ten was dominated by shot-blockers. Five players, headed by Mark Eaton of Utah, totaled more blocked shots than turnovers. Four, led by guards Lafayette Lever and Michael Adams of Denver, registered more steals than turnovers. These were the BEST leaders (formula: blocks plus steals minus turnovers divided by minutes played):

1. Mark Eaton, Utah .... +.078
2. John Williams, Cleveland. .... +.048
3. Akeem Olajuwon, Houston .... +.047
4. Michael Jordan, Chicago .... +.042
5. John Salley, Detroit. .... +.035
6. Larry Nance, Phoenix-Cleveland ..... +.028
7. Benoit Benjamin, LA Clippers .... +.024
8. Patrick Ewing, New York. .... +.023
9. Alvin Robertson, San Antonio .... +.021
10. Randy Breuer, Milwaukee .... +.020

Another significant ball-control statistic is the ratio of assists to turnovers. John Stockton of Utah was the easy leader in this category with 866 more assists than turnovers in 1987–88. His ratio of 4.31 assists to every turnover also was the best in the league. Chart 49 in Section III lists the players with the best ratios of assists to turnovers on the basis of this formula: Assists minus turnovers divided by minutes played. Stockton also lead in this category with a +.305 rating.

Ten players exceeded 3,000 minutes of playing time during 1987–88. These were Michael Jordan of Chicago, 3311; Mark Jackson of New York, 3249; Karl Malone of Utah, 3198; Charles Barkley of Philadelphia, 3170; Otis Thorpe of Sacramento, 3072; Lafayette Lever of Denver, 3061; Clyde Drexler of Portland, 3060; Byron Scott of the Los Angeles Lakers, 3048; Derek Harper of Dallas, 3032; and Danny Ainge of Boston, 3018. Surprises were Ainge leading Bird and the other Celtics, Scott leading Johnson and the rest of the Lakers, and the rookie Jackson placing second overall in the league.

Other 1987–88 individual leaders, all of which are based on per-minute statistics with a 2,000-minute minimum:

- POINTS—Michael Jordan, Chicago 866
- ASSISTS—John Stockton, Utah 397
- REBOUNDS—Roy Tarpley, Dallas 416
- BLOCKED SHOTS—Mark Eaton, Utah 111
- STEALS—John Stockton, Utah 085
- TURNOVERS—Randy Wittman, Atlanta . . .034

Full charts for all individual categories are listed in Section III, as are ratings for teams. According to the TENDEX system, team ratings for 1987–88 were:

1. Boston Celtics 106.4
2. Utah Jazz 105.8
3. Los Angeles Lakers 105.1
4. Chicago Bulls 104.7
5. Portland Trail Blazers 104.5
6. Detroit Pistons 103.9
7. Atlanta Hawks 103.6
8. Seattle Supersonics 103.2
9. Dallas Mavericks 103.0
10. Denver Nuggets 101.8
11. Houston Rockets 101.7
12. Cleveland Cavaliers 101.2
13. Milwaukee Bucks 100.4
14. New York Knicks 99.6
15. Indiana Pacers 99.0

16. Washington Bullets 97.9
17. Philadelphia 76ers 97.2
18. Phoenix Suns 97.0
19. San Antonio Spurs 95.2
20. Sacramento Kings 94.8
21. Golden State Warriors 92.3
22. New Jersey Nets 92.0
23. Los Angeles Clippers 89.4

A team's rating is figured by subtracting from its TENDEX rating its opponents' rating and using 100 as the neutral number. Armed with these team ratings, I was able to predict on a nationally syndicated radio sports talk program that Utah would upset Portland in the playoffs and that the Los Angeles Lakers would have problems with the Jazz in the second round, although the Lakers still had to be favored on the basis of home-court advantage.

Home-court advantage in the NBA is worth four points. At home, against Utah or the Lakers, the Celtics rated as five-point favorites at season's end, according to these ratings, but on the road they were three-point underdogs to these two teams.

The most lopsided potential game at the end of the 1987–88 season would have matched the Celtics (106.4) against the Los Angeles Clippers (89.4) in Boston. To the 17-point differential between the two teams' TENDEX ratings is added a four-point edge for the home court. The Celtics therefore should have been able to beat the Clippers by 21 points at home and by 13 on the road.

I computed the home-court advantage as four points by listing scores of all games for an entire season. This showed an average victory margin of four points for the home teams.

The overall ratings of NBA teams were much closer in 1987–88 than in 1986–87 when three teams exceeded 107, while the Lakers graded out with an awesome 109.0 and easily won the title. However, the Lakers, with Kareem Abdul-Jabbar fading fast and Magic Johnson troubled by injuries, lost four points of their power rating last season and could lose their supremacy in the Western Conference the 1988–89 season unless they make a major trade.

An interesting aspect of the TENDEX system is that it can be used to rate coaches as well as players. Teams that win more games than would be expected based on their player ratings obviously must be either lucky or well-coached. On this basis, the top coaches of 1987–88 were:

1. Pat Riley, Los Angeles Lakers. . . . . +8
2. Doug Moe, Denver Nuggets . . . . +8
3. John MacLeod, Dallas Mavericks . . . . +6
4. Bob Weiss, San Antonio Spurs . . . . +3
5. Bill Fitch, Houston Rockets . . . . +2
6. Chuck Daly, Detroit Pistons . . . . +1

The impact of coaches is perhaps overrated. Riley, Moe, and MacLeod were probably the only ones who significantly improved their team's winning percentage. Twelve of the 23 teams won precisely the number of games they could have been expected to win according to these ratings.

It is noteworthy that all players and coaches mentioned in this section of *The Basketball Abstract* are listed with the teams with which they finished the 1987–88 season. A publishing deadline required the completion of this book before the summer trading season was over. The TENDEX statistics are accurate, but in some cases it may be necessary to switch a recently-traded player from his former team to his current one in order to see the correct perspective for the 1988–89 season.

2

Atlanta Hawks

Coached by Mike Fratello, the Hawks compiled a record of 50–32 in 1987–88, tied for seventh best in the NBA. Their TEN-DEX rating of 103.6 was also the league's seventh best.

Strengths of the Hawks are depth and defense. Complementing all-stars Dominique Wilkins and Glenn (Doc) Rivers is a strong bench. Reserves Cliff Levingston, Antoine Carr, John Battle, Jon Koncak, and Spud Webb were better basketball players last season than starters Tree Rollins, Kevin Willis, and Randy Wittman. Rollins and Wittman no longer are with the team; they have been replaced by All-Star center Moses Malone and Reggie Theus.

Defensively, the Hawks held 1987–88 opponents to 104.3 points per game, nearly four points below the league average. The Hawks' defense was keyed by shot-blockers Rollins, Levingston, Carr, and Koncak. The team ranked second in the NBA in blocking shots.

The corollary of the blocked shot is opponents' field goal percentage. Sparked by the intimidation of the blocked shot, the Hawks held their opponents to a field goal mark of .471. The league average was .480.

Another team strength for the Hawks is ball-control. They ranked No. 2 in the NBA last season in the BEST category comprising blocked shots plus steals minus turnovers.

MOSES MALONE

AGE: 33
HEIGHT: 6-10
WEIGHT: 255
POSITION: Center
EXPERIENCE: 12 Seasons
COLLEGE: None
BIRTHPLACE: Petersburg, VA
1987–88 TENDEX: .677

It was mostly in deference to the popular Julius Erving that the NBA decided to begin counting combined NBA and ABA statistics, but it is Malone who is likely to rewrite the record book as a result of that decision. Turning pro directly out of high school, Malone spent two productive seasons in the ABA before joining the NBA . . . counting the ABA seasons, he already ranks among the all-time top ten in rebounds, blocked shots, and free throws attempted and free throws made . . . at age 33 he is still an excellent player . . . will probably break into the top ten this season in points and games played . . . last season he rated No. 6 in the NBA in rebounds per minute, No. 18 in points per minute, No. 11 in PAR percentage, No. 17 in Shootist percentage, and No. 11 in TENDEX . . . was in the bottom ten in turnovers and ratio of steals to turnovers . . . in the center ratings, Malone was No. 2 in rebounds and PAR percentage, No. 3 in scoring and TENDEX, No. 4 in Shootist percentage, and No. 6 in minutes and free throw percentage . . . ratings ranged from No. 16 to No. 19 in all ball-control categories . . . honors include NBA Playoff MVP in 1983, four first-team All-NBA selections, five rebounding titles, and MVP awards in 1979, 1982, and 1983.

DOMINIQUE WILKINS

AGE: 28
HEIGHT: 6-8
WEIGHT: 200
POSITION: Small Forward
EXPERIENCE: 6 Seasons
COLLEGE: Georgia
BIRTHPLACE: Sorbonne, France
1987–88 TENDEX: .646

An explosive player, exceeded in pure talent by only Michael Jordan and Charles Barkley, Wilkins won an NBA scoring title in 1985–86, and was named to the first All-League team that season . . . lifetime scoring average is 25.8, with a high of 30.7 last season, No. 2 in the league . . . won NBA slam-dunk contest in 1985 and was runnerup to Jordan in controversial competition last year in Chicago . . . has never missed more than four games in a season, twice totaling more than 3,000 minutes played . . . No. 1 among the small forwards last season in scoring, No. 2 in PAR, No. 2 in minutes played, No. 3 in TENDEX rating, No. 5 in steals, No. 7 in free throw percentage . . . Wilkins is a good ball-handler and passer but he sometimes tries to play too much one-on-one offense . . . despite his high scoring, his 1987–88 Shootist rating was only No. 16 out of 22 qualifying small forwards.

MALONE

1987–88	2PFG	3PFG	F.T.	REB.	AST.	STL.	T.O.	BLK.	PTS.
Per Game	.488	.286	.788	11.2	1.4	0.8	3.2	0.9	20.3
Per Minute	.488	.286	.788	.328	.042	.022	.092	.027	.597
Rating	18	2	6	2	16	12	18	16	3

WILKINS

1987–88	2PFG	3PFG	F.T.	REB.	AST.	STL.	T.O.	BLK.	PTS.
Per Game	.476	.295	.826	6.4	2.9	1.3	2.8	0.6	30.7
Per Minute	.476	.295	.826	.170	.076	.035	.074	.016	.813
Rating	19	10	7	14	15	5	17	16	1

GLENN (DOC) RIVERS

AGE: 27
HEIGHT: 6-4
WEIGHT: 185
POSITION: Point Guard
EXPERIENCE: 5 Seasons
COLLEGE: Marquette
BIRTHPLACE: Chicago
1987–88 TENDEX: .652

The only thing that is keeping Rivers from being as much of an impact player as Wilkins is durability; he lacks the physical strength to play 40 minutes, or even 35 minutes per game, but his TENDEX rating the past two seasons has been equal to Wilkins's . . . ranked No. 3 in the NBA in assists last season with .299 per minute, No. 6 on the all-time best list with .318 per minute in 1986–87 . . . in 1987–88 he was No. 3 among the point guards in TENDEX rating, No. 3 in the PAR per-minute category, No. 3 in rebounds, No. 5 in BEST, No. 6 in points, No. 5 in assist-turnover ratio, No. 7 in steals . . . Rivers's major weakness is shooting: He was 20th out of 20 qualifying point guards in the Shootist ratings . . . lack of physical durability is reflected in the fact that he has missed 45 games in his five NBA seasons and never has averaged more than 31 minutes per game.

KEVIN WILLIS

AGE: 26
HEIGHT: 7-0
WEIGHT: 235
POSITION: Power Forward
EXPERIENCE: 4 Seasons
COLLEGE: Michigan State
BIRTHPLACE: Los Angeles
1987–88 TENDEX: .479

After apparently maturing as an NBA player with a .617 TENDEX rating in 1986–87, Willis regressed last season to .479, 18th among the league's power forwards . . . reserve teammate Cliff Levingston had a .530 rating . . . Willis was bothered by an injury, playing 535 fewer minutes than the previous season . . . he dropped off in scoring average from 16.1 to 11.6 and in rebounding from 10.5 to 7.3 . . . finished last in the league in assists, last in PAR, and last among 22 qualifying power forwards in free throw percentage . . . strong points in his game were steals (seventh among power forwards) and two-point field goal percentage (seventh).

RIVERS

1987–88	2PFG	3PFG	F.T.	REB.	AST.	STL.	T.O.	BLK.	PTS.
Per Game	.460	.273	.758	4.6	9.3	1.8	2.6	0.5	14.2
Per Minute	.460	.273	.758	.146	.299	.056	.080	.016	.453
Rating	18	13	20	3	3	7	14	2	6

WILLIS

1987–88	2PFG	3PFG	F.T.	REB.	AST.	STL.	T.O.	BLK.	PTS.
Per Game	.520	.000	.649	7.3	0.4	0.9	1.8	0.5	11.6
Per Minute	.520	.000	.649	.262	.013	.033	.066	.020	.417
Rating	7	16	22	10	20	7	12	10	12

CLIFF LEVINGSTON

AGE: 27
HEIGHT: 6-8
WEIGHT: 210
POSITION: Power Forward
EXPERIENCE: 6 Seasons
COLLEGE: Wichita State
BIRTHPLACE: St. Louis
1987–88 TENDEX: .530

Levingston set a personal career high in minutes played last season with 2,135 because of Kevin Willis' injury and slump . . . led NBA power forwards in lowest turnover percentage, placed No. 3 in blocked shots, No. 3 in Shootist and BEST ratings, No. 5 in two-point field goal percentage, No. 8 in free throw percentage . . . turnover ranking was No. 4 in the league . . . Levingston had one problem in common with Willis, poor passing. He ranked 19th among NBA power forwards in assists and had the sixth worst rating in the league.

REGGIE THEUS

AGE: 31
HEIGHT: 6-7
WEIGHT: 213
POSITION: Shooting Guard
EXPERIENCE: 10 Seasons
COLLEGE: Nevada-Las Vegas
BIRTHPLACE: Inglewood, CA
1987–88 TENDEX: .483

One of the NBA's glamor players, Theus probably could have become a millionaire with product endorsements if he had spent as much of his NBA career playing for teams in New York and Los Angeles as he did in Sacramento and Kansas City . . . excellent scorer, finished No. 13 in the league last season with a 21.6 average, second best of his career . . . also a good play maker, ranked No. 5 among shooting guards in assists . . . other good shooting guard ratings were No. 6 in PAR percentage, No. 6 in scoring, and No. 10 in TENDEX . . . defensive deficiencies were evident with ratings of No. 18 in ratio of steals to turnovers, No. 17 in ratio of blocked shots to turnovers, and No. 18 in BEST—ranked in the NBA's bottom ten in these three categories . . . with 14,771 points, Theus probably will pass 15,000 early this season and could wind up the year with 16,000 or more for his career.

LEVINGSTON

1987–88	2PFG	3PFG	F.T.	REB.	AST.	STL.	T.O.	BLK.	PTS.
Per Game	.557	.500	.772	6.2	0.9	0.6	1.1	1.0	10.0
Per Minute	.557	.500	.772	.236	.033	.024	.044	.039	.384
Rating	5	2	8	14	19	15	1	3	15

THEUS

1987–88	2PFG	3PFG	F.T.	REB.	AST.	STL.	T.O.	BLK.	PTS.
Per Game	.479	.271	.831	3.2	6.3	0.8	3.2	0.2	21.6
Per Minute	.479	.271	.831	.087	.175	.022	.088	.006	.593
Rating	12	10	12	13	5	16	17	11	6

RESERVES

Center Jon Koncak (.478), power forward Cliff Levingston (.530), and shooting guard John Battle (.460) had better ratings than the players they substituted for last season.

Former Wichita State University front-court teammates Levingston and Antoine Carr (.558) probably will continue as reserves, as will point guard Spud Webb (.507).

Carr was the third rated reserve in the NBA last season, while Webb ranked No. 18. Levingston was a contender for sixth-man honors.

Overall, the Hawks' group of reserves was the strongest in the NBA. There were times when they played better as a unit than the starters.

OUTLOOK

At the beginning of the 1987–88 season, Atlanta seemed to be the strongest team in the Central Division of the NBA. The Detroit Pistons took control when three of the Hawks' top eight players missed long periods of time because of injuries.

Atlanta has improved itself at two of its weak positions. One was through the trade of Randy Wittman (TENDEX .354) to Sacramento for Reggie Theus (.483). The other was through the signing of free agent All-Star center, Moses Malone (.677).

Barring another rash of injuries, Atlanta could put up one of the best records in the NBA during the 1988–89 regular season—possibly even *the* best record.

Probable finish: First in Central Division.

3

Boston Celtics

Since Larry Bird brought his clever skills to the NBA in 1979–80, the Celtics have averaged 62 victories per season. Kevin McHale and Robert Parish joined Bird in the Boston frontcourt in 1980–81.

The Celtics led the NBA in five team statistical categories last season, including overall TENDEX power rating, 106.5.

Boston's other areas of leadership were two-point field goal percentage, three-point field goal percentage, Shootist, and assists. The first three are directly related to the last.

By leading in assists the Celtics demonstrated the kind of teamwork necessary to earn high-percentage shots. Of course, it helps when you have good shooters, too. Four of the Celts—Bird, McHale, Parish, and Danny Ainge—were league-leading Shootists at their respective positions. The Shootist statistic is based on points per shot. The Celtics were the only NBA team to average more than one point for every shot. Their 1.012 Shootist percentage was the second highest in NBA history. The Los Angeles Lakers set the record with 1.022 in 1984–85.

Boston also placed high in two other shooting-related stats—No. 3 in points and No. 5 in PAR (points plus assists plus rebounds).

However, the fact that Boston's PAR rating was only No. 5, when the team led in both points and assists, pinpointed a weakness in rebounding. The Celtics ranked only No. 21 out of the NBA's 23 teams in rebounding.

Boston also ranked low in two of the BEST categories, steals (21st) and blocked shots (14th).

The Celtics' decline in physically-demanding aspects of play in which they used to excel is perhaps a sign of the aging of their star players. Parish is 35, Dennis Johnson, 34, Bird, 31, McHale, 30, and Ainge, 29.

LARRY BIRD

AGE: 31
HEIGHT: 6-9
WEIGHT: 220
POSITION: Small Forward
EXPERIENCE: 9 Seasons
COLLEGE: Indiana State
BIRTHPLACE: West Baden, IN
1987–88 TENDEX: .824

In some ways 1987–88 was the best season for Bird, who has been a first-team all-star all nine of his NBA seasons . . . the only player ever to average better than .500 field goal percentage and .900 free throw percentage (1986–87 and 1987–88) . . . last year became the first Celtic ever to score 2,000 points four seasons in a row . . . had personal career highs in scoring (29.9), overall field goal percentage (.527), two-point field goal percentage (.546), free throw percentage (.916), and Shootist percentage (1.071) . . . out of 22 small forwards, ranked among the top three in 11 categories, including first in Shootist, PAR, minutes played, free throw percentage, assists, and TENDEX rating; second in points, steals, and three-point field goal percentage; third in two-point field goal percentage and rebounds . . . PAR-6 rating was just short of career-best PAR-7 . . . the only apparently weak part of his game was turnovers (No. 15), but appearances are deceptive: Every playmaker commits turnovers and Bird is the best playmaking forward in basketball . . . career highlights: NBA Most Valuable Player and TENDEX rating leader 1984, 1985, 1986; Rookie of the Year 1980; playoff MVP 1984 and 1986; All-Star Game MVP 1982: lifetime scoring average 25.0.

KEVIN McHALE

AGE: 30
HEIGHT: 6-10
WEIGHT: 225
POSITION: Power Forward
EXPERIENCE: 8 Seasons
COLLEGE: Minnesota
BIRTHPLACE: Hibbing, MN
1987–88 TENDEX: .665

Win some, lose some: Teammates joke about McHale's reluctance to pass the ball, but he is a pretty good passer, ranking seventh in assists among the NBA's power forwards last season; on the other hand, he is a perennial All-Defensive team choice, an honor he sometimes does not deserve . . . was selected again last season even though his blocked shots dropped off by almost 50 percent . . . strengths are shooting and scoring: No. 1 power forward in both Shootist categories, second in two-point field goal percentage, fourth in free throw percentage, fourth in scoring . . . led NBA in Shootist percentage by making .666 of all his shots . . . in 1986–87 became first player in NBA history to exceed .600 in field goal percentage and .800 in free throw percentage, and had a career-best TENDEX rating of .742 . . . slowed by a foot injury last season, most of his statistics fell off slightly and he finished last in the league in steals.

BIRD

1987–88	2PFG	3PFG	F.T.	REB.	AST.	STL.	T.O.	BLK.	PTS.
Per Game	.546	.414	.916	9.3	6.1	1.6	2.8	0.8	29.9
Per Minute	.546	.414	.916	.237	.158	.042	.072	.019	.767
Rating	3	2	1	3	1	2	15	12	2

McHALE

1987–88	2PFG	3PFG	F.T.	REB.	AST.	STL.	T.O.	BLK.	PTS.
Per Game	.604	.000	.797	8.4	2.7	0.4	2.2	1.4	22.6
Per Minute	.604	.000	.797	.225	.072	.011	.059	.039	.605
Rating	2	11	4	15	7	20	7	4	4

ROBERT PARISH

AGE: 35
HEIGHT: 7-0
WEIGHT: 230
POSITION: Center
EXPERIENCE: 12 Seasons
COLLEGE: Centenary
BIRTHPLACE: Shreveport, LA
1987–88 TENDEX: .579

Parish is a TENDEX 700 Club member who began to show signs of age last season when his rating dropped to a career-low .579, but was still the sixth best center in the NBA . . . No. 1 center in Shootist (1.071) and two-point field goal percentage (.590) ratings . . . field goal percentage was best of his career . . . not quite as dominant underneath basket as in the past, with rebounding average falling to 8.5 per game and blocked shots dipping to 1.1 per game . . . still runs floor well on fast break and has defensive quickness (No. 7 center in steals) . . . a durable player, he never has missed more than 10 games in any of his 12 seasons . . . played four years with Golden State before joining Celtics in 1980–81 . . . in eight seasons with Celts his scoring average is two points higher and his field goal percentage is 57 points higher than they were with Golden State.

DANNY AINGE

AGE: 29
HEIGHT: 6-5
WEIGHT: 185
POSITION: Shooting Guard
EXPERIENCE: 7 Seasons
COLLEGE: Brigham Young
BIRTHPLACE: Eugene, OR
1987–88 TENDEX: .463

TENDEX rating underestimates Ainge's value to Celtics . . . had career-high 3,018 minutes played in 1987–88, leading team; one of ten NBA players to play 3,000 minutes . . . led NBA in Shootist points-per-shot with 1.093 rating . . . led league with a record 144 three-point field goals and finished fourth in three-point percentage (.415) . . . high ratings among shooting guards included second-lowest turnover ratio, No. 4 in two-point field goal percentage, No. 5 in free throw percentage, No. 6 in assists, No. 8 in BEST, No. 10 in steals . . . ranked only No. 16 in scoring, but Celtics concentrate on working ball inside to big men . . . a tough defensive player, as good as any Celtic.

PARISH

1987–88	2PFG	3PFG	F.T.	REB.	AST.	STL.	T.O.	BLK.	PTS.
Per Game	.590	.000	.734	8.5	1.6	0.7	2.1	1.1	14.3
Per Minute	.590	.000	.734	.272	.050	.024	.067	.036	.459
Rating	1	11	13	7	11	7	10	14	12

AINGE

1987–88	2PFG	3PFG	F.T.	REB.	AST.	STL.	T.O.	BLK.	PTS.
Per Game	.534	.415	.878	3.1	6.2	1.4	1.9	0.2	15.7
Per Minute	.534	.415	.878	.083	.167	.038	.051	.006	.421
Rating	4	3	5	14	6	10	2	12	16

DENNIS JOHNSON

AGE: 34
HEIGHT: 6-4
WEIGHT: 202
POSITION: Point Guard
EXPERIENCE: 12 Seasons
COLLEGE: Pepperdine
BIRTHPLACE: San Pedro, CA
1987–88 TENDEX: .440

It would be too easy to declare that D.J. is the most overrated player in the NBA. He certainly is the weak link in the Celtics' starting unit and at times seems to play lackadaisically during the regular season; but then comes playoff time and he turns mean . . . won playoff MVP trophy in 1978–79 as a member of the Seattle Supersonics . . . is the only current Celtic to have earned championship rings with two different teams . . . All-NBA first team in 1981 . . . skills have declined in recent seasons . . . only No. 18 Shootist last season out of 20 point guards, while other four Celtic starters all were positional leaders . . . No. 20 (last place) in two-point field goal percentage, No. 19 in steals, No. 17 in points, and No. 17 in TENDEX rating . . . high rankings were No. 5 in free throw percentage, No. 5 in blocked shots, and No. 8 in assists.

RESERVES

None of the Boston reserves play enough (1,500 or more minutes) to be considered sixth men. They are mostly stopgap substitutes, but a few of them are useful in game situations.

Brad Lohaus (TENDEX rating .461) will probably play a lot more for Robert Parish this season, and Mark Acres (.383) will fill in more for Kevin McHale.

Other reserves who occasionally make good contributions are point guard Dirk Minniefield (.379) and shooting guard Jim Paxson, who scored the 10,000th point of his NBA career last season for Portland before being traded to Boston.

The Celtics also have hopes for Reggie Lewis, their No. 1 draft choice of 1987.

JOHNSON

1987–88	2PFG	3PFG	F.T.	REB.	AST.	STL.	T.O.	BLK.	PTS.
Per Game	.449	.261	.856	3.1	7.8	1.2	2.5	0.4	12.6
Per Minute	.449	.261	.856	.090	.224	.035	.073	.011	.364
Rating	20	14	5	12	8	19	9	5	17

OUTLOOK

The best break the Boston Celtics got in their 1988 playoff series against Detroit was Larry Bird's foul trouble in the fourth game. After Bird committed his fifth foul in the third quarter, he went to the bench for six minutes, his longest rest of the playoffs.

When Bird re-entered the game, rested, he scored seven straight points and the Celtics went on from there to win.

Here's the point: The Celtics aren't as bad as they looked against the Pistons. They shot poorly because they were exhausted. They actually had the best team TENDEX rating in the NBA last season, but got a poor coaching job from K.C. Jones, who, uncharacteristic of Celtic coaches, did not know how to use a bench. Jones "retired" after finishing with the third worst TENDEX rating of the NBA's 23 coaches.

The Celtics have a respectable bench. Otherwise they would not have left Dennis Johnson unprotected in the expansion draft. Brad Lohaus will be the team's starting center some day, and Mark Acres, Reggie Lewis, Jim Paxson, Dirk Minniefield, and rookie Brian Shaw add depth behind the league's best starting lineup.

Don't be surprised if new coach Jim Rodgers brings Danny Ainge off the bench. The Celtics tradition is to use top shooting guards—such as Frank Ramsey and John Havlicek—as sixth men.

Probable finish: First in Atlantic Division.

4

Chicago Bulls

*A*s long as Michael the Archangel is able to make heavenward ascents, the Bulls will be contenders for the NBA championship. With Jordan winning practically every major NBA award last season, Chicago registered its best record (50–32) since 1973–74.

Although the Bulls depend on Jordan for one-third of their scoring, they are a well-balanced team with many fine athletes. Otherwise, they could not have ranked No. 4 in the league last season in TENDEX efficiency rating (1.047), trailing only Boston, Utah, and the Los Angeles Lakers.

Coached by Doug Collins, the Bulls play strong defense, holding opponents to 101.6 points per game last season (No. 1 in the league) and a field goal percentage of .470 (tied for No. 4).

Jordan helped the Bulls outscore their opponents by 3.4 points per game while power forward Charles Oakley helped them outrebound their foes by 4.2 per game.

The Bulls also did well in the BEST ball-control category (No. 3), turnovers (No. 4), two-point field goal percentage (No. 7), blocked shots (No. 8), assists (No. 9), and Shootist (No. 9).

On the negative side, the Bulls lack a balanced offense, relying too much on Jordan. They have the next-to-worst long-range shooting team in the NBA (No. 22 in three-point field goal percentage) and rank No. 20 in scoring, No. 16 in free throw percentage, and No. 15 in PAR.

MICHAEL JORDAN

AGE: 25
HEIGHT: 6-6
WEIGHT: 198
POSITION: Shooting Guard
EXPERIENCE: 4 Seasons
COLLEGE: North Carolina
BIRTHPLACE: Brooklyn, NY
1987–88 TENDEX: .887

Jordan's TENDEX rating in 1987–88 was the second best by a guard in NBA history and the best by a shooting guard. Oscar Robertson holds the backcourt record with .892 in 1961–62 . . . on the basis of position, Jordan's rating was the best of any player in NBA history. His 1.971 easily topped Wilt Chamberlain's 1.885 positional ratio in 1961–62. Chamberlain's TENDEX rating that season was a league record 1.037, but Jordan moved ahead of him when the ratings were divided by positional norms. The norm for a center is .550, while for a shooting guard it is .450 . . . Jordan swept 1987–88 NBA honors, winning MVP, All-Star Game MVP, the slam-dunk contest, and Defensive Player of the Year . . . besides leading the league in scoring (35.0), he was among the leaders in both Shootist statistics, field goal and free throw percentage, BEST, blocked shots, and steals. He was one of four players to compile more steals than turnovers, led the league in minutes played, and was one of seven players to achieve a PAR-5 rating or better . . . had more than 200 steals and 100 blocks for a second straight season, the only NBA player ever to do this . . . career scoring average: 32.7.

DAVE CORZINE

AGE: 32
HEIGHT: 6-11
WEIGHT: 265
POSITION: Center
EXPERIENCE: 10 Seasons
COLLEGE: DePaul
BIRTHPLACE: Chicago
1987–88 TENDEX: .482

The Bulls are like the Hawks in having to surround two exceptional players with three of average or below-average ability in the starting lineup. Corzine is one of the Bulls' below-average starters . . . the best thing about him is stamina. He has played every game in six of the past eight seasons and missed only two games last year . . . a good ball-handler, he had the lowest turnover ratio of the NBA's centers in 1987–88 and ranked sixth in assists and eighth in BEST . . . however, in five important categories he ranked No. 19 out of 22 centers. These were scoring, two-point field goal percentage, Shootist percentage on all shots, PAR, and TENDEX rating. Was No. 20 in steals and No. 17 in rebounding.

JORDAN

1987–88	2PFG	3PFG	F.T.	REB.	AST.	STL.	T.O.	BLK.	PTS.
Per Game	.546	.132	.860	5.5	5.9	3.2	3.1	1.6	35.0
Per Minute	.546	.132	.860	.136	.146	.078	.076	.040	.866
Rating	3	16	8	4	8	2	12	1	1

CORZINE

1987–88	2PFG	3PFG	F.T.	REB.	AST.	STL.	T.O.	BLK.	PTS.
Per Game	.486	.111	.752	6.6	1.9	0.5	1.4	1.1	10.1
Per Minute	.486	.111	.752	.226	.066	.015	.047	.041	.345
Rating	19	5	12	17	6	20	1	10	19

BRAD SELLERS

AGE: 25
HEIGHT: 7-0
WEIGHT: 227
POSITION: Small Forward
EXPERIENCE: 2 Seasons
COLLEGE: Ohio State
BIRTHPLACE: Cleveland
1987–88 TENDEX: .349

To classify a seven-footer as a small forward may seem silly enough, but to make things even sillier, Brad Sellers plays too "small" to be an effective small forward . . . Sellers averaged only three rebounds per game as the Bulls' starting small forward last season and was replaced in the starting lineup during the playoffs by rookie Scottie Pippen, a change that probably will be made permanent this season . . . out of 22 qualifying small forwards, Sellers was 22nd in scoring, 22nd in TENDEX rating, 22nd in PAR, 21st in rebounding, 21st in steals, 20th in Shootist, and 24th in two-point field goal percentage. No, that isn't a mistake: There were two extra players in the two-point field goal category who did not play 2,000 minutes but did reach the qualifying number of 500 shots attempted . . . if ever there was a player ripe for benching, Sellers is that player.

RESERVES

Of the 100 reserves who played between 1,000 and 2,000 minutes last season, Bill Cartwright was the league leader with a TENDEX rating of .627. Cartwright, obtained by the Bulls from New York in the Charles Oakley trade, managed enough field goal attempts in 1987–88 to qualify as No. 15 in the league in that category. He ranks No. 1 on the NBA's all-time field goal percentage list.

Last season's Chicago rookies Scottie Pippen and Horace Grant could be starters this season for the Bulls at the two corner positions. Pippen was drafted higher in 1987 (No. 5 compared to No. 10 for Grant), but Grant had a more consistent first season, achieving the better TENDEX rating, .478 to .451. Both players have the talent to become NBA stars.

Although Sam Vincent didn't play enough minutes to qualify as a regular last season, he took over the point guard job late in the season and maintained a very good .518 rating. He could start from the first game this season.

The other Chicago reserves are guards John Paxson (.393) and Rory Sparrow (.294).

SELLERS

1987–88	2PFG	3PFG	F.T.	REB.	AST.	STL.	T.O.	BLK.	PTS.
Per Game	.460	.143	.790	3.1	1.7	0.4	1.1	0.8	9.5
Per Minute	.460	.143	.790	.113	.064	.015	.041	.030	.351
Rating	24	16	12	21	17	21	2	4	22

OUTLOOK

The Bulls probably have gone as far as they can with essentially a one-player team and, with this in mind, they are striving to improve at other positions.

The trade of Charles Oakley for Bill Cartwright and the drafting of Will Perdue strengthened them at the most important position—center. But did they set themselves back at power forward by dealing Oakley?

Chicago is gambling that Horace Grant can take over the power forward job, and Grant unquestionably is an outstanding athlete. His TENDEX rating of .478 was No. 5 among rookies last season. But he is not as good a rebounder as Oakley, the No. 2 rebounder in the NBA last season.

If the Bulls are to improve this season, it will have to come from development of young players such as Grant, small forward Scottie Pippen, point guard Sam Vincent, and Perdue, and these players will be able to improve only in proportion to the roles they are given in the offense.

Oakley wasn't just being a malcontent last spring when he complained about Chicago's one-dimensional offense. Great as MVP Michael Jordan is, Coach Doug Collins needs to show more confidence in other players. Jordan took 31 percent of the Bulls' total shots last season.

Probable finish: Third in Central Division.

5

Cleveland Cavaliers

*D*uring the telecast of the fifth game of the 1988 Chicago–Cleveland playoff series, when the Bulls held serve, as it were, winning on their home court to advance to the second round, one of the television commentators opined that the Cavaliers had more championship potential than the Bulls.

Although the Bulls have an outstanding young team, with five good players age 25 and under, the commentator probably was correct.

Through shrewd dealing and drafting the past two years, the Cavaliers have managed to stock themselves with one all-star, Larry Nance, and six fine young players. Cleveland already was a team to be reckoned with during the 1987–88 season and could vault into contention for a Central Division title this season as these young players mature.

Coached by Len Wilkens, the Cavs compiled a 42–40 record last season and ranked No. 12 in the league with a TENDEX power rating of 1.012.

Statistically, the Cavs rated No. 2 in the NBA in three-point field goal percentage, No. 3 in blocked shots, No. 7 in steals, No. 8 in two-point field goal percentage, and No. 8 in BEST. Like the Hawks, they were able to translate the intimidation of the blocked shot into good defense. Opposing teams shot only .476 from the field against the Cavaliers, making them the league's ninth best team in this department.

The blocks and steals are reflective of the youth and athleticism of the Cavs, while their low free throw percentage of .744 (No. 20) also could be attributable to the same thing. Young players tend to be nervous at the free throw line.

If the Cavs are to become genuine contenders, they will have to improve in the important categories of rebounding (No. 23), scoring (No. 21), and PAR (No. 21). The acquisition of Nance late last season should help in all three areas.

Cleveland also could use a hard-driving point guard and a muscular big man.

LARRY NANCE

AGE: 29
HEIGHT: 6-10
WEIGHT: 217
POSITION: Forward
EXPERIENCE: 7 Seasons
COLLEGE: Clemson
BIRTHPLACE: Anderson, SC
1987–88 TENDEX: .677

One of the most consistent players in the NBA, Nance has achieved TENDEX ratings of .692, .699, .694, and .677 the past four seasons . . . was hindered last season by an injury that caused him to miss 15 games and by a mid-season trade that sent him from Phoenix to Cleveland . . . is probably the most underrated player in the NBA, certainly the best player in the league not to be a member of the TENDEX 700 Club . . . does not play up to superstar status in any category but is good in every area . . . tied for No. 11 in the NBA in TENDEX rating last season and also finished No. 6 in BEST and No. 8 in blocked shots . . . was one of five NBA players with more blocks than turnovers . . . ranks among the top ten on the NBA's all-time field goal percentage list with mark of .559 . . . among 22 small forwards, had ratings last season of No. 1 in blocks, No. 1 in BEST, No. 2 in TENDEX, No. 2 in rebounds, No. 4 in both Shootist categories, and No. 7 in both PAR categories . . . lowest rating was No. 15 in steals.

BRAD DAUGHERTY

AGE: 23
HEIGHT: 7-0
WEIGHT: 245
POSITION: Center
EXPERIENCE: 2 Seasons
COLLEGE: North Carolina
BIRTHPLACE: Asheville, NC
1987–88 TENDEX: .571

Often compared with other centers drafted No. 1 during the 1980s, but comparisons with David Robinson, Akeem Olajuwon, and Patrick Ewing aren't justified. Daugherty is a solid NBA center who should give the Cavaliers competent play in the pivot for at least a decade, but he is not a great player . . . TENDEX rating of .582 in 1986–87 put him in eighth place among NBA centers and he was named to the All-Rookie team . . . led Cavs in minutes played (2,957), scoring (18.7), and rebounding (665) last season . . . ranked No. 14 in NBA with PAR-4 rating and led centers in that department . . . other high rankings among NBA centers were No. 2 in assists, No. 2 in minutes played, No. 8 in scoring, and No. 8 in TENDEX . . . problem is weak hands enabling opponents to knock the ball away from him. Last year rated a poor No. 16 in steals, No. 17 in turnovers, No. 18 in blocks, and No. 21 in BEST . . . ahead of only two of 101 NBA regular players in BEST . . . below most centers in all three shooting percentages and No. 18 in rebounding.

NANCE

1987–88	2PFG	3PFG	F.T.	REB.	AST.	STL.	T.O.	BLK.	PTS.
Per Game	.531	.333	.779	9.1	3.1	0.9	2.3	2.4	19.1
Per Minute	.531	.333	.779	.255	.087	.026	.065	.067	.537
Rating	6	4	14	2	9	15	10	1	13

DAUGHERTY

1987–88	2PFG	3PFG	F.T.	REB.	AST.	STL.	T.O.	BLK.	PTS.
Per Game	.511	.000	.716	8.4	4.2	0.6	3.4	0.7	18.7
Per Minute	.511	.000	.716	.225	.113	.016	.090	.019	.501
Rating	12	14	15	18	2	16	17	18	8

MARK PRICE

AGE: 24
HEIGHT: 6-1
WEIGHT: 174
POSITION: Point Guard
EXPERIENCE: 2 Seasons
COLLEGE: Georgia Tech
BIRTHPLACE: Bartlesville, OK
1987–88 TENDEX: .533

Price was drafted in the second round the same season that Cavaliers Brad Daugherty, Ron Harper, and John Williams made the NBA's All-Rookie team . . . Price was all but ignored that first season, but with a TENDEX rating 58 points above the positional norm, he ranked best of the four players last season . . . a great shooter, Price joined Craig Hodges in exceeding the previous record for three-point field goals with a .486 percentage on three-pointers . . . No. 2 Shootist among point guards, No. 3 in free throw percentage (No. 8 in the NBA), No. 3 in points per minute, No. 6 in two-point field goals, and No. 6 in turnovers . . . areas where he could stand improvement are assists (No. 18), steals (No. 18), PAR (No. 17), and rebounds (No. 16) . . . tenacious defender who makes up for lack of size with hustle . . . great clutch player, paced Cavs in scoring (21.0) and TENDEX rating (.632) in five-game playoff series against Bulls.

JOHN WILLIAMS

AGE: 26
HEIGHT: 6-11
WEIGHT: 230
POSITION: Power Forward
EXPERIENCE: 2 Seasons
COLLEGE: Tulane
BIRTHPLACE: Sorrento, LA
1987–88 TENDEX: .559

Playing opposite Larry Nance, Williams gives the Cavaliers a second defensive intimidator in the corner to compensate for Brad Daugherty's lack of same in the middle . . . playing sparingly because of lack of stamina, Williams has compiled fine TENDEX ratings of .557 and .559 in his first two NBA seasons . . . last season was the No. 14 rated player in the NBA in least turnovers, No. 2 in BEST, and No. 2 in ratio of blocked shots to turnovers . . . one of five players with more blocks than turnovers in the entire league . . . in comparison with the NBA's other regular power forwards, Williams came out first in blocks, first in BEST, and first in blocks/turnovers ratio . . . weakest aspects of his game are two-point field goal percentage (No. 18) and Shootist (No. 16).

PRICE

1987–88	2PFG	3PFG	F.T.	REB.	AST.	STL.	T.O.	BLK.	PTS.
Per Game	.510	.486	.877	2.3	6.0	1.2	2.3	0.2	16.0
Per Minute	.510	.486	.877	.069	.183	.038	.070	.005	.487
Rating	6	1	3	16	18	18	6	12	3

WILLIAMS

1987–88	2PFG	3PFG	F.T.	REB.	AST.	STL.	T.O.	BLK.	PTS.
Per Game	.477	.000	.756	6.6	1.3	0.8	1.4	1.9	10.9
Per Minute	.477	.000	.756	.240	.049	.029	.049	.069	.400
Rating	18	12	10	13	11	12	5	1	13

RESERVES

Ron Harper, the best athlete in Cleveland's sensational rookie class of '86, should have a page to himself, but a foot injury kept him out of 25 games last season and he did not play 2,000 minutes. A great open-court player, at times resembling Michael Jordan, Harper deserved the Rookie of the Year award that was won by Chuck Person in 1986–87. His TENDEX ratings for his first two seasons were .519 and .522, excellent for a shooting guard. Harper completely recovered from his injury late last season and had a .553 rating against Chicago in the playoffs.

Other Cavalier reserves are forward Mike Sanders (.413) and guard Craig Ehlo (.451).

OUTLOOK

Whatever gains the Cavaliers made last season toward becoming champion contenders were offset by the college and expansion drafts.

While nearly every other team in the NBA was helping itself with one, two, or even three good players in the deepest college draft in history, the Cavaliers got none. They had only one choice in the first 60 and he was forward Randolph Keys of Southern Mississippi. Although Keys was a first-round selection (No. 21), he was one of the lowest rated players in the entire draft (TENDEX .425).

But because of the trade that landed all-star forward Larry Nance late last season, the Cavaliers will be formidable, even without rookie contributions.

Cleveland has stars at four of the five starting positions: Nance, center Brad Daugherty, and guards Ron Harper and Mark Price.

Except for John Williams, however, the bench is thin. Sharpshooting sixth man Dell Curry inexplicably was left unprotected in the expansion draft and Charlotte made him its No. 1 choice.

Probable finish: Fourth in Central Division.

6

Dallas Mavericks

*D*uring the past few seasons the Dallas Mavericks have stayed on a plateau, high above most of the NBA's ordinary teams, but still below a championship peak.

The missing ingredient that could help push them to the top, a superstar, may already be in a Dallas uniform, but now the Mavericks need to find a place for him in the starting lineup. The potential superstar, Roy Tarpley, entered the TENDEX 700 Club last season, but he did not play enough to make the kind of impact a superstar ought to make. Dallas Coach John MacLeod needs to make room for Tarpley, either at center or power forward, on a full-time basis this season.

The rest of the elements for a champion team already are in place, including a solid bench.

MacLeod demonstrated fine coaching last season by guiding the Mavs to 53 victories, fifth best in the league. It was a good coaching job because Dallas' TENDEX power rating of 1.030 was No. 9 in the NBA, four places lower than the team's final position in the standings.

Statistically, the thing that stands out about Dallas is stinginess. In maintaining the sixth best scoring defense in the league, the Mavericks committed fewer personal fouls than any team other than the Los Angeles Lakers and held their opponents to a field goal percentage of .470.

Paced by Tarpley's league-best performance, Dallas out-rebounded its opposition by an average of five per game. The Mavs ranked No. 1 in the NBA in rebounding.

Other Maverick strengths were turnovers (No. 3), free throw shooting (No. 4), BEST (No. 7), and PAR (No. 8).

Except for point guard Derek Harper, the Mavs did poorly in assists (No. 17) and steals (No. 18). They were 17th in three-point field goal percentage. These problems are back-court-related, so it is obvious that their biggest need is another quality guard.

ROY TARPLEY

AGE: 23
HEIGHT: 7-0
WEIGHT: 235
POSITION: Power Forward
EXPERIENCE: 2 Seasons
COLLEGE: Michigan
BIRTHPLACE: New York City
1987–88 TENDEX: .701

The NBA made much ado about the fact that Tarpley became the first non-starter to rank among the league leaders in rebounding when he averaged 11.8 per game last season. Not publicized was the more significant fact that Tarpley's rebounding production of .416 per minute led the league and was the highest percentage in more than a decade in the NBA . . . last player to exceed that figure was Moses Malone with .428 in 1976–77 . . . with a TENDEX rating of .701 in 1987–88, Tarpley ranked No. 8 in the league . . . winner of the league's Sixth Man award . . . three times had 20 or more points and rebounds in a game . . . a versatile player, Tarpley rated No. 3 among power forwards in PAR percentage (points plus assists plus rebounds divided by minutes played), No. 4 in BEST, and was the No. 8 Shootist. He was No. 2 in steals and 5 in blocked shots . . . major weakness was assists: he was No. 17 among power forwards with the ninth worst assists average per minute in the league . . . needs to play more minutes, ranked only No. 6 on the Mavericks with 2,307.

MARK AGUIRRE

AGE: 28
HEIGHT: 6-6
WEIGHT: 232
POSITION: Small Forward
EXPERIENCE: 7 Seasons
COLLEGE: DePaul
BIRTHPLACE: Chicago
1987–88 TENDEX: .615

Aguirre had one of his best seasons in 1987–88, ranking No. 8 in the NBA in scoring with 25.1 points per game, No. 4 in points per minute with .740, and No. 20 in TENDEX with .615. He is the Mavericks' all-time leader with 12,977 points, averaging 24.9 per game, tenth best in league history . . . had career high last season with 57 blocked shots and matched high with .770 free throw percentage . . . was one of nine NBA players with a PAR percentage exceeding 1.000 (1.012), third best among 22 small forwards . . . other good positional ratings were No. 3 in scoring, No. 5 in assists, No. 5 in TENDEX, No. 8 in blocked shots, and No. 9 in three-point field goal percentage . . . not a good ball-handler, he was 20th in turnovers and 17th in BEST.

TARPLEY

1987–88	2PFG	3PFG	F.T.	REB.	AST.	STL.	T.O.	BLK.	PTS.
Per Game	.503	.000	.740	11.8	1.1	1.3	2.1	1.1	13.5
Per Minute	.503	.000	.740	.416	.037	.045	.075	.037	.474
Rating	12	19	13	1	17	2	16	5	8

AGUIRRE

1987–88	2PFG	3PFG	F.T.	REB.	AST.	STL.	T.O.	BLK.	PTS.
Per Game	.496	.302	.770	5.6	3.6	0.9	2.6	0.7	25.1
Per Minute	.496	.302	.770	.166	.107	.027	.078	.022	.740
Rating	13	9	17	15	5	12	20	8	3

DEREK HARPER

AGE: 27
HEIGHT: 6-4
WEIGHT: 203
POSITION: Point Guard
EXPERIENCE: 5 Seasons
COLLEGE: Illinois
BIRTHPLACE: Elberton, GA
1987–88 TENDEX: .511

Harper improved two of his own team records for assists last season. He collected 634 assists to break the season record of 609 he set the previous year and increased his career total to a Dallas-record 2,258 . . . led team in 1987–88 with 3,032 minutes played and 168 steals, while finishing third in scoring with 17.0 average—all three figures being personal career highs . . . was one of ten NBA players to play 3,000 minutes . . . a sure-handed guard, he ranked No. 9 in the NBA in ratio of steals to turnovers but failed to have more steals than turnovers for the first time in three seasons . . . consistent Harper ranked No. 2 among point guards in minutes played, No. 4 in BEST, No. 4 in blocked shots, No. 4 in turnovers, No. 5 in scoring, No. 7 in three-point field goal percentage, No. 8 in steals, No. 8 in PAR percentage, and No. 8 in ratio of assists to turnovers . . . No. 12 point guard in TENDEX.

ROLANDO BLACKMAN

AGE: 29
HEIGHT: 6-6
WEIGHT: 194
POSITION: Shooting Guard
EXPERIENCE: 7 Seasons
COLLEGE: Kansas State
BIRTHPLACE: Panama City, Panama
1987–88 TENDEX: .447

Blackman slipped to the middle of the pack among shooting guards for the first time in his career last season with TENDEX rating of .447 (normal for the position is .450) . . . scoring dropped from 21 points per game to 18.7 and he had career lows in field goal percentage (.473) and rebounds (246) . . . still an explosive offensive player, though, ranking second on the Dallas team in scoring and tenth in the league in free throw percentage (.873) . . . rated last among shooting guards with .476 two-point field goal percentage and last with .000 three-point percentage, missing his only five attempts.

HARPER

1987–88	2PFG	3PFG	F.T.	REB.	AST.	STL.	T.O.	BLK.	PTS.
Per Game	.488	.313	.759	3.0	7.7	2.1	2.3	0.4	17.0
Per Minute	.488	.313	.759	.081	.209	.055	.063	.012	.459
Rating	11	7	19	15	12	8	4	4	5

BLACKMAN

1987–88	2PFG	3PFG	F.T.	REB.	AST.	STL.	T.O.	BLK.	PTS.
Per Game	.476	.000	.873	3.5	3.7	0.9	2.0	0.3	18.7
Per Minute	.476	.000	.873	.095	.102	.025	.056	.007	.514
Rating	18	18	6	12	15	15	4	9	11

SAM PERKINS

AGE: 27
HEIGHT: 6-9½
WEIGHT: 238
POSITION: Power Forward
EXPERIENCE: 4 Seasons
COLLEGE: North Carolina
BIRTHPLACE: New York City
1987–88 TENDEX: .494

Perkins is a respectable but not exceptional power forward, good defensively, below average offensively . . . 1987–88 TENDEX rating of .494 was No. 16 out of 20 power forwards, putting his starting job in jeopardy to third-year pro Roy Tarpley, who was rated 207 percentage points higher . . . Perkins hasn't reached the level of play predicted for him when he was the fourth player drafted in 1984 . . . paradox is shooting: although he ranked No. 2 among power forwards in free throw percentage (.822), he was dead last in two-point field goal percentage (.460), and No. 18 and No. 16 in the two Shootist categories.

JAMES DONALDSON

AGE: 31
HEIGHT: 7-2
WEIGHT: 277
POSITION: Center
EXPERIENCE: 8 Seasons
COLLEGE: Washington State
BIRTHPLACE: Heacham, England
1987–88 TENDEX: .474

For a guy who tried basketball as an afterthought because of his height, and was only a fourth-round draft choice out of college, Donaldson has had a remarkable NBA career . . . biggest asset is stamina, with a streak of six years in a row playing every regular-season game; the streak was broken last year when he played 81 out of 82 . . . it is listed as a four-season streak in Chart 30 of Section III because he played less than the qualifying number of 2,000 minutes in two of the six seasons . . . statistically he hit the skids last season after undergoing surgery for a stress fracture in his right leg . . . minutes played fell from 3,028 to 2,523, field goal percentage from fourth-in-league .586 to .558, free throw percentage from .812 to .778, rebounds from fourth-in-league 11.9 to 9.3, blocked shots from 136 to 104, scoring average from 10.8 to 7.0, and TENDEX rating from .538 to .474 . . . No. 20 rated center in TENDEX.

PERKINS

1987–88	2PFG	3PFG	F.T.	REB.	AST.	STL.	T.O.	BLK.	PTS.
Per Game	.460	.167	.822	8.0	1.6	1.0	1.6	0.7	14.2
Per Minute	.460	.167	.822	.241	.047	.030	.048	.022	.427
Rating	20	8	2	12	12	11	4	9	11

DONALDSON

1987–88	2PFG	3PFG	F.T.	REB.	AST.	STL.	T.O.	BLK.	PTS.
Per Game	.558	.000	.778	9.3	0.8	0.5	1.4	1.3	7.0
Per Minute	.558	.000	.778	.299	.026	.016	.049	.041	.226
Rating	2	6	7	4	20	17	5	9	20

RESERVES

With six players playing enough to be classified as regulars, the Maverick bench may appear thinner than it really is. Count Roy Tarpley as a reserve, and it's probably the best bench in the NBA. Discount him and it's one of the worst.

The only other substitutes with more than 1,000 minutes played in 1987–88 were small forward Detlef Schrempf and point guard Brad Davis.

Schrempf, the No. 8 draft choice in 1985, has had three undistinguished seasons for the Mavericks after being projected as an NBA starter and potential star. Except for fine play making ability for a man his size (6'10"), he does not excel in any aspect of play. His 1987–88 TENDEX rating was .462.

Brad Davis has been a solid NBA player for 11 seasons, but he'll turn 33 this December and may not have many seasons left. His TENDEX rating last season was .464.

OUTLOOK

The Mavericks traded a first-round choice in the 1988 college draft to the Miami Heat to prevent the Heat from taking one of three players Dallas left unprotected in the expansion draft. Because of the exceptional strength of the college draft, the Mavs appear to have given the Heat too much.

Dallas had a fine team in 1986–87, reaching the Western Conference finals and extending the Los Angeles Lakers to seven games. But that was misleading.

The Mavericks would have had little chance to defeat Denver if Nugget guard Lafayette Lever and center Wayne Cooper had not been injured, and they did not play the Lakers nearly as toughly as the Utah Jazz did.

Since the Mavs did not improve themselves in the 1988 college draft, they can hardly be expected to finish ahead of the Nuggets or Jazz, even if they can find 1,000 more minutes for budding superstar Roy Tarpley to play.

The starting backcourt is solid with Derek Harper and Rolando Blackman, although Blackman is aging and should be rested more. Coach John MacLeod may not want to rest Blackman, however, unless reserve Steve Alford shows improvement.

The trouble with the Dallas frontcourt is that Tarpley can't play center and power forward at the same time. Center James Donaldson and power forward Sam Perkins are not top-level players. Mark Aguirre is, but only when he feels like it.

Probable finish: Third in Midwest Division.

7

Denver Nuggets

*D*enver is known among casual observers of the NBA as a run-and-shoot team, but in fact it is tight backcourt defense and ball-control that distinguish the Midwest Division champion Nuggets from ordinary teams.

Other factors cancel each other out. Denver outshot its opponents from the free throw line last season, .806 to .762, but was outshot from the field, .490 to .474. The Nuggets outdid their opponents in assists and three-point field goals, but were outdone in rebounds and blocked shots.

In the last analysis, the reason that they were able to win 54 games and outscore their opponents by a four-point margin per game was their surplus of scoring attempts. A television commentator noted that the Nuggets simply put the ball up more often than their adversaries, but you can't do that unless you have the ball.

The essence of Denver's success resides in two statistical categories—steals and turnovers. By stealing the ball 211 times more than their opponents and losing it 420 fewer times on turnovers, the Nuggets led the league in both categories and acquired the ball possessions necessary to lead the league in scoring and top their division in the standings.

Key players in accomplishing this were guards Lafayette Lever and Michael Adams. Lever and Adams ranked among the top five players at their respective positions in most steals and least turnovers. They were both among the league's top ten in steals and ranked 1–2 in ratio of steals to turnovers. They were two of four players in the NBA to accumulate more steals than turnovers.

Another important part of the Nuggets' success was Coach Doug Moe. According to the TENDEX system, Denver was only the No. 10 team in the league in player strength. Under Moe's leadership, however, the Nuggets compiled the third best record in the league and he was a deserving winner of Coach of the Year honors. It was a timely honor because last year Moe became the 12th coach in NBA history to win 500 games.

LAFAYETTE (FAT) LEVER

AGE: 28
HEIGHT: 6-3
WEIGHT: 175
POSITION: Shooting Guard
EXPERIENCE: 6 Seasons
COLLEGE: Arizona State
BIRTHPLACE: Pine Bluff, AR
1987–88 TENDEX: .642

All that the Nuggets accomplished in the standings last season could be negated if it turns out the price they paid was putting Lever on the meat wagon. Lever, the league's only PAR-7 player last season, played much of the year on an injured knee, and the injury flared up ominously during the playoffs. The circumstances were similar to those that recently wrecked the careers of TENDEX 700 Club member Jeff Ruland, star guard Andrew Toney, and emerging star Derek Smith. These players either were asked or allowed to play through serious injuries and wound up with ruined careers. It may sound courageous to "play hurt," but isn't it much better to do as the Chicago Bulls did with Michael Jordan in 1985–86 and sacrifice a year for the sake of a career? The frail-looking Lever is an amazing player: With a PAR-8 rating in 1986–87, he is tied for third on the all-time best list . . . ranked first among NBA guards in rebounding the past two seasons . . . his total of 729 boards in 1986–87 made him the second best backcourt rebounder in NBA history, trailing Oscar Robertson, who three times had more than that, with a high of 985 in 1961–62 . . . Lever ranked No. 17 among NBA leaders in 1987–88, No. 4 in steals, No. 14 in assists, No. 6 in minutes played, No. 11 in ratio of steals to turnovers, No. 11 in BEST, and No. 1

in PAR. He finished among the top three shooting guards in nine statistical categories . . . earned second-team All-Defensive honors . . . led league in triple-doubles (10 points, assists, and rebounds) . . . twice had 20 points and 20 rebounds in the same game.

ALEX ENGLISH

AGE: 34
HEIGHT: 6-7
WEIGHT: 190
POSITION: Small Forward
EXPERIENCE: 12 Seasons
COLLEGE: South Carolina
BIRTHPLACE: Columbia, SC
1987–88 TENDEX: .569

Despite age, English still ranks among the league's better scorers and is in the top echelon of small forwards . . . tallied exactly 2,000 points in 1987–88 for his seventh straight season of 2,000 or more . . . NBA leading scorer of the decade with 18,843 points . . . for his career he topped the 20,000-point mark last season and finished the year with 21,242, No. 10 on the all-time NBA scoring list . . . amazing durability for a slender player, missing no more than four games in any of the past 11 seasons, five times playing in all 82 games, four times playing at least 3,000 minutes . . . won league scoring title in 1982–83 with 28.4 average, while having best scoring output (29.8) in 1985–86 at the age of 32 . . . ranked No. 9 in NBA with PAR-4 rating last year . . . high 1987–88 ratings among 22 small forwards were No. 2 in PAR and assists, No. 4 in scoring and minutes played, No. 6 in free throw percentage, Shootist and TENDEX rating . . . weaknesses in rebounding (No. 20), shot-blocking (No. 18), and BEST (No. 18).

LEVER

1987–88	2PFG	3PFG	F.T.	REB.	AST.	STL.	T.O.	BLK.	PTS.
Per Game	.484	.211	.785	8.1	7.8	2.7	2.2	0.3	18.9
Per Minute	.484	.211	.785	.217	.209	.073	.059	.007	.505
Rating	11	13	18	1	3	3	5	8	13

ENGLISH

1987–88	2PFG	3PFG	F.T.	REB.	AST.	STL.	T.O.	BLK.	PTS.
Per Game	.496	.000	.828	4.7	4.7	0.9	2.3	2.9	25.0
Per Minute	.496	.000	.828	.132	.134	.025	.064	.008	.710
Rating	12	18	6	20	2	16	8	18	4

DANNY SCHAYES

AGE: 29
HEIGHT: 6-11
WEIGHT: 245
POSITION: Center
EXPERIENCE: 7 Seasons
COLLEGE: Syracuse
BIRTHPLACE: Syracuse, NY
1987–88 TENDEX: .644

Schayes had the best season of his career in 1987–88, ranking No. 4 among NBA centers with a TENDEX rating of .644 . . . did not accumulate high gross totals because he played only 2,166 minutes, but they were quality minutes . . . ranked No. 16 in the league in TENDEX, No. 13 in blocked shots per minute, No. 10 in rebounds per minute, No. 16 in two-point field goal percentage, and No. 2 in Shootist percentage on all shots . . . among centers was rated No. 1 in Shootist percentage; No. 3 in rebounds and free throw percentage; No. 4 in PAR; No. 5 in scoring, steals, and Shootist points per shot; No. 6 in two-point field goal percentage, and No. 8 in blocked shots . . . the only weak point in his game was stamina: he was the No. 17 center in minutes played.

MICHAEL ADAMS

AGE: 25
HEIGHT: 5-11
WEIGHT: 165
POSITION: Point Guard
EXPERIENCE: 3 Seasons
COLLEGE: Boston College
BIRTHPLACE: Hartford, CT
1987–88 TENDEX: .452

Diminutive Adams set an NBA record by sinking three-point shots 43 games in a row at the end of the 1987–88 season, a streak that could carry over into this season . . . ranked No. 16 in the NBA in turnovers last year, best of the league's point guards . . . No. 2 in the league in ratio of steals to turnovers, best of the point guards in this category as well . . . No. 9 in three-point field goal percentage, No. 2 in number of three-pointers made . . . No. 5 in ratio of assists to turnovers, No. 8 in steals, and No. 15 in BEST . . . led all point guards in ratio of blocked shots to turnovers and in BEST . . . weaknesses included No. 16 in PAR percentage, No. 18 in rebounds, and No. 19 in assists . . . became the player with the lowest field goal percentage (.449) ever to average more than one point per shot in the Shootist ratings, but that is misleading because of the number of three-pointers he attempted. He actually was a good shooter with a two-point field goal percentage of .505 and a three-point mark of .367.

SCHAYES

1987–88	2PFG	3PFG	F.T.	REB.	AST.	STL.	T.O.	BLK.	PTS.
Per Game	.542	.000	.836	8.2	1.3	0.8	1.9	1.1	13.9
Per Minute	.542	.000	.836	.306	.049	.028	.072	.042	.521
Rating	6	17	3	3	13	5	12	8	5

ADAMS

1987–88	2PFG	3PFG	F.T.	REB.	AST.	STL.	T.O.	BLK.	PTS.
Per Game	.505	.367	.834	2.2	6.1	2.1	1.8	0.2	13.9
Per Minute	.505	.367	.834	.066	.181	.060	.052	.006	.409
Rating	8	3	10	18	19	4	1	9	9

RESERVES

Denver had four of the NBA's finest reserves last season—offensive threats Blair Rasmussen and Jay Vincent and defensive specialists Bill Hanzlik and T.R. Dunn.

Vincent and Rasmussen gave the Nuggets plenty of scoring in the frontcourt, averaging 15.4 and 12.7 points per game, respectively, while playing only a little more than 20 minutes per game apiece. Rasmussen had the seventh best TENDEX rating of the NBA's reserves at .551. Vincent was the No. 5 rated small forward with a mark of .497.

Hanzlik and Dunn had ratings in the vicinity of .300, but their roles were different. They often were assigned to cool off the hot-shooting players on opposing teams.

In order to protect themselves in case Lafayette Lever's sore knee does not respond to surgery, the Nuggets signed Walter Davis as a free agent. Davis ranked No. 5 in free throw percentage (.887) and No. 16 among reserves with a .512 TENDEX in 1987–88, but he is 34 years old.

OUTLOOK

The Nuggets could finish anywhere from first to fifth in the Midwest Division, depending on the physical condition of all-star guard Lafayette Lever and shot-blocking center Wayne Cooper, and on the signing of free agent Dan Schayes.

If Cooper and Lever return to 100 percent capability, the Nuggets could win the division and contend for the NBA title. If not, they'll fall near the bottom.

Center-forwards Schayes and Blair Rasmussen had good seasons in 1987–88, but neither has the defensive capabilities of Cooper.

Lever, however, is the key. He is as versatile as the Los Angeles Lakers' Magic Johnson, albeit underpublicized. Lever was the only player in the NBA last season to average seven points, seven rebounds, and seven assists or more per game. If he does not recover fully from a knee injury, Denver is in deep trouble.

Point guard Michael Adams is on the small side and is not as good a playmaker as Lever, but he is one of the best three-point field goal shooters in the league.

Small forward Alex English remains a rock of durability and consistency going into his 12th NBA season.

Rookie Jerome Lane adds depth and rebounding strength to the frontcourt.

Probable finish: Second in Midwest Division.

8

Detroit Pistons

*T*he importance of rebounds and field goal percentage is demonstrated by the record of the Detroit Pistons.

These were the only two categories in which the Pistons substantially outdid their opponents last season, and yet they managed to outscore their opposition by five points per game in compiling one of the best records (54–28) in the NBA.

Detroit lagged in three-point field goal percentage, free throw percentage, turnovers, steals, blocked shots, and BEST and was only average in the assists, PAR, and Shootist statistics.

The Pistons manufactured their fine record with powerful inside play that translated into a surplus of three rebounds per game.

They made use of the extra shots acquired through the rebounding advantage by shooting .493 from the field and holding their opponents to .467. The discrepancy of .026 between the Pistons' shooting percentage and their opponents' was the fourth largest in the NBA, behind Utah, Boston, and the Los Angeles Lakers.

The other noteworthy thing about Coach Chuck Daly's team is its physical play, calculated to intimidate opponents, or at the very least to make them black-and-blue.

The team's front line consists of bruisers Rick Mahorn and Bill Laimbeer, young lions Dennis Rodman and John Salley, and veteran Adrian Dantley, who at 6′4″ is no pushover in the low-post area.

The Pistons' media guide last season was perhaps a sign of things to come. On the front cover was a photo of Dantley hitting an opponent in the chest with his right forearm while shooting the ball with his left hand.

ISIAH THOMAS

AGE: 27
HEIGHT: 6-1
WEIGHT: 185
POSITION: Point Guard
EXPERIENCE: 7 Seasons
COLLEGE: Indiana
BIRTHPLACE: Chicago
1987–88 TENDEX: .562

Since peaking in 1984–85 with a TENDEX rating of .681, Thomas has fallen into a pattern of cruising through early-season games before stepping on the accelerator around mid-season. His early-season holidays have become longer and longer in recent seasons as evidenced by decreasing ratings at a point in his career when he should be peaking (.635 in 1985–86, .588 in 1986–87, .562 in 1987–88). Last season his name did not appear on the top-10 list of point guards until the final month of the season . . . but Thomas can still play when he wants to, always doing well in playoffs and All-Star games . . . All-Star Game MVP in 1984 and 1986 . . . holds league record for assists, averaging 13.9 per game in 1984–85, although his total of 1,123 that season was broken last year by John Stockton of Utah . . . once scored 16 points in 96 seconds during a playoff game . . . ranked No. 18 last season in steals and No. 8 in the NBA in assists; but was in the league's bottom ten in turnovers . . . rated No. 1 out of 20 point guards in scoring, No. 4 in PAR and minutes played, No. 6 in TENDEX rating, and No. 7 in assists . . . low ratings were No. 19 in turnovers and No. 18 in BEST.

BILL LAIMBEER

AGE: 31
HEIGHT: 6-11
WEIGHT: 245
POSITION: Center
EXPERIENCE: 8 Seasons
COLLEGE: Notre Dame
BIRTHPLACE: Boston
1987–88 TENDEX: .583

The consistency of Laimbeer is remarkable. He has played every game in each of the past six seasons to tie for fifth place on the all-time NBA list with Jim Chones. In those six seasons his minutes played have never been more than 2,897 or less than 2,854. Last season's 2,897 was a personal high . . . rebounds dropped off the past two seasons to 955 and 832 after he pulled down more than 1,000 three years in a row; but strong young frontcourt teammates competing on boards could have something to do with that . . . consistency carries over to other areas of play as he ranks among the top ten centers in 12 out of 18 statistical departments . . . high ratings are No. 1 in three-point field goal percentage and ratio of steals to turnovers; No. 2 in free throw percentage and turnovers; No. 3 in minutes played; No. 4 in assists; and No. 5 in rebounds and TENDEX rating . . . only rating below the top 15 last season was No. 17 in points per minute.

THOMAS

1987–88	2PFG	3PFG	F.T.	REB.	AST.	STL.	T.O.	BLK.	PTS.
Per Game	.475	.309	.774	3.4	8.4	1.7	3.4	0.2	19.5
Per Minute	.475	.309	.774	.095	.232	.048	.093	.006	.539
Rating	15	9	16	9	7	11	19	7	1

LAIMBEER

1987–88	2PFG	3PFG	F.T.	REB.	AST.	STL.	T.O.	BLK.	PTS.
Per Game	.500	.333	.874	10.2	2.4	0.8	1.7	1.0	13.5
Per Minute	.500	.333	.874	.287	.069	.023	.047	.027	.383
Rating	14	1	2	5	4	8	2	15	17

DENNIS RODMAN

AGE: 27
HEIGHT: 6-8
WEIGHT: 210
POSITION: Small Forward
EXPERIENCE: 2 Seasons
COLLEGE: Southeastern Oklahoma State
BIRTHPLACE: Dallas
1987–88 TENDEX: .618

Rodman could be referred to as an NBA star of the future, but the truth is he probably already is one and lacks only the acknowledgment . . . TENDEX rating last season was 19th best in the NBA and fourth best among small forwards, three places higher on the list than more-publicized teammate Adrian Dantley, who plays the same position . . . an excellent athlete, Rodman ranked No. 5 in the league in rebounding percentage and No. 5 in two-point field goal percentage, leading small forwards in both categories . . . Shootist rating was No. 7 among small forwards, even though his free throw percentage of .535 was the worst in the league . . . winner of the Wilt Chamberlain award as the only regular NBA player with a higher field goal percentage (.561) than free throw percentage (.535) . . . has a chance to become a 700 Club member if he can learn to cope with free throw line jitters.

ADRIAN DANTLEY

AGE: 32
HEIGHT: 6-4
WEIGHT: 210
POSITION: Small Forward
EXPERIENCE: 12 Seasons
COLLEGE: Notre Dame
BIRTHPLACE: Washington, DC
1987–88 TENDEX: .569

Missing 13 games because of injury, Dantley actually played less minutes at the small forward position last season than teammate Dennis Rodmam, but reclaimed the regular job before the playoffs . . . averaged exactly 20 points per game, his ninth season in a row reaching the 20-point plateau . . . passed the 20,000-point mark for his career and wound up with 21,058 for 11th place on the all-time NBA scoring list . . . career scoring average of 25.5 is good for ninth place . . . won scoring titles in 1980–81 and 1983–84 . . . Rookie of the Year in 1976–77 . . . ranked No. 11 in the NBA last season in points per minute and was No. 4 in the Shootist category computed by dividing total number of shots made by total number of shots taken . . . good shooter but below average in other phases of play, his ratings among 22 small forwards ranged from No. 1 in Shootist statistic to No. 22 in rebounding. Other highs were No. 2 in free throw percentage, No. 5 in points, and No. 7 in TENDEX rating.

RODMAN

1987–88	2PFG	3PFG	F.T.	REB.	AST.	STL.	T.O.	BLK.	PTS.
Per Game	.568	.294	.535	8.7	1.3	0.9	1.9	0.5	11.6
Per Minute	.568	.294	.535	.333	.051	.035	.073	.021	.444
Rating	1	11	23	1	20	6	16	10	18

DANTLEY

1987–88	2PFG	3PFG	F.T.	REB.	AST.	STL.	T.O.	BLK.	PTS.
Per Game	.516	.000	.860	3.3	2.5	0.6	2.0	0.1	20.0
Per Minute	.516	.000	.860	.106	.080	.018	.063	.005	.644
Rating	8	20	2	22	13	19	7	19	5

JOE DUMARS

AGE: 25
HEIGHT: 6-3
WEIGHT: 195
POSITION: Shooting Guard
EXPERIENCE: 3 Seasons
COLLEGE: McNeese State
BIRTHPLACE: Natchitoches, LA.
1987–88 TENDEX: .417

Of the 11 players cited this past season for All-Defensive first- and second-team honors, ten achieved more offensively than defensively and several of them probably didn't deserve defensive recognition. Dumars is a player who did deserve it, but lack of publicity for offensive achievements cost him. A good passer, Dumars ranked No. 10 among shooting guards in assists, even though Isiah Thomas controlled the ball most of the time . . . not a good shooter, Dumars rated only No. 17 out of 18 shooting guards in two-point field goal percentage and PAR . . . was also No. 17 in rebounding and No. 16 in TENDEX, ranking in league's bottom ten in both of these statistics.

JOHN SALLEY

AGE: 24
HEIGHT: 6-11
WEIGHT: 231
POSITION: Power Forward
EXPERIENCE: 2 Seasons
COLLEGE: Georgia Tech
BIRTHPLACE: Brooklyn, NY
1987–88 TENDEX: .516

An inconsistent basketball personality, Salley is excellent in some phases of play, lousy in others . . . No. 3 in the league in ratio of blocked shots to turnovers, No. 5 in BEST, No. 7 in blocks, and No. 11 in Shootist percentage; but stuck in the NBA's bottom ten in the important scoring and PAR statistics . . . played in all 82 games each of first two NBA seasons . . . last season, out of 20 power forwards, rated No. 2 in blocked shots and BEST, No. 3 in field goal percentage, No. 4 in Shootist, but No. 19 in PAR, No. 18 in scoring, No. 17 in free throw percentage, and No. 17 in rebounding . . . could push Rick Mahorn for a starting job this season.

DUMARS

1987–88	2PFG	3PFG	F.T.	REB.	AST.	STL.	T.O.	BLK.	PTS.
Per Game	.477	.211	.815	2.4	4.7	1.1	2.1	0.2	14.2
Per Minute	.477	.211	.815	.073	.142	.032	.063	.005	.425
Rating	17	14	14	17	10	13	8	13	15

SALLEY

1987–88	2PFG	3PFG	F.T.	REB.	AST.	STL.	T.O.	BLK.	PTS.
Per Game	.566	.000	.709	4.9	1.4	0.6	1.5	1.7	8.5
Per Minute	.566	.000	.709	.201	.056	.027	.060	.068	.350
Rating	3	10	17	17	10	13	9	2	18

RESERVES

Rick Mahorn actually started 64 games last season, but an injury caused him to miss 15 games and he failed to play the qualifying number of 2,000 minutes to be classified as a regular. Mahorn is the Pistons' physical enforcer, and he isn't a bad basketball player when he sets his mind to it. His TENDEX rating of .546 was eighth best of the NBA's reserves.

Other quality Detroit reserves were center James Edwards, obtained in a trade with Phoenix, and guard Vinnie Johnson. Edwards, an 11-year veteran, had a .464 TENDEX rating, but he played more for the Suns than the Pistons. Johnson, a prolific scorer, had one of his poorest seasons with a .433 rating.

This is a good bench when it is considered that Rodman and Salley seldom started.

OUTLOOK

It was June 20, 1988 and the New York Yankees were playing the Detroit Tigers for first place in the American League's Eastern Division. But most of the spectators in Tiger Stadium had another sport on their minds. Several times during the baseball game a chant spread through the stands: "Beat L.A. . . . Beat L.A. . . . Beat L.A. . . ." Banners appeared reading, "Go Pistons & Tigers."

Television commentator Al Michaels observed: "It's as if the Tigers are an afterthought."

The Tigers defeated the Yankees that night, but 24 hours later, when the Lakers edged the Pistons for the NBA title, with Piston hero Isiah Thomas hobbled by an injury, there was no joy in Detroit for the first-place Tigers. There was only sadness for the Pistons.

The Pistons will make another try to win an NBA title this season with essentially the same team as last season, although third-year players Dennis Rodman and John Salley could be starters instead of reserves. Salley is likely to start at power forward in place of Rick Mahorn, and Rodman could take over at small forward for Adrian Dantley, a defensive liability who was victimized by James Worthy in the final game of the 1988 playoffs. Center Bill Laimbeer and guards Thomas and Joe Dumars have starting jobs secured.

Probable finish: Second in Central Division.

9

Golden State Warriors

*I*n the alphabetical listings of the NBA, it is coincidental that the first seven teams all had winning records in 1987–88. But after discussing those seven, what can you say about a team like Golden State, which lost more games than any of the seven won?

The Warriors used a league-high total of 22 players in a futile effort to find a winning combination, and none of the 22 played as many as 2,200 minutes.

Solitary bright spots were guards Chris Mullin and Winston Garland, both of whom displayed star potential.

Warriors ranked 21st out of 23 teams in won–lost record and TENDEX rating. They proved in reverse that blocked shots influence opponents' field goal percentage by ranking last in the league in blocks and having their opponents shoot .501 against them—second best behind San Antonio's opposition.

Golden State also rated 20th or worse in two-point field goal percentage, rebounding, and BEST. Their only high rankings were No. 3 in free throw percentage and No. 5 in steals.

The Warriors were outscored by 8.3 points per game, next to last in the league.

CHRIS MULLIN

AGE: 25
HEIGHT: 6-7
WEIGHT: 220
POSITION: Shooting Guard
EXPERIENCE: 3 Seasons
COLLEGE: St. John's
BIRTHPLACE: Brooklyn, NY
1987–88 TENDEX: .578

We have said that Mullin has star potential, but it is arguable that he became one in 1987–88, his third NBA season . . . achieved a TENDEX rating of .578, fourth best among shooting guards . . . ranked No. 6 in the league in free throw percentage, No. 8 in the primary Shootist statistic (points per shot), No. 13 in steals, and No. 19 in points per minute . . . scoring average was 20.2 . . . despite missing 22 games because of injury, Mullin led the Warriors in scoring and free throw percentage and was second on the team in field goal percentage, assists and steals . . . versatility enabled him to rank among the top ten shooting guards in 15 of 18 categories, with highs of No. 3 Shootist; No. 4 in TENDEX rating and blocked shots; No. 5 in points, steals, and three-point field goal percentage; No. 6 in BEST and two-point field goals; and No. 7 in PAR . . . weakest stat was No. 15 in ratio of blocks to turnovers.

ROD HIGGINS

AGE: 28
HEIGHT: 6-7
WEIGHT: 210
POSITION: Small Forward
EXPERIENCE: 6 Seasons
COLLEGE: Fresno State
BIRTHPLACE: Monroe, LA
1987–88 TENDEX: .503

In his sixth NBA season, Higgins became a respectable player . . . ranked among the league's top 20 in both Shootist statistics and two turnover-related categories . . . led Warriors with a field goal percentage of .526 and averaged 15.5 points per game . . . among small forwards he was rated No. 1 in three-point field goal percentage, No. 3 Shootist, No. 3 in turnovers, No. 4 in free throw percentage, No. 7 in two-point field goal percentage, and No. 7 in BEST . . . weak points were rebounding (No. 19), PAR (No. 18), and blocked shots (No. 17).

MULLIN

1987–88	2PFG	3PFG	F.T.	REB.	AST.	STL.	T.O.	BLK.	PTS.
Per Game	.526	.351	.885	3.4	4.8	1.9	2.6	0.5	20.2
Per Minute	.526	.351	.885	.101	.143	.056	.063	.016	.597
Rating	6	5	3	10	9	5	13	4	5

HIGGINS

1987–88	2PFG	3PFG	F.T.	REB.	AST.	STL.	T.O.	BLK.	PTS.
Per Game	.528	.487	.848	4.3	2.8	1.0	1.6	0.5	15.5
Per Minute	.528	.487	.848	.134	.086	.032	.051	.014	.482
Rating	7	1	4	19	10	8	3	17	15

WINSTON GARLAND

AGE: 23
HEIGHT: 6-2
WEIGHT: 170
POSITION: Point Guard
EXPERIENCE: 1 Season
COLLEGE: Southwest Missouri State
BIRTHPLACE: Gary, IN
1987–88 TENDEX: .453

Signed by Golden State after being cut by two other teams, Garland surprised by taking over the regular point job and achieving the sixth best TENDEX rating of the 1987–88 rookies . . . ranked No. 17 in the league in assists per minute and had a free throw percentage of .879, good enough to rank eighth if he had attempted enough shots to qualify . . . on the negative side, he was in the NBA's bottom ten in blocked shots and Shootist percentage . . . ranked among the top ten point guards in rebounding, steals, free throw percentage, three-point field goal percentage, and BEST . . . but was last in two-point field goal percentage and low in most other categories . . . a good penetrator, with point-guard cockiness, expect him to improve this season.

BEN McDONALD

AGE: 26
HEIGHT: 6-8
WEIGHT: 225
POSITION: Power Forward
EXPERIENCE: 3 Seasons
COLLEGE: California-Irvine
BIRTHPLACE: Torrance, CA
1987–88 TENDEX: .344

There is no gentle way to phrase it: McDonald was the worst regular player in the NBA last season, dead last in TENDEX rating with his .344 . . . also finished among the bottom ten in points, blocked shots, and PAR . . . last in five categories out of 20 power forwards, 19th in three other categories . . . the only good aspect of his play was turnovers, No. 6 in the NBA, but when you don't have the ball you can't lose it.

GARLAND

1987–88	2PFG	3PFG	F.T.	REB.	AST.	STL.	T.O.	BLK.	PTS.
Per Game	.444	.333	.879	3.4	6.4	1.7	2.5	0.1	12.4
Per Minute	.444	.333	.879	.107	.202	.055	.079	.003	.392
Rating	21	6	2	8	14	9	13	17	12

McDONALD

1987–88	2PFG	3PFG	F.T.	REB.	AST.	STL.	T.O.	BLK.	PTS.
Per Game	.482	.257	.784	4.1	1.7	0.5	1.1	0.1	7.6
Per Minute	.482	.257	.784	.164	.068	.019	.046	.004	.300
Rating	17	5	5	20	8	19	3	20	20

RESERVES

The Warriors' primary reserve—no, their primary player among regulars or reserves, is Ralph Sampson. The team is putting its hopes for future respectability on the condition of the 7'4" Sampson's knees. With injuries to both knees last season, Sampson had a terrible time, winding up with a TENDEX rating of .508 while playing only 1,663 minutes in 48 games. But if he can get his knees sound this fall, he could be ready for his best season since he joined the TENDEX 700 Club five years ago. The reason for optimism is that the Warriors intend to use Sampson exclusively at center. He played out of position at power forward for four seasons in Houston before being traded to the Warriors.

Golden State also obtained 7'6" Manute Bol from Washington as a backup for Sampson.

Tellis Frank, a 6'10" player who was Golden State's first draft choice last year, developed reasonably well with a .403 TENDEX rating his rookie season and has potential to start at either forward position.

If it weren't for Mullin, shooting guard Otis Smith also might have a chance to start. Smith's TENDEX rating of .553 was the sixth best of the NBA reserves last season.

OUTLOOK

The Warriors went into the 1988 college draft with a solid backcourt and a flimsy frontcourt. So why did they select two backcourtmen?

With Winston Garland showing potential at point guard as a rookie last season, and Chris Mullin developing into an excellent shooting guard, the Warriors appeared set in backcourt. So what do they do with top draft choices Mitch Richmond and Keith Smart?

Richmond, drafted No. 5 overall, and Mullin could be the best two players on the Golden State team, but unfortunately they play the same position.

Smart has the ability to compete with Garland, although these two are not as good as the Mullin–Richmond tandem.

It's up front where the problems are.

Golden State is counting on center Ralph Sampson to make a complete recovery from injuries to both knees. Even if he does so, he probably won't see the ball much, because opposing teams will surround him with players who normally would be assigned to guard the Warrior forwards.

The Warriors do not have a forward who can even be considered average.

Probable finish: Sixth in Pacific Division.

10

Houston Rockets

*T*he payoff question is this: Why did they wait so long?

The twin-towers experiment, destined for failure from the beginning, as other such experiments with two superstar seven-footers in the same lineup have failed, was sustained for four seasons before the Rockets finally gave up on it and traded Ralph Sampson to Golden State.

The remaining big guy, Akeem Olajuwon, is the best center in the league since Kareem Abdul-Jabbar's heyday during the 1970s, but the Rockets are still lacking in quality players, both in the starting lineup and on the bench, to support their awesome big man. Imbalance is shown by the fact that in 1987–88 Olajuwon led the team in every statistical category other than assists, free throw percentage, and three-point field goal percentage.

In TENDEX power rating, Houston placed 11th in the NBA but performed a little better than that with a record of 46–36, tenth best in the league.

The Rockets matched their opponents statistically in most categories. Their winning edge was gained in blocked shots (No. 5 in the league). The intimidation factor associated with shot-blocking helped them hold opponents to a field goal percentage of .465, making Houston the second best team in the league in that category.

Rockets rated No. 2 in the NBA in rebounding, No. 6 in blocked shots and BEST, and No. 7 in free throw percentage and scoring. Negative areas were three-point field goal percentage (No. 21), Shootist (No. 19), and two-point field goal percentage (No. 18).

AKEEM OLAJUWON

AGE: 25
HEIGHT: 7-0
WEIGHT: 250
POSITION: Center
EXPERIENCE: 4 Seasons
COLLEGE: Houston
BIRTHPLACE: Lagos, Nigeria
1987–88 TENDEX: .782

Olajuwon is probably the second or third best player in the NBA in terms of overall impact on his team . . . All-NBA choice at center the last two seasons and probably should have been so honored all four of his years in the league . . . All-Defensive first team past two seasons . . . consistent and versatile, he did not lead the league in any major statistical category last season but finished among the leaders in most of them: No. 3 in BEST; No. 4 in blocked shots, rebounds, and overall TENDEX rating; No. 7 in PAR; No. 10 in steals and ratio of blocks to turnovers; and No. 12 in scoring (points per minute) . . . led the league with six 20–20 games (20 rebounds and 20 points) . . . one of four players with more than 100 steals and 100 blocked shots . . . second player in NBA history to rank among the top ten in both steals and blocks . . . always a great playoff player, he outdid himself in a four-game series against Dallas, averaging 37.5 points and 16.8 rebounds, with an .884 free throw percentage and a .571 field goal percentage for an incredible TENDEX rating of 1.170; even more incredibly, the Rockets still lost . . . in regular season led Rockets in scoring average, blocked shots, steals, rebounds, and field goal percentage . . . among NBA centers

centers achieved No. 1 ratings in TENDEX, steals, rebounds, and PAR; No. 2 in BEST; No. 4 in blocked shots and minutes played.

ERIC (SLEEPY) FLOYD

AGE: 28
HEIGHT: 6-3
WEIGHT: 175
POSITION: Shooting Guard
EXPERIENCE: 6 Seasons
COLLEGE: Georgetown
BIRTHPLACE: Gastonia, NC
1987–88 TENDEX: .501

Floyd became a little too sleepy last season and at times seemed to be sleepwalking on the basketball court after ranking among the NBA's best backcourtmen the previous two years . . . TENDEX rating dropped more than 100 points and led to his being traded by Golden State to Houston . . . was accused in both Golden State and Houston of failing to pass to open teammates, a severe criticism to be levied against a guy who averaged 10.3 assists the previous season; last season that figure dropped to 7.1 . . . but in terms of physical ability he is Rockets' second most talented player, capable of averaging 20 points and ten assists if he plays to potential . . . holds NBA record for points in one half (39) and one quarter (29) in a playoff game . . . his streak of three years in a row playing all 82 games was broken last season . . . No. 12 in NBA in assists per minute and No. 18 in PAR, nearly achieving a PAR-4 rating; but was among the league's ten worst players in BEST and Shootist points per shot.

OLAJUWON

1987–88	2PFG	3PFG	F.T.	REB.	AST.	STL.	T.O.	BLK.	PTS.
Per Game	.516	.000	.695	12.1	2.1	2.1	3.1	2.7	22.8
Per Minute	.516	.000	.695	.339	.058	.057	.086	.076	.639
Rating	10	20	17	1	7	1	16	4	2

FLOYD

1987–88	2PFG	3PFG	F.T.	REB.	AST.	STL.	T.O.	BLK.	PTS.
Per Game	.453	.194	.850	3.8	7.1	1.2	2.9	0.2	15.0
Per Minute	.453	.194	.850	.118	.216	.038	.089	.005	.459
Rating	21	15	11	6	2	11	18	15	14

RODNEY McCRAY

AGE: 27
HEIGHT: 6-8
WEIGHT: 235
POSITION: Small Forward
EXPERIENCE: 5 Seasons
COLLEGE: Louisville
BIRTHPLACE: Mount Vernon, NY
1987–88 TENDEX: .518

McCray is a player who receives more credit than his overall performance warrants . . . a sound all-around player, but not exceptional at either end of the court, in spite of being voted to All-Defensive team last season . . . set Houston field goal percentage record with .552 in 1986–87, but dropped off to .481 last season . . . ranked No. 20 in the league in least turnovers, but that was his only ranking among leaders . . . second on Rockets in minutes played, but did not lead team in a single statistical category . . . among small forwards had good ratings of No. 4 in rebounds and turnovers, and No. 6 in assists; poor ratings of No. 21 in scoring, No. 18 in steals and Shootist, and No. 17 in PAR and two-point field goal percentage; below-average TENDEX of No. 13.

ALLEN LEAVELL

AGE: 31
HEIGHT: 6-2
WEIGHT: 190
POSITION: Point Guard
EXPERIENCE: 9 Seasons
COLLEGE: Oklahoma City
BIRTHPLACE: Muncie, IN
1987–88 TENDEX: .448

One thing you can say about Leavell: He makes things happen, some good, some bad . . . ranked among NBA leaders last season in ratio of steals to turnovers (seventh), free throw percentage (11th), steals (11th), and assists (20th) . . . but was in the bottom ten in rebounds, blocked shots, and PAR . . . like backcourt teammate Sleepy Floyd, he has been accused of shooting too much and not too well; both players shot under 44 percent from the field last season . . . had good ratings among 20 NBA point guards of No. 3 in turnovers, No. 4 in free throw percentage, No. 5 in BEST and No. 6 in steals, but ranked No. 15 or below in ten other categories.

McCRAY

1987–88	2PFG	3PFG	F.T.	REB.	AST.	STL.	T.O.	BLK.	PTS.
Per Game	.484	.000	.785	7.8	3.3	0.7	1.8	0.6	12.4
Per Minute	.484	.000	.785	.235	.098	.021	.054	.019	.374
Rating	17	19	13	4	6	18	4	13	21

LEAVELL

1987–88	2PFG	3PFG	F.T.	REB.	AST.	STL.	T.O.	BLK.	PTS.
Per Game	.471	.216	.869	1.9	5.1	1.6	1.6	0.1	10.2
Per Minute	.471	.216	.869	.069	.188	.058	.060	.004	.381
Rating	16	16	4	17	17	6	3	16	14

JOE BARRY CARROLL

AGE: 30
HEIGHT: 7-1
WEIGHT: 255
POSITION: Center
EXPERIENCE: 7 Seasons
COLLEGE: Purdue
BIRTHPLACE: Pine Bluff, AR
1987–88 TENDEX: .492

Carroll probably should be listed as a reserve, because his days as a starter in the NBA are probably over; but he played 2,004 minutes last season, just enough to qualify as a regular . . . was a 20-point scorer for his first seven seasons, but career average dropped to 19.4 when he averaged only 12.7 in limited playing time last season for Golden State and Houston . . . surpassed the 10,000-point mark during 1987–88 and now has 10,755 for his career . . . rated No. 10 in the NBA in blocked shots last season, but was in the bottom ten in field goal percentage and both Shootist categories . . . among the league's centers who played 2,000 or more minutes, he had good ratings of No. 6 in steals and blocked shots, No. 8 in PAR, and No. 9 in scoring . . . bad ratings of No. 21 in two-point field goal percentage, No. 20 in both Shootist statistics, No. 15 in rebounds and turnovers, and No. 16 in TENDEX.

RESERVES

The only good thing about the Rockets' reserves is that they didn't have to worry about losing anyone important in the expansion draft for the two new teams last spring.

Able to protect eight players from the draft, the Rockets had no problem because they didn't have more than that many players who merited protection.

Purvis Short is a good one. He averaged 14.3 points per game as the sixth man last season and had a good TENDEX rating of .486, above the norm of .450 for a shooting guard.

Forward–center Jim Petersen was respectable with a .463 rating in 1,793 minutes.

Second-year forward Buck Johnson showed improvement with a .498 rating that could earn him more playing time than the 879 minutes he had in 1987–88.

CARROLL

1987–88	2PFG	3PFG	F.T.	REB.	AST.	STL.	T.O.	BLK.	PTS.
Per Game	.436	.000	.764	6.4	1.5	0.7	2.1	1.4	12.7
Per Minute	.436	.000	.764	.244	.056	.025	.082	.053	.487
Rating	21	13	10	15	10	6	15	6	9

OUTLOOK

The Rockets need to send their management back to college for a course in Chemistry 101. They can't be faulted for the players they have drafted during the 1980s, but they always seem to duplicate strengths and fail to deal with weaknesses. They have terrible chemistry.

The selection of Derrick Chievous as this year's No. 1 pick won't change the situation much, if at all.

Chievous is a guard–forward who does a lot of things like Rodney McCray. Chievous is versatile and plays well in the open court, but doesn't shoot well from long range.

Outside shooting remains the Rockets' biggest need to ease the pressure of collapsing defenses around the NBA's best big man, Akeem Olajuwon.

Olajuwon's achievements during the past four seasons have been remarkable considering this team's poor balance. Akeem probably shouldn't have been chosen at all by Houston in 1984 when they had a healthy Ralph Sampson and a chance to complement Sampson with Michael Jordan.

The twin towers got in each other's way for three and a half seasons before Sampson finally was traded last year for Sleepy Floyd. Then the Rockets learned to their surprise that Floyd could not shoot well from long range and was not a good playmaker, so they still need a point guard.

Also, they could use a power forward.

Probable finish: Fifth in Midwest Division.

11

Indiana Pacers

*I*t's a case of too many shooters and not enough basketballs to go around.

Except for point guard Vern Fleming and center Steve Stipanovich, all of the Pacers' other top players shoot at least once from the field for every three minutes of playing time; some of them shoot a lot more than that and, if it were possible, they'd probably like to shoot even more.

And Fleming and Stipanovich aren't exactly shy to shoot either.

The 1987–88 season was disappointing for the Pacers and head coach Jack Ramsay, who expected better things after qualifying for the playoffs in 1986–87 for the first time in six years. They failed to make the 1988 playoffs.

Ramsay, in second place on the all-time list of winning NBA coaches, moved closer to Red Auerbach's record 938 regular-season victories with the 38 Pacer wins in 1987–88.

Ramsay-coached teams have won 864 games in 20 seasons.

Eagerness to shoot from outside hurts the Pacers' inside game and as a consequence they don't get to the free throw line enough. They were the only NBA team to shoot fewer than 2,000 free throws last season.

As might be expected, the strongest part of the Pacers' game in 1987–88 was shooting. They ranked No. 3 in the league in the Shootist statistic computed by dividing total points by total shots. They were No. 5 in three-point field goal percentage, No. 6 in free throw percentage, and No. 11 in two-point field goal percentage.

Except for turnovers (No. 8), Indiana finished below average in all other statistical departments, the worst being blocked shots (No. 22), steals (No. 20), BEST (No. 18), assists (No. 18), points (No. 17), PAR (No. 17), and TENDEX (No. 15).

VERN FLEMING

AGE: 27
HEIGHT: 6-5
WEIGHT: 195
POSITION: Point Guard
EXPERIENCE; 4 Seasons
COLLEGE: Georgia
BIRTHPLACE: New York City
1987–88 TENDEX: .572

Yes, I know scorers Chuck Person and Wayman Tisdale receive more nationwide publicity, but Fleming is Indiana's best player . . . trouble is, he is not good enough to be the best player on a good team; all of the league's ten best teams had at least one player in the superstar (TENDEX .700) or star (.600) classification last season . . . an excellent backcourtman, Fleming was No. 12 in the NBA in 1987–88 with a PAR-4 rating and No. 16 in assists . . . led the Pacers in steals, assists, and field goal percentage . . . among point guards was rated in the top ten in 14 statistical categories, with high rankings of No. 4 in TENDEX and two-point field goal percentage, and No. 5 in rebounds, turnovers and Shootist . . . only real weakness is long-range shooting as he missed all 13 of his three-point field goal attempts.

STEVE STIPANOVICH

AGE: 28
HEIGHT: 7-0
WEIGHT: 250
POSITION: Center
EXPERIENCE: 5 Seasons
COLLEGE: Missouri
BIRTHPLACE: St. Louis
1987–88 TENDEX: .549

A workmanlike player, Stipanovich doesn't rank among the NBA leaders in any area of play—but he doesn't rank among the losers either . . . for his position Stipanovich plays with more quickness than power, shoots well from outside, and perhaps is better suited to power forward, if the Pacers could find a legitimate intimidating center . . . led Pacers in rebounds, but was only No. 12 of the league's 21 regular centers in that department . . . among centers graded No. 2 in ratio of steals to turnovers, No. 3 in steals, No. 3 in three-point field goal percentage, No. 4 in free throw percentage, No. 5 in assists, and No. 10 in TENDEX rating . . . far down the list at No. 17 in blocked shots and No. 16 in PAR.

FLEMING

1987–88	2PFG	3PFG	F.T.	REB.	AST.	STL.	T.O.	BLK.	PTS.
Per Game	.531	.000	.802	4.6	7.1	1.4	2.2	0.1	13.9
Per Minute	.531	.000	.802	.133	.208	.042	.064	.004	.407
Rating	4	20	14	5	13	14	5	14	10

STIPANOVICH

1987–88	2PFG	3PFG	F.T.	REB.	AST.	STL.	T.O.	BLK.	PTS.
Per Game	.502	.200	.809	8.3	2.3	1.1	2.0	0.9	13.5
Per Minute	.502	.200	.809	.246	.068	.033	.058	.026	.401
Rating	13	3	4	12	5	3	8	17	14

WAYMAN TISDALE

AGE: 24
HEIGHT: 6-9
WEIGHT: 240
POSITION: Power Forward
EXPERIENCE: 3 Seasons
COLLEGE: Oklahoma
BIRTHPLACE: Tulsa, OK
1987–88 TENDEX: .535

In three seasons in the NBA Tisdale has shown very little of the explosive power around the basket that he was noted for as an All-American at the University of Oklahoma. He isn't a bad pro player, but he isn't really a very good one either . . . not rated among the NBA leaders or the bottom ten in any statistical category last season . . . did not lead the Pacers in any category either . . . among power forwards his high rating was No. 5 Shootist . . . also was No. 6 in scoring and free throw percentage . . . low ratings were No. 17 in steals and blocked shots . . . most of his other marks were around the middle of the pack, including a TENDEX rating of No. 12.

CHUCK PERSON

AGE: 24
HEIGHT: 6-8
WEIGHT: 225
POSITION: Small Forward
EXPERIENCE: 2 Seasons
COLLEGE: Auburn
BIRTHPLACE: Brantley, AL
1987–88 TENDEX: .477

Person is a mystifying player, who burst into the NBA with talent that seemed comparable to former Auburn teammate Charles Barkley, winning Rookie of the Year award in 1986–87; but last season he fell right on his tush . . . as a rookie he boasted that he would become the dominant small forward in the Central Division, surpassing Dominique Wilkins; last season he not only failed to overtake Wilkins, but regressed to rate as only the No. 6 small forward in the six-team division . . . essentially a shooter, he took 1,449 shots and yet finished next to last in the league in Shootist percentage, beating out only brickthrower Mark Eaton of Utah . . . also finished in the league's bottom ten in BEST and blocked shots, with the worst rating of any frontcourt player . . . lack of defensive effort and concentration were evident in his tailspin as the rookie award seemed to go to his head . . . No. 18 rated small forward out of 22 qualifiers, but he has the physical talent to become Indiana's best player, potentially.

TISDALE

1987–88	2PFG	3PFG	F.T.	REB.	AST.	STL.	T.O.	BLK.	PTS.
Per Game	.513	.000	.783	6.2	1.3	0.7	1.8	0.4	16.1
Per Minute	.513	.000	.783	.206	.043	.023	.061	.014	.533
Rating	8	15	6	16	14	17	11	17	6

PERSON

1987–88	2PFG	3PFG	F.T.	REB.	AST.	STL.	T.O.	BLK.	PTS.
Per Game	.480	.333	.670	6.8	3.9	0.9	2.7	0.1	17.0
Per Minute	.480	.333	.670	.191	.110	.026	.075	.003	.478
Rating	18	3	21	9	3	14	18	22	16

JOHN LONG

AGE: 32
HEIGHT: 6-5
WEIGHT: 200
POSITION: Shooting Guard
EXPERIENCE: 10 Seasons
COLLEGE: Detroit
BIRTHPLACE: Romulus, MI
1987–88 TENDEX: .415

Long's TENDEX rating last season was the seventh worst among the 101 NBA players who played 2,000 or more minutes, but Coach Ramsay can't be faulted for keeping him in the lineup because his eventual replacement, rookie Reggie Miller, didn't do much better; Miller had a .419 rating and plenty of defensive lapses . . . Long's free throw percentage of .907 gave him the No. 3 ranking in official NBA statistics, although in the TENDEX system listings he was omitted because he fell 17 short of the qualifying number of 200 attempts . . . Long's top ranking among 18 shooting guards was No. 1 in three-point field goal percentage; conversely, he was No. 17 in assists, and No. 17 in TENDEX rating.

RESERVES

Herb Williams has been a full-time player for so long that it feels strange to have to list him among the Pacers' reserves. But the 30-year-old Williams failed last season for the first time in his seven-year NBA career to play 2,000 minutes and so he must be listed here. Still a fair rebounder and shot-blocker, Williams' TENDEX rating slipped to .473 primarily because of abysmal shooting. He ranked in the NBA's bottom ten with a field goal percentage of .425.

While Williams appears to be on the way down, Reggie Miller and Ron Anderson are on the way up.

Last season Miller demonstrated great shooting range and was rated as the NBA's tenth best rookie with a TENDEX rating of .419. Although he has a lot to learn about fundamentals, he could become an excellent player. He probably will win the regular shooting guard job this season.

Anderson has averaged about 1,000 minutes of playing time for his first four NBA seasons, but on the strength of his performance last year he should be given a chance to play much more as a reserve for forwards Wayman Tisdale and Chuck Person. His 1987–88 TENDEX rating of .518 was actually better than Person's last season. He was the 13th rated reserve in the league.

LONG

1987–88	2PFG	3PFG	F.T.	REB.	AST.	STL.	T.O.	BLK.	PTS.
Per Game	.478	.442	.907	2.8	2.1	1.0	1.6	0.1	12.8
Per Minute	.478	.442	.907	.113	.086	.042	.063	.005	.511
Rating	16	1	1	8	17	9	7	16	12

OUTLOOK

Like the Rockets, the Pacers have drafted some good players, but haven't been able to formulate the right chemistry. They have too many players trying to maintain high scoring averages and no dominant rebounders.

With the selection of 7'3" center Rik Smits in the first round of the 1988 draft, the Pacers took a step in the right direction. But Indiana fans need to be patient with Smits, who probably won't make much impact in 1988–89, jumping all the way from the lowest level of college competition (Marist) to the best division in the NBA.

The next step may be to trade one of the two hotshot forwards, Chuck Person or Wayman Tisdale, for a versatile guard. Steve Stipanovich has done an unselfish job as the Pacers' center the past few seasons, but he is better suited to be a forward.

Behind standout point guard Vern Fleming, the Pacers have little backcourt strength.

Probable finish: Sixth in Central Division.

12

Los Angeles Clippers

*T*he Clippers get a break this season: They won't be the worst team in the NBA for the first time in three years. That dubious distinction will be earned by one of the expansion teams, either Miami or Charlotte.

Unlike other poor teams, such as Golden State and New Jersey, the Clippers don't even have a nucleus of developing players from which to build for the future. Their best players—rebounder Michael Cage, shot-blocker Benoit Benjamin, and scorer Mike Woodson—are one-dimensional. The rest of the Clippers are zero-dimensional.

Realistically, though, the Clippers or any other team can turn the corner and become a contender with one or two excellent draft years, as Cleveland did. They may already be on the right track by landing Danny Manning this season.

It is easy to pick out the team strengths of the Clippers, because they have only one, shot-blocking. Led by Benjamin, they blocked more shots than their opponents last season; but in all other categories, offensive and defensive, they were buried. They were outscored by an average of 109–99 in losing 65 of 82 games.

Perhaps the ultimate mark of the Clippers' futility was that, even though they had the official rebounding champion of the NBA, Cage, they lost the battle of the boards by an average of 4.4 rebounds per game to their opposition.

The Clippers ranked last in the league in two-point field goal percentage, free throw percentage, Shootist, points, turnovers, and TENDEX rating. They were 22nd in PAR, 21st in assists, and 20th in three-point field goal percentage.

BENOIT BENJAMIN

AGE: 24
HEIGHT: 7-0
WEIGHT: 245
POSITION: Center
EXPERIENCE: 3 Seasons
COLLEGE: Creighton
BIRTHPLACE: Monroe, LA
1987-88 TENDEX: .562

The same question can be asked about Benjamin's legitimacy as a player that was asked about Cage, although it is a little more difficult to accumulate blocked shots in a vacuum than it is rebounds . . . No. 2 in the league in blocks, No. 7 in BEST, but finished in the bottom ten in turnovers with poor ball-handling in the low post . . . out of 21 centers, ranked No. 9 in TENDEX . . . also had high ratings of No. 3 in assists, No. 3 in BEST, and No. 3 in PAR . . . downside stats were No. 21 in ratio of steals to turnovers, No. 20 in turnovers, No. 16 in free throw percentage, No. 16 in scoring, and No. 15 in two-point field goal percentage.

MIKE WOODSON

AGE: 30
HEIGHT: 6-5
WEIGHT: 198
POSITION: Shooting Guard
EXPERIENCE: 8 Seasons
COLLEGE: Indiana
BIRTHPLACE: Indianapolis
1987-88 TENDEX: .448

Woodson is the regular shooting guard in the NBA's creakiest backcourt . . . led the Clippers in scoring in 1987-88 with an 18.0 average; also led in 1986-87 with 17.1 . . . with career total of 9,477 points, he could reach 10,000-point mark this season . . . rated No. 12 in the league last year in free throw percentage, but was in the bottom ten in rebounds . . . No. 5 among shooting guards in blocked shots, No. 7 in free throw percentage, No. 8 in steals, and No. 8 in scoring . . . lows were No. 20 in two-point field goal percentage, No. 17 Shootist, No. 16 in PAR, No. 16 in rebounds, and No. 13 in TENDEX rating.

BENJAMIN

1987–88	2PFG	3PFG	F.T.	REB.	AST.	STL.	T.O.	BLK.	PTS.
Per Game	.496	.000	.706	8.0	2.6	0.8	3.4	3.4	13.0
Per Minute	.496	.000	.706	.244	.079	.023	.103	.104	.396
Rating	15	21	16	13	3	9	20	2	16

WOODSON

1987–88	2PFG	3PFG	F.T.	REB.	AST.	STL.	T.O.	BLK.	PTS.
Per Game	.459	.231	.868	2.4	3.4	1.4	2.3	0.3	18.0
Per Minute	.459	.231	.868	.075	.108	.043	.073	.010	.567
Rating	20	11	7	16	14	8	11	5	8

LARRY DREW

AGE: 30
HEIGHT: 6-2
WEIGHT: 190
POSITION: Point Guard
EXPERIENCE: 8 Seasons
COLLEGE: Missouri
BIRTHPLACE: Kansas City
1987-88 TENDEX: .388

Drew is a very weak player, last in the NBA in 1987–88 in rebounds and blocked shots; in bottom ten in PAR percentage, Shootist, and TENDEX rating . . . highest ranking was No. 19 in assists . . . the only regular player in the league who did not rate higher than tenth in any category for his position . . . rankings compared with other point guards ranged from No. 10 in turnovers to last in rebounds, steals, blocked shots, Shootist percentage, PAR, and TENDEX rating.

RESERVES

Substitute guards Quentin Dailey (.495) and Darnell Valentine (.463) actually had higher TENDEX ratings than the starters, but maybe that was because they played a lot against other teams' subs. All four guards are well past their primes as players.

Although none of the Clippers' three first-round draft choices from last year played well in their rookie seasons, they haven't given up on Reggie Williams (No. 4 pick in the first round), Joe Wolf (No. 13), or Ken Norman (No. 19). Norman's TENDEX rating of .389 was the best of the three.

DREW

1987–88	2PFG	3PFG	F.T.	REB.	AST.	STL.	T.O.	BLK.	PTS.
Per Game	.479	.289	.769	1.6	5.2	0.9	2.1	0.0	10.3
Per Minute	.479	.289	.769	.059	.189	.032	.075	.000	.378
Rating	14	12	18	20	16	20	10	20	16

OUTLOOK

The Clippers are ready to make a big move upward.

They are likely to jump from last place to at least fourth in the seven-team Pacific Division this season, and third place is a possibility.

This was a team that had just one good player in 1987–88, rebounding champion Michael Cage. Cage was involved in a multiplayer draft-day deal that wound up with the Clippers receiving forward Charles Smith and guard Gary Grant.

And then, of course, there is Danny Manning.

With three first-round draft choices two seasons in a row, the Clippers probably will start four of them this season around center Benoit Benjamin. Benjamin is not as bad as his detractors contend and could show improvement now that opponents will have to play honest defense instead of sagging around him.

The other four starters likely will be forwards Manning and Smith, and guards Grant and/or Norm Nixon and Reggie Williams.

They may not jell early in the season, but this is a team with playoff potential this season and championship potential within three years.

The 1987 first-rounders Joe Wolf and Ken Norman fortify the bench, along with 1988 second-rounder Tom Garrick.

Probable finish: Fourth in Pacific Division.

13

Los Angeles Lakers

*T*he Lakers led the NBA standings for the second season in a row in 1987–88, but a few nicks began to appear in their furnishings.

The Lakers' Big Three—Magic Johnson, Kareem Abdul-Jabbar, and James Worthy—all experienced declines in level of play. But intelligent coaching by Pat Riley, improvement by Byron Scott, and a strong bench kept the Lakers on top. Their 62–20 record gave a winning season for a league-high 12th year in a row.

According to the TENDEX rating system, the Lakers had only one individual player among the league's top 20 (Johnson, No. 7) and ranked behind Boston and Utah in overall player talent. But thanks to the clever leadership of Riley, the team won 62 games—eight more than it should have won according to its ability—and then squeaked past Utah in a quarter-final playoff series that was decided by the home-court advantage.

The eight-game boost Riley gave the team with his coaching equaled Coach of the Year Doug Moe of Denver as the best in the league.

Statistics showed that the Lakers excelled in shooting and playmaking while holding their own in other aspects of play. They ranked No. 2 in two-point field goal percent-

age, No. 2 in Shootist (points per shot), No. 3 in assists, No. 4 in PAR, and No. 5 in scoring. Their lowest ratings were No. 16 in three-point field goal percentage, No. 15 in steals, and No. 15 in blocked shots.

And, despite having a comparatively old team, the Lakers played good defense, holding their opponents to 107.0 points per game—1.2 points under the league average. Riley deserves credit for this too, because he made sure the older players got plenty of rest. Only the 27-year-old Scott was called on for a workhorse season with more than 3,000 minutes of court time. None of the other regulars played as many as 2,700 minutes.

Another factor in the Lakers' success was intimidation—not of opposing teams but of referees. With the help of nervous whistle-blowers, they were awarded 22.8 percent more free throws than their opponents, profiting also from foul trouble of key opposing players, even though they did not have the muscle to be as aggressive in the low-post as teams like Detroit and Atlanta. It is in the low-post area, of course, where most fouls normally are committed.

The Lakers may be vulnerable now, but they are still formidable.

EARVIN (MAGIC) JOHNSON

AGE: 29
HEIGHT: 6-9
WEIGHT: 226
POSITION: Point Guard
EXPERIENCE: 9 Seasons
COLLEGE: Michigan State
BIRTHPLACE: Lansing, MI
1987–88 TENDEX: .721

One of the all-time great backcourtmen, Johnson had another TENDEX 700 Club season in 1987–88, although his rating dropped off by 90 points from his Most Valuable Player season of 1986–87 . . . injury caused him to miss ten games last season and may have affected his play in other games as his rating fell from No. 2 in the league to No. 7 . . . All-NBA six times, playoff MVP three times . . . led league in assists four times, steals twice . . . third on career list for assists with 7,037 and should pass Lenny Wilkens (7,211) early this season and move into the No. 2 spot behind Oscar Robertson (9,887) . . . No. 2 in the NBA last year in assists and also No. 2 with a PAR-6 rating . . . No. 12 in Shootist percentage and No. 17 in free throw percentage . . . but a few alarming negatives began to appear in his game, as he finished in the league's bottom ten in turnovers, ratio of blocked shots to turnovers, and BEST . . . in point guard listings, out of 20 qualifying players, he was No. 1 in rebounds, No. 1 in PAR, No. 2 in assists, No. 2 in Shootist percentage, No. 2 in scoring, and No. 2 in TENDEX (behind John Stockton of Utah) . . . conversely, he finished last among point guards in turnovers, BEST, and ratio of steals and blocked shots to turnovers.

BYRON SCOTT

AGE: 27
HEIGHT: 6-4
WEIGHT: 195
POSITION: Shooting Guard
EXPERIENCE: 5 Seasons
COLLEGE: Arizona State
BIRTHPLACE: Ogden, UT
1987–88 TENDEX: .550

After four disappointing seasons, Scott matured last season when he became one of the most consistent players in the NBA, although he was also one of the most underrated . . . was the only player in the league to have single-digit ratings (No. 9 or better) in 17 of 18 statistical categories at his position . . . No. 1 shooting guard in two-point field goal percentage, No. 2 and 3 in Shootist categories, No. 5 and 8 in PAR statistics, No. 3 in turnovers, No. 3 in ratios of steals and blocked shots to turnover, No. 4 in BEST, No. 4 in minutes played, No. 6 in blocked shots, No. 6 in steals, No. 6 in three-point field goal percentage, No. 7 in scoring, No. 9 in free throw percentage, No. 9 in rebounds, and No. 7 in TENDEX . . . finished among the league's top 20 in seven categories: Shootist, steals, PAR, free throw percentage, two-point field goal percentage, minutes played, and ratio of steals to turnovers . . . while Magic Johnson was hurt he had more opportunity to handle the ball and stepped up his play . . . led Lakers in scoring, steals, free throw percentage, three-point field goal percentage, and minutes . . . No. 4 on NBA lifetime list in three-point field goal percentage (.379).

JOHNSON

1987–88	2PFG	3PFG	F.T.	REB.	AST.	STL.	T.O.	BLK.	PTS.
Per Game	.510	.196	.853	6.2	11.9	1.6	3.7	0.2	19.6
Per Minute	.510	.196	.853	.170	.325	.043	.102	.005	.534
Rating	5	18	6	1	2	13	20	11	2

SCOTT

1987–88	2PFG	3PFG	F.T.	REB.	AST.	STL.	T.O.	BLK.	PTS.
Per Game	.554	.346	.858	4.1	4.1	1.9	2.0	0.3	21.7
Per Minute	.554	.346	.858	.109	.110	.051	.053	.009	.575
Rating	1	6	9	9	13	6	3	6	7

JAMES WORTHY

AGE: 27
HEIGHT: 6-9
WEIGHT: 235
POSITION: Small Forward
EXPERIENCE: 6 Seasons
COLLEGE: North Carolina
BIRTHPLACE: Gastonia, NC
1987–88 TENDEX: .541

Worthy is a steady player, excellent scorer, and weak rebounder, who always seems to be at his best around playoff time . . . No. 9 on NBA lifetime field goal percentage list (.558) . . . he had a so-so season in 1987–88 by his standards, with career highs in assists (3.9) and free throw percentage (.796), career lows in rebounds (5.0) and field goal percentage (.531) . . . the No. 13 Shootist in the NBA last season and No. 19 in two-point field goal percentage . . . among small forwards had good ratings of No. 2 Shootist, No. 4 in PAR (just short of a PAR-4 rating), No. 4 in assists, No. 6 in turnovers, No. 7 in ratio of steals to turnovers, and No. 9 in minutes played, blocked shots and ratio of blocks to turnovers . . . weaknesses were three-point field goal percentage (No. 17) and rebounds (No. 17) . . . rated No. 12 out of 22 small forwards with TENDEX of .541.

KAREEM ABDUL-JABBAR

AGE: 41
HEIGHT: 7-2
WEIGHT: 267
POSITION: Center
EXPERIENCE: 19 Seasons
COLLEGE: UCLA
BIRTHPLACE: New York City
1987–88 TENDEX: .525

It may be time to quit. This is not a suggestion, but an observation based on knowledge of what happened to other great athletes when they overstayed their time, and Abdul-Jabbar's 1987–88 statistics indicate that time may be at hand . . . holder of many NBA career records, including points, minutes and seasons played, field goals attempted and made, personal fouls, and blocked shots . . . six-time league MVP, ten-time first team All-NBA, five-time All-Defensive team choice, four-time league leader in blocked shots, two-time leader in scoring, and two-time playoff MVP . . . but last season was a bummer . . . ranked No. 12 out of 21 centers in TENDEX and could have been much lower if he played for a weaker team . . . the only thing that kept him respectable was legendary sky-hook, which enabled him to rate No. 4 among centers as Shootist, No. 6 in points per minute, No. 8 in field goal percentage, and No. 9 in PAR . . . was in lower half of the ratings in nearly all categories unrelated to shooting, with a personal worst ranking of No. 21 (last place) in rebounds per minutes played.

WORTHY

1987–88	2PFG	3PFG	F.T.	REB.	AST.	STL.	T.O.	BLK.	PTS.
Per Game	.537	.125	.796	5.0	3.9	1.0	2.1	0.7	19.7
Per Minute	.537	.125	.796	.141	.109	.027	.058	.021	.557
Rating	5	17	10	17	4	11	6	9	12

ABDUL-JABBAR

1987–88	2PFG	3PFG	F.T.	REB.	AST.	STL.	T.O.	BLK.	PTS.
Per Game	.532	.000	.762	6.0	1.7	0.6	2.0	1.2	14.6
Per Minute	.532	.000	.762	.207	.058	.021	.069	.040	.505
Rating	8	12	11	21	8	13	11	12	6

A. C. GREEN

AGE: 25
HEIGHT: 6-9
WEIGHT: 230
POSITION: Power Forward
EXPERIENCE: 3 Seasons
COLLEGE: Oregon State
BIRTHPLACE: Portland, OR
1987–88 TENDEX: .487

An unobtrusive but valuable player for the Lakers, Green doesn't hurt them with any pronounced weaknesses but he does help on the boards, ranking first on the team last season in rebounding . . . rated among league leaders in four categories: No. 5 in lowest turnover percentage, No. 15 in ratio of steals to turnovers, No. 16 in Shootist percentage, and No. 17 in rebounds . . . was in the bottom ten in assists and PAR . . . among power forwards ranked No. 2 in ratio of steals to turnovers, No. 5 in Shootist percentage, No. 6 in BEST and steals, No. 7 in free throw percentage and ratio of blocked shots to turnovers, and No. 9 in rebounds . . . a reluctant shooter and ball-handler, he was No. 18 in assists and No. 17 in scoring, PAR, and TENDEX rating.

MYCHAL THOMPSON

AGE: 33
HEIGHT: 6-10
WEIGHT: 235
POSITION: Center
EXPERIENCE: 9 Seasons
COLLEGE: Minnesota
BIRTHPLACE: Nassau, Bahamas
1987–88 TENDEX: .487

Thompson is a valuable replacement for Abdul-Jabbar and also can play the power forward position . . . often is in the lineup in place of A.C. Green during critical minutes of important games . . . ranked No. 20 in the NBA last season in blocked shots and No. 16 in ratio of blocks to turnovers . . . in bottom ten in assists, free throw, percentage and PAR . . . among centers had ratings of No. 7 in turnovers, No. 8 in ratio of steals to turnovers, and No. 9 in ratio of blocked shots to turnovers . . . most other listings were low, including No. 20 in field goal percentage, No. 18 in assists, and No. 18 in TENDEX rating . . . has scored 11,078 points during nine-year NBA career.

GREEN

1987–88	2PFG	3PFG	F.T.	REB.	AST.	STL.	T.O.	BLK.	PTS.
Per Game	.505	.000	.773	8.7	1.1	1.1	1.5	0.5	11.4
Per Minute	.505	.000	.773	.269	.035	.033	.046	.017	.355
Rating	11	14	7	9	18	6	2	13	17

THOMPSON

1987–88	2PFG	3PFG	F.T.	REB.	AST.	STL.	T.O.	BLK.	PTS.
Per Game	.515	.000	.634	6.1	0.8	0.5	1.4	1.0	11.6
Per Minute	.515	.000	.634	.244	.033	.019	.056	.039	.461
Rating	11	19	20	16	18	15	7	13	11

RESERVES

With principal substitute Mychal Thompson having played just enough minutes (2,007) to be classified as a regular, the Lakers' reserves appear to be thin, but they are basically a seven-man team anyway.

The versatility of Thompson and Michael Cooper, who can play the three positions Thompson can't, enables the Lakers to cover all bases. Cooper averages nearly 30 minutes a game in giving rest to Magic Johnson, Byron Scott, and James Worthy.

Cooper is the best man-to-man defensive player in the NBA and usually plays the opposing team's best scorer. He has been an NBA All-Defensive team selection five times and was Defensive Player of the Year in 1986–87. He probably would have repeated last season, but he missed 21 games because of an injury. TENDEX rating of .389 is misleading because his roles are defense and shooting three-point shots.

In case of injuries to any of the Lakers' top seven players, forwards Kurt Rambis and Tony Campbell are competent reserves. They'd play a lot more as members of weaker teams.

OUTLOOK

Now that Portland has solidified its team with the drafting of power forward Mark Bryant, the Lakers are no better than even with the Trail Blazers in player matchups.

But Portland can't match up with Pat Riley.

The Lakers' coach was the best in the NBA last season and was a major factor as they won playoff series in which they were physically outplayed by Utah and Detroit.

He can be a factor this season in the Pacific Division.

With Kareem Abdul-Jabbar having slipped from superstardom to mediocrity in three seasons, and with no one to replace him, the Lakers have become a vulnerable team.

James Worthy played the best game of his career in the seventh game of the 1988 championship series, but even Worthy has been only slightly better than average at his position during the past few seasons, and his forward counterpart, A.C. Green, is barely adequate.

Fortunately for the Lakers, their backcourt more than makes up for the weak frontline. Not only do Magic Johnson and Byron Scott lead the team in scoring and assists most of the time, but they often out-rebound Worthy and Abdul-Jabbar. They're the best backcourt tandem in the NBA.

The bench isn't bad, with rookie David Rivers added to veterans Michael Cooper and Mychal Thompson.

Probable finish: First in Pacific Division.

14

Milwaukee Bucks

*A*fter winning seven straight divisional titles, the Bucks seem to be fading toward the bottom of the NBA's Central Division.

Milwaukee won the Midwest Division championship with a record of 49–33 in 1979–80 and then won 50 or more games in capturing the Central Division title the next six seasons.

But in 1986–87 they slipped to third place in the division, although still winning 50 games. And last season they dropped into a tie for fourth with a 42–40 mark.

The plunge coincides with the aging and knee woes of Sidney Moncrief, one of the best all-around backcourtmen in NBA history. Some of the other Bucks—notably Terry Cummings, Ricky Pierce, Paul Pressey, and Jack Sikma—could be in the latter stages of their careers as well.

At the moment the Bucks are just average.

Older players usually take care of the ball without turning it over, and shoot well from the free throw line; but they don't fare so well in categories that require exceptional athletic talent, such as rebounds, steals, and blocked shots.

This was precisely the pattern of the Buck's play last season. They ranked a very good No. 5 in turnovers, No. 8 in free throw percentage, and No. 8 in assists. But they were far down the list at No. 19 in rebounds, No. 19 in blocks, and No. 16 in steals.

Their TENDEX rating of 1.004 was No. 13 in the league, and they matched that by tying for 12th and 13th places in the overall standings.

JACK SIKMA

AGE: 33
HEIGHT: 7-0
WEIGHT: 250
POSITION: Power Forward
EXPERIENCE: 11 Seasons
COLLEGE: Illinois Wesleyan
BIRTHPLACE: Kankakee, IL
1987–88 TENDEX: .614

A TENDEX 700 Club member, Sikma played center for ten seasons before being moved into the corner after having a down year in 1986–87. He responded well to the move, leading the Bucks last season in TENDEX rating and rebounds . . . led the NBA in free throw percentage (.922) . . . with 9,260 rebounds, he has a chance to reach the 10,000 plateau near the end of this season . . . played in all 82 games last season for the eighth time in his career . . . ranks among the top ten active players in minutes played, rebounds and free throw percentage . . . last season, in addition to winning the NBA free throw title, he finished No. 18 in minutes, No. 19 in turnover percentage, and No. 21 in TENDEX rating . . . among power forwards was consistent with 16 single-digit ratings out of 18 categories, including No. 1 in free throw percentage, No. 1 and No. 9 in the two PAR categories, No. 3 in assists, No. 5 in BEST, No. 6 Shootist, and No. 6 in TENDEX.

PAUL PRESSEY

AGE: 29
HEIGHT: 6-5
WEIGHT: 205
POSITION: Point Guard
EXPERIENCE: 6 Seasons
COLLEGE: Tulsa
BIRTHPLACE: Richmond, VA
1987–88 TENDEX: .567

Pressey settled at point guard last season after dividing time between guard and forward in seasons past . . . NBA All-Defensive team selection 1984–85 and 1985–86 . . . had PAR-5 rating last year, seventh best in the league; also finished No. 13 in the league in assists . . . led Milwaukee in assists and steals . . . in point guard listings, ranked No. 2 in rebounds, No. 3 in blocked shots, No. 4 in Shootist percentage, No. 7 in two-point field goal percentage, and No. 5 in TENDEX rating . . . did not finish lower than No. 15 in any statistical category.

SIKMA

1987–88	2PFG	3PFG	F.T.	REB.	AST.	STL.	T.O.	BLK.	PTS.
Per Game	.489	.214	.922	8.7	3.4	1.1	1.9	1.0	16.5
Per Minute	.489	.214	.922	.243	.095	.032	.054	.027	.463
Rating	14	7	1	11	3	8	6	7	9

PRESSEY

1987–88	2PFG	3PFG	F.T.	REB.	AST.	STL.	T.O.	BLK.	PTS.
Per Game	.508	.205	.798	5.0	7.0	1.5	2.6	0.5	13.1
Per Minute	.508	.205	.798	.151	.211	.045	.080	.014	.396
Rating	7	17	15	2	11	12	15	3	11

TERRY CUMMINGS

AGE: 27
HEIGHT: 6-9
WEIGHT: 235
POSITION: Small Forward
EXPERIENCE: 6 Seasons
COLLEGE: DePaul
BIRTHPLACE: Chicago
1987–88 TENDEX: .557

Former Rookie of the Year (1982–83) and TENDEX 700 Club member, Cummings had the worst season of his career in 1987–88 with a TENDEX rating of .557, with career lows in rebounds, steals, and blocked shots. He led the Bucks in scoring with 21.3 average, 15th best in the league . . . ranked No. 20 in the NBA in PAR . . . in a five-game playoff series against Atlanta, averaged 25.8 points with a TENDEX rating of .637 . . . rated No. 9 in TENDEX out of 22 small forwards . . . other high ratings were No. 5 in PAR, No. 6 in rebounds, No. 7 in points, and No. 9 in steals . . . finished far down the list with ratings of No. 19 and No. 18 in the two Shootist categories, No. 22 in free throw percentage, No. 16 in two-point field goal percentage, and No. 16 in assists.

RANDY BREUER

AGE: 28
HEIGHT: 7-3
WEIGHT: 263
POSITION: Center
EXPERIENCE: 5 Seasons
COLLEGE: Minnesota
BIRTHPLACE: Lake City, MN
1987–88 TENDEX: .522

Breuer became a regular for the first time last season and his height helped him rank among the league leaders in four statistical categories: BEST (No. 10), blocked shots (No. 11), least turnovers (No. 9), and ratio of blocked shots to turnovers (No. 6) . . . finished among the bottom ten in free throw percentage . . . out of 21 centers rated No. 13 in TENDEX . . . best ratings were No. 3 in turnovers and ratios of blocks and steals to turnovers . . . worst were No. 19 in free throw percentage and No. 18 Shootist.

CUMMINGS

1987–88	2PFG	3PFG	F.T.	REB.	AST.	STL.	T.O.	BLK.	PTS.
Per Game	.485	.333	.665	7.3	2.4	1.0	2.2	0.6	21.3
Per Minute	.485	.333	.665	.210	.069	.030	.065	.017	.617
Rating	16	6	22	6	16	9	11	15	7

BREUER

1987–88	2PFG	3PFG	F.T.	REB.	AST.	STL.	T.O.	BLK.	PTS.
Per Game	.495	.000	.657	6.8	1.3	0.6	1.3	1.3	12.0
Per Minute	.495	.000	.657	.244	.046	.020	.047	.047	.429
Rating	17	7	19	14	15	14	3	7	13

RESERVES

The Bucks were deep in backcourt reserves but thin in the frontcourt last season.

Ricky Pierce, who missed half of the season because of an injury, and John Lucas were guards who had TENDEX ratings of exactly .500.

Jay Humphries, a point guard obtained in a trade with Phoenix, had a rating of .485 and took enough shots to rank No. 17 in the league in two-point field goal percentage and No. 2 among point men.

Although knee trouble sidelined the 31-year-old Sidney Moncrief for 26 games, he played well at times with a rating of .491.

Jerry Reynolds, another guard, had a .432 rating with sparse playing time.

The only frontcourt reserve to play as many as 1,000 minutes was second-year man Larry Krystkowiak, and he barely made it with 1,050. His TENDEX was .428.

OUTLOOK

The Bucks solved one problem, drafting Jeff Grayer as a likely successor to dimming star Sidney Moncrief.

But this is an aging team. Forwards Terry Cummings and Jack Sikma, both TENDEX 700 Club members, aren't close to being the players they once were.

Center Randy Breuer and point guard Paul Pressey aren't aging, but they aren't champion level players either. Breuer is just adequate as a center and Pressey, a fine player, is better suited to be a small forward than a point guard. He is not one of the better penetrating point men in the league.

Ricky Pierce is a great sixth man, but this is a team with too many problems to be a contender in the league's toughest division.

Probable finish: Fifth in Central Division.

15

New Jersey Nets

*T*he plight of the Nets is not quite as desperate as that of the Clippers. They have one star player, Buck Williams, another good frontcourt player, Roy Hinson, and a potentially good backcourtman, Dennis Hopson.

They are a point guard and a center away from being a playoff team.

Williams had a typical season in 1987–88, finishing as the 18th best player in the league with a TENDEX rating of .635. But after seven seasons of toiling for the Nets, the intensely-competitive power forward wouldn't be blamed if he started becoming discouraged. Only once in those seven seasons have the Nets advanced beyond the first round of the playoffs. The last two seasons they haven't made the playoffs at all.

The easy way out is to blame the coach, and so the New Jersey management "blamed" two of them during the 1987–88 season. After firing two head coaches, the Nets wound up the season with Willis Reed as head man, but how long that will last is anyone's guess.

The Nets' total of coach firings amounted to exactly one-third of the cannings in the league during the season.

What the Nets really wish is that they could win one-third of their games during the season. That is a possibility in 1988–89, if they can clean up on the two expansion teams.

Statistically, the Nets are almost as bad as the Clippers, with eight ratings of No. 20 or worse out of 13 categories. In 1987–88 they ranked No. 23 (last place) in assists, PAR, and BEST; No. 22 in free throw percentage, rebounds points and TENDEX rating; and No. 21 in Shootist and turnovers.

Their only respectable rating was No. 8 in steals.

Defensively, they were almost as bad as offensively. They allowed their opponents to outdo them in every statistical area, with the most obvious discrepancies in scoring (100.4 points for the Nets and 108.5 for their opponents) and field goal percentage (.468 and .497).

BUCK WILLIAMS

AGE: 28
HEIGHT: 6-8
WEIGHT: 225
POSITION: Power Forward
EXPERIENCE: 7 Seasons
COLLEGE: Maryland
BIRTHPLACE: Rocky Mount, NC
1987–88 TENDEX: .635

A model of strength and stamina, Williams missed only one game during his first six seasons, but missed 12 in 1987–88 because of an injury . . . one of eight players in league history to pull down 1,000 rebounds each of his first four seasons . . . NBA Rookie of the Year in 1981–82 . . . lifetime field goal percentage of .552 puts him in 11th place on the all-time NBA list . . . had four 20–20 games last season (20 rebounds and 20 points) . . . NBA All-Defensive second team . . . No. 7 in league in rebounds, No. 7 in two-point field goal percentage, No. 8 in minutes per game, and No. 20 in Shootist percentage . . . led Nets in points, rebounds, and field goal percentage . . . out of 20 power forwards, had ratings of No. 4 in rebounds and field goal percentage; No. 5 TENDEX; and No. 7 in PAR percentage, Shootist, and scoring . . . should score his 10,000th NBA point this season.

ROY HINSON

AGE: 27
HEIGHT: 6-9
WEIGHT: 220
POSITION: Small Forward
EXPERIENCE: 5 Seasons
COLLEGE: Rutgers
BIRTHPLACE: Trenton, NJ
1987–88 TENDEX: .508

After being traded from Philadelphia to New Jersey midway through last season, Hinson began to show signs of returning to the good form of his first three NBA campaigns with Cleveland . . . getting away from low-post dominator Charles Barkley might have helped . . . a good defensive intimidator, Hinson ranked No. 9 in the league in blocked shots, No. 11 in ratio of blocks to turnovers, and No. 14 in BEST . . . was in the bottom ten in assists . . . among the league's small forwards rated No. 2 in blocks, No. 3 in BEST, No. 7 in rebounds, and No. 9 in Shootist percentage . . . low rankings were No. 22 in assists, No. 21 in PAR, and No. 17 in scoring . . . TENDEX rating was 14th for small forward position.

WILLIAMS

1987–88	2PFG	3PFG	F.T.	REB.	AST.	STL.	T.O.	BLK.	PTS.
Per Game	.560	1.000	.668	11.9	1.6	1.0	2.7	0.6	18.3
Per Minute	.560	1.000	.668	.316	.041	.026	.072	.017	.485
Rating	4	1	20	4	16	14	13	14	7

HINSON

1987–88	2PFG	3PFG	F.T.	REB.	AST.	STL.	T.O.	BLK.	PTS.
Per Game	.488	.000	.775	6.7	1.3	0.9	2.2	1.8	15.3
Per Minute	.486	.000	.775	.199	.038	.027	.065	.054	.454
Rating	15	21	15	7	22	13	12	2	17

TIM McCORMICK

AGE: 26
HEIGHT: 7-0
WEIGHT: 240
POSITION: Center
EXPERIENCE: 4 Seasons
COLLEGE: Michigan
BIRTHPLACE: Detroit
1987–88 TENDEX: .488

Still young enough to develop into a competent pro pivotman, McCormick has been hindered by having to adjust to three teams in his first four NBA seasons . . . improved noticeably after being traded from Philadelphia to New Jersey last season . . . ranked No. 18 in NBA in two-point field goal percentage and No. 18 in turnovers, but was in bottom ten in steals . . . did not compare well with other centers, having low grades of No. 21 in blocked shots, No. 19 in rebounds and steals, No. 18 in free throw percentage, and No. 17 in PAR percentage, BEST, and TENDEX rating.

JOHN BAGLEY

AGE: 28
HEIGHT: 6-0
WEIGHT: 192
POSITION: Point Guard
EXPERIENCE: 6 Seasons
COLLEGE: Boston College
BIRTHPLACE: Bridgeport, CT
1987–88 TENDEX: .413

The Nets thought they had solved their point guard problem with the drafting of Pearl Washington in 1986, and their shooting guard problem with the drafting of Dennis Hopson in 1987 . . . they still have some hope for Hopson but gave up on Washington, which is why journeyman Bagley became a regular last season . . . barely adequate, Bagley ranked in the NBA's bottom ten in Shootist percentage, PAR percentage, and TENDEX rating . . . led Nets in assists . . . among point guards was in the top ten in only one category, turnover percentage . . . poor ratings were No. 20 in assists and PAR percentage, No. 19 in Shootist percentage, and No. 18 in scoring and TENDEX.

McCORMICK

1987–88	2PFG	3PFG	F.T.	REB.	AST.	STL.	T.O.	BLK.	PTS.
Per Game	.539	.000	.674	6.7	1.7	0.5	1.6	0.3	12.0
Per Minute	.539	.000	.674	.221	.056	.015	.053	.011	.398
Rating	7	15	18	19	9	19	6	21	15

BAGLEY

1987–88	2PFG	3PFG	F.T.	REB.	AST.	STL.	T.O.	BLK.	PTS.
Per Game	.471	.292	.822	3.1	5.8	1.3	2.5	0.1	12.0
Per Minute	.471	.292	.822	.093	.173	.040	.072	.004	.354
Rating	17	11	12	11	20	16	8	13	18

RESERVES

Dudley Bradley is a twin of the Lakers' Michael Cooper, except that, playing in Los Angeles, Cooper's talents are appreciated. A standout defender, one of the best in the NBA, Bradley led the Nets in steals last season even though he played fewer than 1,500 minutes. Also led in three-point field goal percentage. TENDEX rating of .390, like Cooper's similarly low rating, is not a good indicator of his value to the team.

Walter Berry (TENDEX .563) is a third-year player with potential to develop into a fine cornerman.

Hopson (.334) is going to have to forget the college-draft hype and start playing better or find himself in the CBA.

OUTLOOK

New Jersey is another team with management that must have flunked chem lab.

The Nets had respectable cornermen in Buck Williams and Roy Hinson last season, but were especially bad at center and in the backcourt.

So, in the expansion draft they surrendered guard Pearl Washington, and in the college draft they selected three cornermen.

How do you figure it?

Maybe rookie Chris Morris is going to be as great a forward as the Nets believe, but unless Williams or Hinson is traded, he probably won't start in his rookie season.

Second-round draft choice Charles Shackleford probably won't get much playing time at all.

For now, unless the undersized Hinson or Shackleford is converted from forward to center, Tim McCormick starts in the pivot. John Bagley is the regular point guard, and just maybe Dennis Hopson will show enough improvement after a disappointing rookie season to take over the shooting guard job.

Probable finish: Fourth in Atlantic Division.

16

New York Knicks

*A*fter the Nets' failure with Pearl Washington in 1986, the Knicks weren't to be blamed when they were hesitant in 1987 to draft another New York backcourt product who had starred in the Big East Conference. If it hadn't been for a clamorous crowd roaring the name of Mark Jackson on draft day in New York, it is unlikely that the Knicks would have selected him.

And it is unlikely that they would have made the playoffs in 1987–88 or that their future prospects would be any brighter than the Nets'.

But they did and they are.

Jackson not only won Rookie of the Year on his own merits (breaking Oscar Robertson's rookie assists record), but he also provided the missing element in Patrick Ewing's game.

The big center for the first time showed that the Knicks were justified in making him the No. 1 lottery choice in 1985, upgrading his TENDEX rating by more than 100 points.

Ewing's improvement was simply a matter of having somebody, Jackson, who could get the ball to him at the right place and time.

With Jackson and Ewing to build around, the Knicks have the two most important ingredients (point guard and center) in putting together a team reminiscent of the Walt Frazier–Willis Reed units that won two NBA championships during the early 1970s. As a matter of fact, Jackson is very similar to Frazier in personality and style of play and, with imagination, similarities can be pointed out between Reed and Ewing.

Under Coach Rick Pitino, the Knicks got into the playoffs in 1987–88. With a 38–44 record, they were not a dominant team statistically, but did match up evenly against most opponents and ranked No. 2 in the league in steals, a category in which both Ewing and Jackson happened to excel.

Plug in a DeBusschere and a Monroe and New York will be a team to reckon with for the first time in 15 years.

PATRICK EWING

AGE: 26
HEIGHT: 7-0
WEIGHT: 240
POSITION: Center
EXPERIENCE: 3 Seasons
COLLEGE: Georgetown
BIRTHPLACE: Kingston, Jamaica
1987–88 TENDEX: .760

There are still nits that can be picked from Ewing's game. He is probably never going to be a Wilt Chamberlain, a Kareem Abdul-Jabbar, or even an Akeem Olajuwon. But he was, without question, the second best center in the NBA in 1987–88 when he joined the TENDEX 700 Club . . . NBA Rookie of the Year in 1985–86 . . . broke his own Knick record for blocked shots with 245 in 1987–88 . . . named to NBA All-Defensive second team . . . one of four players in the league with more than 100 steals and 100 blocked shots . . . ranked among NBA leaders in numerous categories, including No. 3 in blocked shots, No. 5 in TENDEX rating, No. 8 in BEST, No. 9 in two-point field goal percentage, No. 10 in points per minute, No. 12 in PAR percentage, No. 15 in ratio of blocks to turnovers, No. 18 in rebounds, and No. 18 in both Shootist statistics . . . but he still had two major flaws, ball-handling and durability . . . rated last in the league in turnover percentage and averaged only 31 minutes per game, well below normal for a player of his caliber . . . by contrast, Olajuwon, the top-rated center, averaged nearly 36 minutes and rookie teammate Jackson averaged 39.6 . . . high ratings among NBA centers were No. 1 in points, No. 2 in steals, No. 3 in blocked shots, No. 3 in field goal percentage, No. 3 in PAR percentage, and No. 3 Shootist . . . No. 2 behind Olajuwon in TENDEX.

MARK JACKSON

AGE: 23
HEIGHT: 6-3
WEIGHT: 205
POSITION: Point Guard
EXPERIENCE: 1 Season
COLLEGE: St. John's
BIRTHPLACE: Brooklyn, NY
1987–88 TENDEX: .545

Jackson's amazing stamina (39.6 minutes per game) made him even more valuable to the Knicks than his .545 TENDEX rating indicates . . . Rookie of the Year in a landslide, with 77 of the 80 first-place votes, the lowest draft choice (No. 18) in 30 years to win rookie honors . . . shattered Oscar Robertson's rookie record for assists, surpassing the Big O's total of 690 a month before the end of the season and finishing with 868, third best in the league behind John Stockton and Magic Johnson . . . had great season in steals, ranking No. 6 in official league statistics and falling only six short of the rookie record . . . No. 2 in minutes played, trailing only Player of the Year Michael Jordan . . . No. 8 with a PAR-4 rating, and No. 10 in ratio of assists to turnovers . . . negatives were bottom ten listings in blocked shots, points per minute, and both Shootist statistics . . . ratings among point guards included the good (No. 1 in minutes, No. 3 in steals, No. 3 in PAR) and the bad (No. 19 in field goal percentage, No. 19 in points, No. 19 Shootist), but nothing ugly: Jackson is a fluid player with grace, intelligence, and intensity.

EWING

1987–88	2PFG	3PFG	F.T.	REB.	AST.	STL.	T.O.	BLK.	PTS.
Per Game	.556	.000	.716	8.2	1.5	1.3	3.5	3.0	20.2
Per Minute	.556	.000	.716	.266	.049	.041	.113	.096	.649
Rating	3	18	14	8	12	2	21	3	1

JACKSON

1987–88	2PFG	3PFG	F.T.	REB.	AST.	STL.	T.O.	BLK.	PTS.
Per Game	.458	.254	.774	4.8	10.6	2.5	3.2	0.1	13.6
Per Minute	.458	.254	.774	.122	.267	.063	.079	.002	.343
Rating	19	15	17	7	6	3	12	18	19

CHARLES OAKLEY

AGE: 24
HEIGHT: 6-9
WEIGHT: 245
POSITION: Power Forward
EXPERIENCE: 3 Seasons
COLLEGE: Virginia Union
BIRTHPLACE: Cleveland
1987–88 TENDEX: .611

Oakley was the only player in the NBA to pull down more than 1,000 rebounds last season. He also exceeded 1,000 rebounds in 1986–87 when he led the league in rebounding average . . . a great defensive rebounder, his 775 defensive rebounds in 1986–87 set a Chicago Bulls record and his total of 1,079 was the second highest in team history . . . Oakley had a league-high 35 rebounds in one game last season . . . his TENDEX rating was 21st overall in the league and seventh among the power forwards . . . also rated No. 5 for his position in PAR, minutes played, and assists . . . drawback is limited offensive ability, ranking No. 17 in Shootist, No. 16 in scoring, No. 15 in field goal percentage, and No. 15 in free throw percentage . . . had a poor BEST ball-control rating, last among 20 qualifying power forwards.

GERALD WILKINS

AGE: 25
HEIGHT: 6-6
WEIGHT: 190
POSITION: Shooting Guard
EXPERIENCE: 3 Seasons
COLLEGE: Tennessee-Chattanooga
BIRTHPLACE: Atlanta
1987–88 TENDEX: .434

Gerald is no Dominique, but he sometimes resembles his famous brother with soaring open-court moves . . . the Knicks' No. 2 scorer during the 1987–88 regular season, he led the team with a 20-point average in the playoffs . . . a steady player, Wilkins did not rank among the leaders or the bottom ten in any statistical category . . . rated no higher than No. 7, no lower than No. 19 in shooting guard listings . . . top ratings No. 7 in blocked shots and three-point field goal percentage, and No. 9 in PAR and minutes played . . . lows were No. 19 in two-point field goal percentage, No. 18 in Shootist percentage, and No. 17 in free throw percentage . . . was No. 15 shooting guard in TENDEX rating.

OAKLEY

1987–88	2PFG	3PFG	F.T.	REB.	AST.	STL.	T.O.	BLK.	PTS.
Per Game	.487	.250	.727	13.0	3.0	0.8	2.9	0.3	12.4
Per Minute	.487	.250	.727	.379	.088	.024	.086	.010	.360
Rating	15	6	15	2	5	16	18	19	16

WILKINS

1987–88	2PFG	3PFG	F.T.	REB.	AST.	STL.	T.O.	BLK.	PTS.
Per Game	.462	.302	.786	3.3	4.0	1.1	2.6	0.3	17.4
Per Minute	.462	.302	.786	.100	.121	.033	.078	.008	.522
Rating	19	7	17	11	12	12	15	7	10

KENNY WALKER

AGE: 24
HEIGHT: 6-8
WEIGHT: 210
POSITION: Small Forward
EXPERIENCE: 2 Seasons
COLLEGE: Kentucky
BIRTHPLACE: Roberta, GA
1987–88 TENDEX: .447

Too much may have been expected from Walker when the Knicks made him their No. 1 choice and the fifth pick overall in the 1986 draft. He had been a glamor player at the University of Kentucky and was expected to step right into the Knicks' lineup as a big scorer and rebounder. Lack of shooting range has prevented him from putting up big offensive numbers for the Knicks, but he has played exceptionally well on defense, better than at least three of the 11 players who received All-Defensive team first- or second-team citations last season . . . good defense is reflected by his top 20 ratings in the league in BEST and ratios of blocked shots and steals to turnovers . . . ranked No. 2 in the NBA in lowest turnover percentage . . . but in the bottom ten in both PAR statistics . . . among small forwards ranked among the top three in four categories, but was among the bottom three in six, including 20th in overall TENDEX rating.

SIDNEY GREEN

AGE: 27
HEIGHT: 6-9
WEIGHT: 220
POSITION: Power Forward
EXPERIENCE: 5 Seasons
COLLEGE: Nevada-Las Vegas
BIRTHPLACE: Brooklyn, NY
1987–88 TENDEX: .476

Green is a basic role player whose role is rebounding . . . the fifth-rated rebounder among power forwards last season and No. 8 overall in the league in rebounds per minute played . . . but ranked No. 13 or lower in 16 other statistical categories for power forwards, including No. 21 in field goal percentage, No. 20 in both Shootist statistics, No. 19 in scoring, No. 19 in TENDEX rating, No. 16 in blocked shots, and No. 16 in both PAR categories . . . one of bottom ten NBA players in the two Shootist statistics and two-point field goal percentage.

WALKER

1987–88	2PFG	3PFG	F.T.	REB.	AST.	STL.	T.O.	BLK.	PTS.
Per Game	.473	.000	.775	4.7	1.1	0.8	1.0	0.7	10.1
Per Minute	.473	.000	.775	.182	.040	.029	.039	.028	.386
Rating	21	22	16	12	21	10	1	5	19

GREEN

1987–88	2PFG	3PFG	F.T.	REB.	AST.	STL.	T.O.	BLK.	PTS.
Per Game	.443	.000	.663	7.8	1.1	0.8	1.8	0.4	7.8
Per Minute	.443	.000	.663	.313	.045	.031	.072	.016	.313
Rating	21	17	21	5	13	9	14	16	19

RESERVES

The Knicks are beginning to develop a respectable bench.

The acquisition of Charles Oakley from Chicago puts last season's starting power forward, Sidney Green (TENDEX .476) on the bench.

Another good substitute is second-year man John Newman, who played poorly for most of the 1987–88 season but improved toward the end and was the Knicks' No. 2 playoff scorer with a 19-point average.

In the backcourt New York has Trent Tucker, the top-rated three-point field goal shooter in NBA history. Tucker ranked No. 6 in the league in his three-point specialty last season.

OUTLOOK

At first look, the Knicks' choice of Rod Strickland in the 1988 college draft appeared to be a poor one; on second thought, maybe it wasn't so bad.

With a .663 TENDEX rating, Strickland was the No. 8 rated player in the draft and the No. 1 point guard. The Knicks landed him with the No. 19 choice, so they got a tremendous athlete considering their location in the draft.

The trouble is, Strickland plays the same position as Mark Jackson, Rookie of the Year in 1987–88. But Jackson averaged nearly 40 minutes per game in 1987–88—too many for a point guard who must work hard at both ends of the court.

Strickland will give Jackson a breather in 1988–89 and eventually may challenge him for a starting job.

The Knicks solved their power forward problem by trading reserve center Bill Cartwright to Chicago for Charles Oakley, one of the league's best rebounders.

With Patrick Ewing finally coming into his prime as one of the NBA's best centers, this is a team to reckon with, even though it could stand improvement at the shooting guard and small forward positions.

Probable finish: Second in Atlantic Division.

17

Philadelphia 76ers

*C*areer-ending injuries to Jeff Ruland and Andrew Toney have set the 76ers back, and Charles Barkley's attitude that the entire focus of the team should be on him could set it back even more.

The 76ers had the longest streak of winning seasons (12) in the NBA going into the 1987–88 campaign; but it ended last season and so did an identical streak of playoff appearances, even though Barkley had a career-best .829 TENDEX rating.

The other side of the story is that Barkley is awesome enough that he actually can win some games practically by himself. The 76ers missed the 1988 playoffs by only two games and had a not-so-awful record of 36–46. It just seemed awful by ordinary Philadelphia standards.

The 76ers' critical weakness was in the area of assists, but it shouldn't be that way because they have one of the top point guards in NBA history, Mo Cheeks. With Barkley controlling the offense, Cheeks simply didn't have the ball as much as he should have to set up teammates. Thus, the 76ers did poorly in assists (No. 20) and also in two-point field goal percentage (No. 14) because they weren't being set up for good shots. Even that below-average No. 14 is misleadingly high. Excluding Barkley's league-leading .630 two-point field goal percentage, the 76ers were No. 22 in this category.

Philadelphia placed among the top ten in only two team categories—No. 9 in three-point field goal percentage and No. 10 in blocked shots. The 76ers were No. 16 or worse in nine categories, including No. 17 in overall TENDEX rating.

CHARLES BARKLEY

AGE: 25
HEIGHT: 6-6
WEIGHT: 263
POSITION: Power Forward
EXPERIENCE: 4 Seasons
COLLEGE: Auburn
BIRTHPLACE: Leeds, AL
1987–88 TENDEX: .829

Excluding Michael Jordan, Barkley is the most talented player in the NBA. He is an outstanding rebounder and low-post scorer, but also can fill a lane on the fast break as well as anyone in the league . . . No. 1 in TENDEX rating in 1986–87 (.828) and No. 2 last season with a personal-best .829 . . . led NBA in rebounding in 1986–87, led in two-point field goal percentage the past two seasons . . . ranks No. 3 lifetime in field goal percentage (.577) . . . had four 20–20 games last season (20 rebounds and 20 points) . . . was one of four players in the league with 100 steals and 100 blocked shots . . . rated No. 3 in PAR percentage, No. 3 in Shootist percentage, No. 4 in minutes played, No. 5 in points per minute, and No. 11 in rebounds per minute . . . slipped into the bottom ten in turnovers and ratio of steals to turnovers . . . dominated power forward listings: No. 1 in TENDEX, points, two-point field goal percentage, and PAR; No. 2 in minutes, Shootist, and Shootist percentage . . . only problem was turnovers (No. 19), but that was to be expected of a player who handled the ball so much.

MO CHEEKS

AGE: 32
HEIGHT: 6-1
WEIGHT: 180
POSITION: Point Guard
EXPERIENCE: 10 Seasons
COLLEGE: West Texas State
BIRTHPLACE: Chicago
1987–88 TENDEX: .534

In ten seasons Cheeks has quietly accumulated the highest total of steals in NBA history, 1,837. He was named to the league's All-Defensive team four times . . . ranked No. 2 last season in ratio of assists to turnovers (3.97 to 1), trailing only John Stockton of Utah . . . other 1987–88 NBA ratings: No. 3 in ratio of steals to turnovers, No. 9 in steals, No. 10 in assists, and No. 19 in BEST . . . led 76ers in steals and assists for the tenth season in a row . . . consistency is reflected in his ratings last season compared to 19 other point guards: No. 2 in turnovers, No. 2 in ratios of steals and blocked shots to turnovers, No. 3 in BEST, No. 5 in minutes played and steals, No. 6 in blocked shots, No. 7 in both Shootist categories, No. 9 in assists and two-point field goal percentage, No. 10 in PAR, and No. 10 in TENDEX rating . . . only poor effort was No. 19 in three-point field goal percentage.

BARKLEY

1987–88	2PFG	3PFG	F.T.	REB.	AST.	STL.	T.O.	BLK.	PTS.
Per Game	.630	.280	.751	11.9	3.2	1.3	3.8	1.3	28.3
Per Minute	.630	.280	.751	.300	.080	.032	.096	.033	.714
Rating	1	3	12	7	6	10	19	6	1

CHEEKS

1987–88	2PFG	3PFG	F.T.	REB.	AST.	STL.	T.O.	BLK.	PTS.
Per Game	.504	.136	.825	3.2	8.0	2.1	2.0	0.3	13.7
Per Minute	.504	.136	.825	.088	.221	.058	.056	.008	.378
Rating	9	19	11	13	9	5	2	6	15

MIKE GMINSKI

AGE: 29
HEIGHT: 6-11
WEIGHT: 260
POSITION: Center
EXPERIENCE: 8 Seasons
COLLEGE: Duke
BIRTHPLACE: Monroe, CT
1987–88 TENDEX: .575

Essentially a high-post center, Gminski seemed to mesh talents well with Charles Barkley after being traded last season by New Jersey to the 76ers. Barkley dominates the low-post area and had not been able to blend his skills with Roy Hinson and Tim Mc-Cormick, who were involved in the trade for Gminski . . . finished No. 3 in the NBA last season in free throw percentage, No. 14 in minutes played, No. 17 in rebounds per minute, and No. 17 in ratio of blocked shots to turnovers . . . no bottom ten ratings . . . among centers had rankings of No. 1 in minutes played, No. 1 in free throw percentage, No. 6 in rebounds, No. 7 in TENDEX rating, No. 8 in PAR, No. 9 in turnovers, and No. 10 in points . . . low ratings were No. 19 Shootist and No. 20 in two-point field goal percentage.

CLIFF ROBINSON

AGE: 28
HEIGHT: 6-9
WEIGHT: 240
POSITION: Small Forward
EXPERIENCE: 9 Seasons
COLLEGE: Southern Cal
BIRTHPLACE: Oakland, CA
1987–88 TENDEX: .493

In his ninth season Robinson reached 10,000 points, finishing with 10,582 . . . ranked in the bottom ten in Shootist (points per shot) . . . missed 20 games because of injury . . . was rated No. 4 in steals and No. 8 in rebounds among small forwards . . . between No. 11 and No. 22 in the other 16 categories, with worsts of 22nd in two-point field goal percentage and Shootist, and No. 20 in free throw percentage . . . No. 16 small forward in overall TENDEX rating.

GMINSKI

1987-88	2PFG	3PFG	F.T.	REB.	AST.	STL.	T.O.	BLK.	PTS.
Per Game	.449	.000	.906	10.0	1.7	0.8	2.2	1.5	16.9
Per Minute	.449	.000	.906	.275	.047	.022	.060	.040	.461
Rating	20	16	1	6	14	11	9	11	10

ROBINSON

1987-88	2PFG	3PFG	F.T.	REB.	AST.	STL.	T.O.	BLK.	PTS.
Per Game	.466	.222	.717	6.5	2.1	1.3	2.6	0.6	19.0
Per Minute	.466	.222	.717	.192	.062	.037	.076	.018	.558
Rating	22	13	20	8	18	4	19	14	11

RESERVES

Philadelphia has a poor bench. Only forward Ben Coleman, obtained from New Jersey in the Gminski deal, exceeded .400 in TENDEX rating (.472) in 1987–88, and he played only 841 minutes for the 76ers.

The bench players with 1,000 or more minutes were guard Gerald Henderson (.395), forward Albert King (.287), and guard David Wingate (.263). Wingate and King had the worst and next-to-worst ratings of all reserves in the NBA.

Wingate had enough attempts to qualify in the two-point field goal percentage listings and finished last with a .412 percentage. Interestingly, this percentage would have been good enough to lead the league in its first two seasons.

The only bright spot among the reserves was Gerald Henderson's rating of No. 3 among the NBA's three-point field goal shooters with a percentage of .423.

OUTLOOK

Maybe rookie Hersey Hawkins will take some pressure off Charles Barkley, if Barkley really wants some pressure taken off.

The 76ers' dive during the past few seasons has coincided with Barkley's individual rise to pre-eminence, and there are some observers who believe Barkley's personality demands that he be the dominant player on his team, even at the expense of teammates and overall team cohesiveness.

Moses Malone was traded because of low-post clashes with Barkley, and so was Roy Hinson.

Hawkins isn't a low-post player, but he likes to possess the basketball and shoot the basketball, and he may not be as deferential to Barkley as point guard Mo Cheeks is.

Cheeks' willingness to subordinate himself to Barkley was perhaps the only thing that kept the 76ers in the race for a playoff berth last season.

For this team to be successful, the ball must be put into Cheeks' hands, and Barkley and Hawkins must be willing to work without the ball. If the three of them can get together, the 76ers will challenge New York for second place in the Atlantic Division. If not, they'll challenge Washington and New Jersey for fifth.

Probable finish: Third in Atlantic Division.

18

Phoenix Suns

*P*hoenix fans won't be able to tell the team without a program anymore, and even with a program it won't be easy.

The Suns underwent almost a complete overhaul in 1987–88 and at season's end there wasn't a member of the starting team who had been a starter the year before.

At first glance it might appear that the Suns merely exchanged mediocre players for other mediocre players through a series of trades. But it wasn't as simple as that. It was a calculated gamble.

One of the traded players, Larry Nance, is anything but mediocre. The Suns' gamble consisted of the hope that one player they got for the All-Star Nance, Kevin Johnson, eventually would become nearly as good as Nance and that they could build for the future with the help of draft choices, including a first-rounder obtained from Cleveland in the Nance deal.

However, the Suns' management gave their fans one disturbing thought to consider: After deliberately giving up on the 1987–88 season in order to plan for the future, why did they fire Coach John Wetzel? By firing Wetzel, Suns executives were delivering the illogical message that, in the middle of the chaos of players coming and going, they thought he should have led the Suns to a better record than 28–54. They were fortunate they didn't do worse.

The thing that saved their public image was Johnson's sudden improvement in a Phoenix uniform. After having a TENDEX rating in the middle of the rookie class for two-thirds of the season in Cleveland, Johnson, after joining the Suns, suddenly began to play like Rookie of the Year Mark Jackson.

Because of the turnover in personnel, it is difficult to make any sense out of statistics related to the Suns' performance. Their best category, thanks in large part to Johnson and Jeff Hornacek, was assists (No. 5 in the NBA). And with good backcourt playmaking, they were above average in most shooting statistics, although they did not do as well late in the season when their best shooter, Nance, was gone and their second best, Walter Davis, was benched.

The luck of the draft in the next year or two probably will determine whether the Suns made a good gamble with the Nance trade or not.

KEVIN JOHNSON

AGE: 22
HEIGHT: 6-1
WEIGHT: 180
POSITION: Point Guard
EXPERIENCE: 1 Season
COLLEGE: California
BIRTHPLACE: Sacramento, CA
1987–88 TENDEX: .517

The hotshot Suns' rookie last season was supposed to be Armon Gilliam, the No. 2 overall draft choice. Gilliam, being well-publicized, was selected for the All-Rookie team. But at season's end the future of the Suns was clearly in Johnson's hands . . . Johnson wound up with the second best TENDEX rating among rookies, behind Rookie of the Year Mark Jackson . . . after being traded to Phoenix, Johnson played as well as Jackson, with a .582 rating . . . Johnson said he felt like a "new person" with Phoenix and he certainly played like one . . . in 28 games with the Suns, he averaged 31.2 minutes, 12.6 points, 8.7 assists, and had a free throw percentage of .859 . . . How well can he play this season after going through a training camp with his new teammates? The Suns can't wait to find out.

TOM CHAMBERS

AGE: 29
HEIGHT: 6-10
WEIGHT: 230
POSITION: Small Forward
EXPERIENCE: 7 Seasons
COLLEGE: Utah
BIRTHPLACE: Ogden, UT
1987–88 TENDEX: .543

With a field goal percentage that has declined every year but one since he entered the NBA seven years ago, Chambers needs to start shooting more selectively, but if he does that his game might dry up altogether because it is totally centered around scoring . . . rated No. 18 in the NBA last season in scoring average (20.4) and No. 13 in points per minute . . . averaged 25.8 points to lead Sonics in five-game playoff series against Denver . . . passed 10,000-point mark last season and has 10,811 going into this season . . . best ratings among NBA small forwards last year were No. 6 in scoring and PAR percentage, No. 7 in steals, No. 8 in three-point field goal percentage, and No. 9 in free throw percentage . . . last place in two-point field goal percentage, No. 21 Shootist, and No. 21 in turnovers . . . in middle of pack with No. 10 TENDEX rating.

JOHNSON

1987–88	2PFG	3PFG	F.T.	REB.	AST.	STL.	T.O.	BLK.	PTS.
Per Game			unrated: did not play 2,000 minutes						
Per Minute									
Rating									

CHAMBERS

1987–88	2PFG	3PFG	F.T.	REB.	AST.	STL.	T.O.	BLK.	PTS.
Per Game	.461	.303	.807	6.0	2.6	1.1	2.6	0.6	20.4
Per Minute	.461	.303	.807	.183	.079	.032	.078	.020	.625
Rating	23	8	9	11	14	7	21	11	6

JEFF HORNACEK

AGE: 25
HEIGHT: 6-4
WEIGHT: 190
POSITION: Shooting Guard
EXPERIENCE: 2 Seasons
COLLEGE: Iowa State
BIRTHPLACE: Elmhurst, IL
1987–88 TENDEX: .515

After a nondescript rookie season, Hornacek was the surprise of the Suns in 1987–88 . . . playing both guard positions, he shot well (.528 in two-point field goal percentage), and passed well, leading team with 540 assists (6.6 per game) . . . among the league's shooting guards he had surprisingly strong ratings of No. 1 in assists per minute, No. 5 in two-point field goal percentage and Shootist percentage, No. 7 in rebounds and steals, and No. 8 in three-point field goal percentage . . . No. 8 in TENDEX rating . . . lows were No. 18 in blocked shots and No. 17 in scoring . . . barring injuries, Hornacek should combine successfully in backcourt with Johnson until the mid-1990s.

MARK WEST

AGE: 28
HEIGHT: 6-10
WEIGHT: 230
POSITION: Center
EXPERIENCE: 5 Seasons
COLLEGE: Old Dominion
BIRTHPLACE: Petersburg, VA
1987–88 TENDEX: .500

While with Cleveland, West was regarded as one of the best reserve centers in the NBA, but it is another matter to be in the starting lineup opposite the likes of Akeem Olajuwon, Patrick Ewing, and Moses Malone . . . based on his performance last season, in his first chance to play regularly, the Suns probably need a stronger offensive center to become a competitive post-season team . . . good ratings of No. 5 in the NBA in blocked shots per minute, No. 11 in two-point field goal percentage, and No. 14 in ratio of blocks to turnovers were more than offset by bottom ten listings in PAR, assists, free throw percentage, and ratio of steals to turnovers . . . among centers he was rated in the upper half only in field goal percentage (No. 4) and all statistics related to blocked shots (No. 5) . . . far down the list in everything else, with a TENDEX standing of No. 15.

HORNACEK

1987–88	2PFG	3PFG	F.T.	REB.	AST.	STL.	T.O.	BLK.	PTS.
Per Game	.528	.293	.822	3.2	6.6	1.3	1.9	0.1	9.5
Per Minute	.528	.293	.822	.117	.241	.048	.070	.004	.348
Rating	5	8	13	7	1	7	10	18	17

WEST

1987–88	2PFG	3PFG	F.T.	REB.	AST.	STL.	T.O.	BLK.	PTS.
Per Game	.552	.000	.596	6.3	0.9	0.6	0.2	1.8	9.7
Per Minute	.552	.000	.596	.249	.035	.022	.082	.070	.382
Rating	4	10	22	11	17	10	14	5	18

EDDIE JOHNSON

AGE: 29
HEIGHT: 6-7
WEIGHT: 215
POSITION: Small Forward
EXPERIENCE: 7 Seasons
COLLEGE: Illinois
BIRTHPLACE: Chicago
1987–88 TENDEX: .473

Like many other basketball players who grew up in the Chicago area, Eddie Johnson has a one-track mentality, which is to shoot the basketball . . . led Suns in scoring last season after Nance was traded and Davis was benched, winding up with 17.7 average . . . but scoring is about all the Suns are going to get from him . . . No. 20 in the NBA in points per minute and No. 20 in free throw percentage, but weak defense was exposed by bottom ten standards in steals, blocked shots, and BEST . . . among small forwards had low ratings in rebounds (No. 16), Shootist percentage (No. 16), and TENDEX (No. 19).

RESERVES

Including Armon Gilliam among Phoenix reserves seems almost as strange as doing the same with Golden State's Ralph Sampson. But we did make one exception for Kevin Johnson, who, like Sampson and Gilliam, failed to play 2,000 minutes last season. We made the exception for Johnson because he is clearly the Suns' best player going into the 1988–89 season.

About Gilliam one thing is certain: He will be a full-time regular this season, if he can avoid the kind of serious injury that sidelined him for one-third of the 1987–88 campaign. TENDEX rating of .445 (No. 8 among rookies) was misleadingly low because, with his injury and with player personnel changing all around him, he never really had a chance to get settled.

Alvan Adams, a TENDEX 700 Club member, has retired, so the rest of the Suns' bench is weak.

Craig Hodges did set an NBA record last season for three-point field goal percentage (.491), but his TENDEX rating was only .368.

Tyrone Corbin, a forward obtained in the Nance trade, could be helpful. He had a .450 rating while averaging 21 minutes of playing time.

JOHNSON

1987–88	2PFG	3PFG	F.T.	REB.	AST.	STL.	T.O.	BLK.	PTS.
Per Game	.501	.255	.850	4.4	2.5	0.5	1.9	0.1	17.7
Per Minute	.501	.255	.850	.146	.083	.015	.064	.004	.594
Rating	11	12	3	16	12	22	9	21	8

OUTLOOK

Phoenix is a difficult team to figure. The personnel on this team has changed almost as much as the Los Angeles Clippers during the 1986–87 and 1987–88 seasons, but the Suns' new players aren't quite as good as the Clippers'.

The Suns do have some good ones. They have two of the top ten players from the 1987 rookie crop and two more first-rounders from the 1988 draft. All four of these players may start in 1988–89.

Point guard Kevin Johnson (1987) and power forward Armon Gilliam (1987) are sure starters, while rookie small forward Tim Perry and rookie shooting guard Dan Majerle are possible starters. Perry will probably spend his rookie season as a substitute for Chambers.

Andrew Lang and Dean Garrett, chosen in the second round of the 1988 college draft, will compete with Mark West for the starting center job, and Jeff Hornacek is a solid guard who can back up both Johnson and Majerle, if he doesn't start ahead of Majerle.

Once these players get to know each other, in another year or two, this is going to be a good team. If in the meantime, through the luck of the lottery, Phoenix lands a star center, a future league championship is not out of the question.

Probable finish: Fifth in Pacific Division.

19

Portland Trail Blazers

The Trail Blazers took some criticism after being upset by Utah in the first round of the 1988 playoffs, but it eased up somewhat when Utah played the Los Angeles Lakers to the hilt in the second round.

The Trail Blazers are actually only a power forward away from being the best team in the NBA, and if center Kevin Duckworth improves as much this year as he did last, they could move to the top even without a rugged rebounder in the corner.

They are set at the other positions with new TENDEX 700 Club member Clyde Drexler and a pair of all-star quality players, point guard Terry Porter and small forward Jerome Kersey.

In compiling a 53–29 record, Coach Mike Schuler's team did well last season in nearly all team statistics. The Blazers were No. 1 in PAR, No. 2 in scoring, No. 3 in rebounding and No. 4 in two-point field goal percentage—four of the most important categories.

They were also No. 5 in Shootist, No. 6 in assists, and No. 5 in the most significant statistic—overall TENDEX efficiency rating.

With the inexperienced Duckworth still not an effective defensive player, they rated only No. 21 in blocked shots, but that was their only really weak area of performance.

This is a young team with an NBA championship in its near future.

167

CLYDE DREXLER

AGE: 26
HEIGHT: 6-7
WEIGHT: 215
POSITION: Shooting Guard
EXPERIENCE: 5 Seasons
COLLEGE: Houston
BIRTHPLACE: New Orleans, LA
1987–88 TENDEX: .700

Drexler ascended to superstardom in 1987–88, joining the TENDEX 700 Club with the ninth highest rating in the NBA. He also was No. 5 in the league in PAR (PAR-5), No. 6 in points per game (27.0), No. 6 in points per minute (.714), No. 6 in steals, No. 6 in PAR percentage, No. 7 in minutes played, and No. 12 in ratio of steals to turnovers . . . had PAR-6 rating in 1986–87 . . . the blazer of Blazers, Drexler raced to the second best rating among shooting guards last season, behind Michael Jordan . . . out of 18 statistical categories, he was among the top five shooting guards in 11 of them: No. 2 in rebounds, points, PAR percentage, and TENDEX; No. 3 in minutes played, blocked shots, and PAR; No. 4 in steals and Shootist percentage; and No. 5 in BEST and ratio of steals to turnovers . . . lowest rating was No. 15 in free throw percentage, but at .811 he wasn't exactly bad.

TERRY PORTER

AGE: 25
HEIGHT: 6-3
WEIGHT: 195
POSITION: Point Guard
EXPERIENCE: 3 Seasons
COLLEGE: Wisconsin-Stevens Point
BIRTHPLACE: Milwaukee
1987–88 TENDEX: .561

A perfect complementary backcourt teammate for Drexler, Porter broke his own Portland assists record last season, finishing with 831 for an average of 10.1, fourth in the NBA . . . ranked No. 10 in the league in PAR (PAR-4), No. 11 in minutes played, No. 17 in steals, and No. 9 in ratio of assists to turnovers . . . remarkably, the Portland backcourt of Drexler and Porter had 12 statistical rankings among the league leaders between them, without slipping into the bottom ten in a single category . . . Porter had 14 top-ten ratings in point guard statistics: No. 3 in minutes played, two-point field goal percentage, and Shootist percentage; No. 4 in Shootist and PAR; No. 5 in assists, PAR percentage, and three-point field goal percentage; No. 6 in rebounds; No. 7 in free throw percentage and TENDEX; No. 8 in scoring; and No. 10 in steals and blocked shots . . . had a problem with turnovers (rating No. 16) and was burned on defense by penetrating point guards.

DREXLER

1987–88	2PFG	3PFG	F.T.	REB.	AST.	STL.	T.O.	BLK.	PTS.
Per Game	.515	.212	.811	6.6	5.8	2.5	2.9	0.6	27.0
Per Minute	.515	.212	.811	.174	.153	.066	.077	.017	.714
Rating	8	12	15	2	7	4	14	3	2

PORTER

1987–88	2PFG	3PFG	F.T.	REB.	AST.	STL.	T.O.	BLK.	PTS.
Per Game	.533	.348	.846	4.6	10.1	1.8	3.0	0.2	14.9
Per Minute	.533	.348	.846	.126	.278	.050	.082	.005	.409
Rating	3	5	7	6	5	10	16	10	8

JEROME KERSEY

AGE: 26
HEIGHT: 6-7
WEIGHT: 222
POSITION: Small Forward
EXPERIENCE: 4 Seasons
COLLEGE: Longwood
BIRTHPLACE: Clarksville, VA
1987–88 TENDEX: .566

When Kiki Vandeweghe became injured early last season, in a way it was a good break for the Trail Blazers, because it enabled Coach Mike Schuler to replace the popular Vandeweghe with Kersey. Not as good a scorer as Vandeweghe, Kersey is better in almost every other aspect of play, especially defense and rebounding . . . his defense was typified by NBA ratings of No. 18 in BEST and No. 14 in ratio of steals to turnovers . . . No. 20 in minutes played . . . among small forwards Kersey ranked No. 1 in steals, No. 2 in ratio of steals to turnovers, No. 3 in minutes, No. 4 in BEST, No. 5 in rebounds, No. 5 in turnovers, No. 6 in ratio of blocked shots to turnovers, No. 7 in blocked shots, and No. 8 in TENDEX . . . poor free throw shooter, ranked No. 19 in that category, the only weak part of his game.

KEVIN DUCKWORTH

AGE: 24
HEIGHT: 7-0
WEIGHT: 280
POSITION: Center
EXPERIENCE: 2 Seasons
COLLEGE: Eastern Illinois
BIRTHPLACE: Harvey, IL
1987–88 TENDEX: .512

An awkward rookie in 1986–87, Duckworth made excellent improvement last year after replacing the injured Steve Johnson . . . increases in points (from 5.4 to 15.8 per game) and rebounds (from 3.4 to 7.4) were the primary reasons that he was named the NBA's Most Improved Player, although a big increase in minutes played (from 875 to 2,223) had a lot to do with it . . . an excellent athlete, he needs only to learn the game's finer points in order to become an all-star player . . . weaknesses were pinpointed last season by five bottom ten ratings: steals, assists, BEST, PAR, and ratio of steals to turnovers . . . a weak defensive player, he rated No. 20 among centers in blocked shots, No. 20 in BEST, and No. 21 in steals . . . No. 14 center in TENDEX rating.

KERSEY

1987–88	2PFG	3PFG	F.T.	REB.	AST.	STL.	T.O.	BLK.	PTS.
Per Game	.502	.200	.735	8.3	3.1	1.6	2.0	0.8	19.2
Per Minute	.502	.200	.735	.227	.084	.044	.056	.023	.525
Rating	10	14	19	5	11	1	5	7	14

DUCKWORTH

1987–88	2PFG	3PFG	F.T.	REB.	AST.	STL.	T.O.	BLK.	PTS.
Per Game	.496	.000	.770	7.4	0.9	0.4	2.3	0.4	15.8
Per Minute	.496	.000	.770	.259	.030	.014	.080	.014	.554
Rating	16	8	8	10	19	21	13	20	4

RESERVES

The development of Kersey as a starter improves the Trail Blazers' bench, because it puts Vandeweghe there. A great scorer, ideal as a sixth man, Vandeweghe had a TENDEX rating of .557 last season, tied for No. 4 among the league's reserves. Missed 45 games because of injuries but averaged 20.2 points per game in the 37 games he played.

Center Steve Johnson probably also will do better as a substitute than he did as a starter. Lacking stamina at age 31, he missed 39 games because of injuries last year, but showed he could still play respectably with a .500 TENDEX rating. He ranks No. 2 on the all-time NBA field goal list with a career percentage of .580.

Other reserves are Michael Holton (TENDEX .400), Caldwell Jones (.376), and Richard Anderson (.398). Jones actually was a starter last season, but didn't play 2,000 minutes. He's the weak link who must be replaced for the Blazers to win the title.

OUTLOOK

Mark it down: Mark Bryant was the steal of the 1988 college draft.

With a TENDEX rating of .691 for his senior season at Seton Hall, Bryant was the No. 7 rated player in the draft and the second best power forward. With a body like Karl Malone, he could wind up being better than several of the players who were rated ahead of him, and the Trail Blazers landed him with the 21st pick in the draft.

Portland is a team with no excuses any more. The ingredients are all here for an NBA championship within the next two or three years. Now it's up to Coach Mike Schuler to put them together.

With Bryant the likely starter at power forward, the Blazers will have a 1988–89 lineup with good athletes at every position and none of them more than 26 years old.

The backcourt consisting of new 700 Club member Clyde Drexler and Kevin Porter matches up well with the Los Angeles Lakers' backcourt; and the frontline of Jerome Kersey, Kevin Duckworth, and Bryant is potentially better than the Lakers'.

If Kiki Vandeweghe is willing to accept the role of sixth man, which he is ideally suited for, this team should challenge the Lakers in 1988–89.

Probable finish: Second in Pacific Division.

20

Sacramento Kings

*T*he best break the Kings get in 1988–89 is moving out of the tough Midwest Division and into the Pacific Division, where they could be competitive with three other teams.

Last season the Kings finished last in the Midwest Division with a record (24–58) that was good enough to rank ahead of two Pacific Division teams and wasn't much worse than a third, Phoenix (28–54).

Concurrent with NBA expansion from 23 teams to 25, the Kings move in 1988–89 to the Pacific Division because of their geographic proximity to other teams in that division. Miami replaces the Kings in the Midwest Division and the teams will be reshuffled in 1989–90 when two more expansion teams are added.

Sacramento has one excellent young player, Otis Thorpe, and one potentially good one, Kenny Smith. But the team gives Thorpe little help in the frontcourt, and it is especially evident at the defensive end of the court. Last season the Kings allowed 113.7 points per game, third worst in the league, and allowed opponents to shoot .498 from the field, also the third worst.

Paced by Thorpe and centers Joe Kleine and LaSalle Thompson, the Kings ranked No. 4 in rebounding, but they had low listings of No. 23 in steals, No. 21 in BEST, No. 19 in turnovers, No. 17 in two-point field goals percentage, and No. 20 in TENDEX rating.

OTIS THORPE

AGE: 26
HEIGHT: 6-11
WEIGHT: 236
POSITION: Power Forward
EXPERIENCE: 4 Seasons
COLLEGE: Providence
BIRTHPLACE: Boynton Beach, FL
1987–88 TENDEX: .603

Thorpe isn't as well known as James Worthy or Xavier McDaniel, but he is just as good a basketball player, if not better, and he'll get a chance to prove it when he plays in the same division with these prominent cornermen this season. Last season was the best of Thorpe's four-year NBA career as he registered personal highs in minutes played, rebounds, assists, steals, and points . . . average of 20.8 points per game was 16th best in the league . . . led Kings in minutes, field goal percentage, and rebounds . . . No. 5 in the league in minutes, No. 9 in rebounds per game, No. 15 in PAR percentage . . . among power forwards Thorpe ranked No. 3 in minutes and PAR, No. 4 in assists and PAR percentage, No. 5 in points, No. 8 in Shootist percentage and rebounds, and No. 9 in two-point field goal percentage . . . he was No. 8 in TENDEX with a .600-plus rating that put him in the "star" category . . . lifetime field goal percentage is .547, and he could be listed in the NBA's top 20 all-time players in this category if he reaches the qualifying number of 2,000 field goals during the 1988–89 season.

RANDY WITTMAN

AGE: 29
HEIGHT: 6-6
WEIGHT: 210
POSITION: Shooting Guard
EXPERIENCE: 5 Seasons
COLLEGE: Indiana
BIRTHPLACE: Indianapolis
1987–88 TENDEX: .354

Wittman was the third lowest rated player among NBA regulars in 1987–88 and the lowest of the shooting guards. He made a misnomer of the shooting guard position by failing to attempt a single three-point field goal and by averaging only ten points per game . . . shot under 50 percent from the field for the first time in his career . . . ranked last among the shooting guards in PAR . . . the one strong point of his game was ball-handling: He led the league in lowest turnover percentage and finished fourth with a ratio of 3.68 assists for every turnover.

THORPE

1987–88	2PFG	3PFG	F.T.	REB.	AST.	STL.	T.O.	BLK.	PTS.
Per Game	.510	.000	.755	10.2	3.2	0.8	2.8	0.7	20.8
Per Minute	.510	.000	.755	.272	.087	.020	.074	.018	.555
Rating	9	20	11	8	4	18	15	12	5

WITTMAN

1987–88	2PFG	3PFG	F.T.	REB.	AST.	STL.	T.O.	BLK.	PTS.
Per Game	.478	.000	.798	2.1	3.7	0.6	1.0	0.2	10.0
Per Minute	.478	.000	.798	.070	.125	.021	.034	.007	.341
Rating	15	17	16	18	11	17	1	10	18

KENNY SMITH

AGE: 23
HEIGHT: 6-3
WEIGHT: 170
POSITION: Point Guard
EXPERIENCE: 1 Season
COLLEGE: North Carolina
BIRTHPLACE: Queens, NY
1987–88 TENDEX: .408

After a good start, Smith had a disappointing finish to his rookie NBA season. He was playing well when he was sidelined for 21 games with an injury and, although he recovered from the injury, he didn't recover his early-season playing form . . . named to the All-Rookie team, but was only the No. 11 rookie, according to TENDEX ratings . . . finished No. 18 in the league in assists, but in the bottom ten among regulars in blocked shots, ratio of blocks to turnovers, and TENDEX . . . highest rating among 20 point guards was No. 9 in the two Shootist statistics . . . in bottom ten point guards in all other stats, with worsts of No. 19 in rebounds and TENDEX.

HAROLD PRESSLEY

AGE: 25
HEIGHT: 6-8
WEIGHT: 210
POSITION: Small Forward
EXPERIENCE: 2 Seasons
COLLEGE: Villanova
BIRTHPLACE: Bronx, NY
1987–88 TENDEX: .433

Pressley made some improvement in his second NBA season, but was still a long way from being the player the Kings hoped he'd be when they drafted him in the first round in 1986 . . . finished in NBA's bottom ten in TENDEX . . . No. 20 or worse in small forward stats in five categories: No. 20 in PAR percentage, No. 20 in two-point field goal percentage, No. 20 in scoring, No. 21 in TENDEX, and No. 21 in Shootist percentage . . . good ball-control player, with ratings of No. 3 in steals, No. 4 in ratio of steals to turnovers, No. 6 in blocked shots, and No. 6 in BEST.

SMITH

1987–88	2PFG	3PFG	F.T.	REB.	AST.	STL.	T.O.	BLK.	PTS.
Per Game	.487	.308	.819	2.3	7.1	1.5	3.0	0.1	13.8
Per Minute	.487	.308	.819	.064	.200	.042	.085	.004	.388
Rating	12	10	13	19	15	15	17	15	13

PRESSLEY

1987–88	2PFG	3PFG	F.T.	REB.	AST.	STL.	T.O.	BLK.	PTS.
Per Game	.476	.327	.792	4.6	2.3	1.1	1.7	0.7	9.7
Per Minute	.476	.327	.792	.182	.091	.041	.067	.027	.382
Rating	20	7	11	13	8	3	13	6	20

RESERVES

None of the three Kings' centers—LaSalle Thompson, Joe Kleine, or Jawann Oldham—played enough minutes to be considered a regular, but among them they gave the Kings adequate play in the pivot, with 1,648 points, 1,310 rebounds, and 242 blocked shots. Thompson's TENDEX rating of .586 was No. 2 of all NBA reserves who played between 1,000 and 2,000 minutes. Kleine ranked No. 19 with a .503 rating.

Other respectable reserves were Ed Pinckney (.463), Terry Tyler (.409), and three-point field goal specialist Mike McGee (.414).

Derek Smith showed occasional flashes of his great 1984–85 form, when he averaged 22.1 points per game before being hobbled by a knee injury early in 1985–86.

OUTLOOK

The Kings had a bad team in 1987–88, and in 1988–89 they could be even worse.

The trade of Reggie Theus for Randy Wittman weakened their backcourt, and they did nothing to strengthen their equally weak frontcourt in the draft. Forward–guard Ricky Berry, their first-round choice, appeared overmatched in post-season play against other college seniors and should be even more overmatched in the NBA.

Up front, Sacramento has one star player, Otis Thorpe, who could start for any team in the NBA except the Boston Celtics.

LaSalle Thompson is an underrated center, who always does a workmanlike job, but he seldom plays more than 25 minutes per game. The other center, Joe Kleine, is inadequate.

Like Thompson, point guard Kenny Smith has durability problems which are aggravated by the fact that the Kings have no one to replace him.

This is a team that could lose a few games to Miami and Charlotte.

Probable finish: Seventh in Pacific Division.

21

San Antonio Spurs

*T*he missing piece is David Robinson.

With everything but an intimidating center, the Spurs edged into the playoffs last season with a record of 31–51, but were blitzed in the first round by the Los Angeles Lakers.

After Robinson joins the team in 1989–90, the Spurs probably won't be blitzed by anybody.

This is already a good offensive team, averaging 113.6 points per game, No. 4 in the league, in 1987–88. The problems were rebounding and defense, which just happen to be the best parts of Robinson's game. The Spurs ranked last in the NBA in scoring defense in 1987–88, with a yield of 118.5 points. On the boards they were No. 21, allowing opponents 46.4 rebounds per contest.

The Spurs have good starters at four positions and a good bench, but must use natural forwards Frank Brickowski and Greg Anderson in the pivot. With Robinson patrolling the middle, Anderson and Brickowski will be able to share time at their natural position, power forward.

In the meantime, the Spurs will have to try to score enough points to eke into the playoffs.

Besides being a good scoring team in 1987–88, they also excelled in PAR (No. 3 in the NBA), assists (No. 4), two-point field goal percentage (No. 5), steals (No. 6), Shootist (No. 7), three-point field goal percentage (No. 8), and blocked shots (No. 9).

Poor stats were free throw percentage (No. 21) and TENDEX (No. 19).

ALVIN ROBERTSON

AGE: 26
HEIGHT: 6-4
WEIGHT: 190
POSITION: Shooting Guard
EXPERIENCE: 4 Seasons
COLLEGE: Arkansas
BIRTHPLACE: Barberton, OH
1987–88 TENDEX: .571

Robertson is one Spur who knows how to play defense and for that reason is an even better player than his good TENDEX rating indicates . . . NBA Defensive Player of the Year 1985–86, All-Defensive team past two seasons . . . set league record for steals with 301 in 1985–86, led league again in 1986–87 . . . league's Most Improved Player 1985–86 . . . All-NBA second team 1985–86 . . . led Spurs in minutes played, assists, steals, and scoring in 1987–88, with personal highs in points (19.6) and assists (6.8) . . . ranked No. 2 in the league in steals, No. 4 in PAR, No. 6 in ratio of steals to turnovers, and No. 9 in BEST . . . averaged 22.3 points in playoff series against Los Angeles Lakers . . . among NBA shooting guards had excellent ratings of No. 1 in steals; No. 2 in blocked shots, BEST, and PAR (PAR-6); No. 3 in rebounds; No. 4 in assists; and No. 5 in TENDEX . . . only problem was so-so free throw shooting (No. 20).

FRANK BRICKOWSKI

AGE: 29
HEIGHT: 6-10
WEIGHT: 240
POSITION: Center/Forward
EXPERIENCE: 4 Seasons
COLLEGE: Penn State
BIRTHPLACE: Bayville, NY
1987–88 TENDEX: .532

One of the ironies of last season was the play of Brickowski for the Spurs after sitting on the Los Angeles Lakers' bench in 1986–87 . . . Lakers traded Brickowski to Spurs and he proceeded to finish ahead of Laker center Kareem Abdul-Jabbar in the TENDEX rating for centers. Brickowski placed No. 11 with a .532 rating, while Jabbar was No. 12 with .525 . . . Brickowski ranked No. 1 among centers in assists per minute, No. 2 in PAR, No. 4 in steals, No. 6 in Shootist percentage and PAR percentage, No. 7 in scoring, No. 8 Shootist, and No. 9 in free throw percentage and two-point field goal percentage . . . poor facets of play were rebounds (No. 20), turnovers (No. 19), blocked shots (No. 19), and BEST (No. 18) . . . in NBA league-wide ratings Brickowski was No. 19 in PAR and Shootist percentage, but in the bottom ten in turnovers and ratio of blocked shots to turnovers.

ROBERTSON

1987–88	2PFG	3PFG	F.T.	REB.	AST.	STL.	T.O.	BLK.	PTS.
Per Game	.478	.284	.748	6.1	6.8	3.0	3.1	0.8	19.6
Per Minute	.478	.284	.748	.167	.187	.082	.084	.023	.541
Rating	13	9	20	3	4	1	16	2	9

BRICKOWSKI

1987–88	2PFG	3PFG	F.T.	REB.	AST.	STL.	T.O.	BLK.	PTS.
Per Game	.530	.200	.768	6.9	3.8	1.1	3.0	0.5	16.0
Per Minute	.530	.200	.768	.217	.119	.033	.093	.016	.502
Rating	9	4	9	20	1	4	19	9	7

JOHNNY DAWKINS

AGE: 25
HEIGHT: 6-2
WEIGHT: 165
POSITION: Point Guard
EXPERIENCE: 2 Seasons
COLLEGE: Duke
BIRTHPLACE: Washington, DC
1987–88 TENDEX: .495

Dawkins improved his TENDEX rating by 54 percentage points over his 1986–87 rookie rating of .441. He ranked No. 4 in the NBA in free throw percentage and No. 11 in assists per minute . . . improved scoring average from 10.3 to 15.8 . . . in point guard rankings placed No. 1 in free throw percentage, No. 4 in scoring, No. 6 in PAR percentage and Shootist, No. 7 in turnovers, and No. 8 in three-point field goal percentage . . . downside stats reflected poor defense: No. 19 in blocked shots, No. 17 in steals, and No. 16 in BEST . . . rated No. 13 point guard in TENDEX.

RESERVES

Rookie Greg Anderson and second-year man Walter Berry comprised the starting corner tandem for the Spurs for about half of the 1987–88 season, but neither player managed to play the 2,000 minutes necessary to qualify as a regular.

Berry has been traded to New Jersey for forward Dallas Comegys (TENDEX .408).

Anderson, who started a few games at center late in the season, led the Spurs in rebounds and blocked shots. He had one game in which he scored 20 points and pulled down 20 rebounds. TENDEX rating of .490 was No. 4 among rookies and he was voted to the All-Rookie team. Like Berry, the big negative in Anderson's game was free throw percentage (.604).

Other San Antonio substitutes are center Petur Gudmundsson (TENDEX .543, No. 9 on the NBA's list of reserves), forwards Mike Mitchell (.444) and David Greenwood (.408).

DAWKINS

1987–88	2PFG	3PFG	F.T.	REB.	AST.	STL.	T.O.	BLK.	PTS.
Per Game	.499	.311	.896	3.1	7.4	1.4	2.4	0.0	15.8
Per Minute	.499	.311	.896	.094	.220	.040	.071	.001	.471
Rating	10	8	1	10	10	17	7	19	4

OUTLOOK

All the engine parts are in place now except the carburetor.

The signing of Larry Brown to coach the Spurs and a great crop of 1988 draft choices gives San Antonio everything it needs to reach the .500 mark or better in 1988–89 and move to the top of the league in 1989–90 when David Robinson joins the team.

Brown may have difficulty deciding who to cut. He may have to agonize over the starting lineup for this deep team.

One of the starters will be guard Alvin Robertson, but there will be competition at every other position.

Rookie point guard Willie Anderson could depose Johnny Dawkins from his starting role.

Rookie small forward Shelton Jones could muster a challenge for a starting job.

Second-year man Greg Anderson probably will start at power forward or center. If he's the center, Frank Brickowski will likely be the power forward. If he's the power forward, rookie Barry Sumpter could be the center.

Probable finish: Fourth in Midwest Division.

22

Seattle Supersonics

*E*ven with three of the NBA's top 20 scorers, Seattle was unable to mount a serious challenge for a league title during the 1986–87 and 1987–88 seasons.

One reason is that the Sonics, like the San Antonio Spurs, are a center away from excellence. Unlike the Spurs, they don't have a good center signed to a contract.

Shooting guard Dale Ellis and forwards Xavier McDaniel and Tom Chambers are standout scorers (Nos. 7, 14, and 18, respectively, last season). But Chambers is no longer a Sonic, and McDaniel and Ellis probably are not the team's best players. For that distinction you can choose between point guard Nate McMillan and forward Michael Cage, both of whom have serious limitations in their games.

Maybe that is what is wrong with the Sonics: They have nobody whom they can turn to with confidence, game after game. McDaniel is erratic. Ellis is a pure shooter who does not excel in other areas of play. McMillan is hesitant to shoot. Cage is erratic offensively.

When a team doesn't measure up to expectations, there is a tendency to blame the coach, but Bernie Bickerstaff is probably doing the best he can with the talent—some of it overrated—that he has on hand.

In compiling the 11th best record in the NBA last season (44–38), the Sonics got the better of most statistics but, ironically, shot worse from the field (.476 to .485) than their opponents.

In statistical comparisons with the league as a whole, the Sonics had good ratings of No. 3 in three-point field goal percentage (thanks to Ellis), No. 4 in steals, No. 6 in scoring and BEST, No. 7 in PAR, and No. 8 in rebounds and TENDEX. The most severe team weakness was free throw shooting (No. 19).

179

DALE ELLIS

AGE: 28
HEIGHT: 6-7
WEIGHT: 213
POSITION: Shooting Guard
EXPERIENCE: 5 Seasons
COLLEGE: Tennessee
BIRTHPLACE: Marietta, GA
1987–88 TENDEX: .552

The least spectacular of the Sonics' three high scorers but, considering the position he plays, the best of the three. Ellis' TENDEX rating of .552 last season made him the only Sonic to exceed the average for his position (.450) by 100 or more percentage points. Playing the more opportune forward positions, McDaniel and Chambers actually wound up the 1987–88 season less than 50 points above the norms for their positions, well down the rating list of regular cornermen . . . a smooth player with outstanding size for his position, Ellis is an excellent long-range shooter. With his .413 percentage in three-point shots during the 1987–88 season, Ellis vaulted from seventh place to third on the all-time NBA list . . . selected the NBA's Most Improved Player in 1986–87 . . . in 1987–88 he was rated the No. 10 Shootist in the NBA (1.013) . . . led Sonics in scoring with seventh best average in the league (25.8) . . . among shooting guards he had ratings of No. 3 in scoring, No. 4 Shootist, No. 4 in three-point field goal percentage, No. 5 in rebounds, No. 5 in PAR percentage, No. 6 in turnovers, No. 7 in minutes played, No. 7 in two-point field goal percentage, and No. 6 in TENDEX . . . weaknesses were No. 19 in free throw percentage, No. 18 in assists, and No. 17 in blocked shots.

MICHAEL CAGE

AGE: 26
HEIGHT: 6-9
WEIGHT: 230
POSITION: Power Forward
EXPERIENCE: 4 Seasons
COLLEGE: San Diego State
BIRTHPLACE: West Memphis, AR
1987–88 TENDEX: .591

Is Cage a legitimate NBA star or are his statistics, especially rebounds, inflated by the fact that he plays for a poor team? This is a question that probably won't be answered until he plays for a good team, but a case can be made both ways on the evidence of 1987–88 statistics. Cage actually finished No. 3, not No. 1, on the basis of rebounds per minute instead of gross average per game, but his board strength is impressive either way . . . he had three games in which he scored 20 points and pulled down 20 rebounds . . . also did well with a No. 5 ranking among power forwards in steals and No. 8 in blocked shots . . . but his strengths were counterbalanced by bad shooting, with No. 19 ratings in field goal percentage, free throw percentage, and Shootist . . . finished one notch above the middle of the pack with a No. 9 TENDEX rating out of 20 full-time power forwards.

ELLIS

1987–88	2PFG	3PFG	F.T.	REB.	AST.	STL.	T.O.	BLK.	PTS.
Per Game	.521	.413	.767	4.5	2.6	1.0	2.3	0.1	25.8
Per Minute	.521	.413	.767	.122	.071	.027	.062	.004	.695
Rating	7	4	19	5	18	14	6	17	3

CAGE

1987–88	2PFG	3PFG	F.T.	REB.	AST.	STL.	T.O.	BLK.	PTS.
Per Game	.471	.000	.688	13.0	1.5	1.3	2.2	0.8	14.5
Per Minute	.471	.000	.688	.353	.041	.034	.060	.022	.393
Rating	19	13	19	3	15	5	10	8	14

XAVIER McDANIEL

AGE: 25
HEIGHT: 6-8
WEIGHT: 205
POSITION: Power Forward
EXPERIENCE: 3 Seasons
COLLEGE: Wichita State
BIRTHPLACE: Columbia, SC
1987–88 TENDEX: .571

The X Man at times is one of the NBA's most spectacular players, but at other times he seems to disappear . . . his scoring in the NBA has been better than expected (No. 14 last season), but after leading the NCAA in rebounds two years in a row for Wichita State, his board work as a professional has been disappointing; averaged only 6.6 rebounds per game last season, No. 18 out of 20 regular power forwards . . . a good passer, McDaniel had the best percentage of assists per minutes among power forwards . . . other good ratings were No. 2 in PAR, No. 3 in points, No. 4 in three-point field goal percentage and steals, and No. 6 in minutes played . . . not a standout ball-control player, he was only No. 17 in turnovers, No. 17 in ratio of steals to turnovers, No. 15 in ratio of blocked shots to turnovers, and No. 15 in BEST . . . ranked No. 16 in free throw percentage.

NATE McMILLAN

AGE: 24
HEIGHT: 6-5
WEIGHT: 190
POSITION: Point Guard
EXPERIENCE: 2 Seasons
COLLEGE: North Carolina State
BIRTHPLACE: Raleigh, NC
1987–88 TENDEX: .558

McMillan achieved the second best TENDEX rating on the Sonics last season; also, the second best rating relative to his position, 83 points above the point guard norm of .475. An excellent defender, he gives Magic Johnson as much trouble as any opponent in the league and deserves All-Defensive team recognition . . . an outstanding ballhandler, McMillan ranked No. 3 in the NBA in 1987–88 in ratio of assists to turnovers, No. 4 in assists, No. 5 in steals, No. 10 in ratio of steals to turnovers, and No. 17 in BEST . . . with 702 assists he fell 64 short of Len Wilkens's Seattle record . . . No. 14 rating in the league in PAR (PAR-4) . . . among point guards did well in all important aspects of play unrelated to shooting and scoring: No. 1 in blocked shots, No. 2 in BEST and steals, No. 4 in rebounds and assists, No. 7 in PAR, and No. 8 in TENDEX . . . needs to shoot more and better, ranked last among point guards in free throw percentage and scoring.

McDANIEL

1987–88	2PFG	3PFG	F.T.	REB.	AST.	STL.	T.O.	BLK.	PTS.
Per Game	.496	.280	.715	6.6	3.4	1.2	2.9	0.7	21.4
Per Minute	.496	.280	.715	.192	.097	.036	.083	.019	.617
Rating	13	4	16	18	1	4	17	11	3

McMILLAN

1987–88	2PFG	3PFG	F.T.	REB.	AST.	STL.	T.O.	BLK.	PTS.
Per Game	.479	.375	.707	4.1	8.6	2.1	2.3	0.6	7.6
Per Minute	.479	.375	.707	.138	.286	.069	.077	.019	.254
Rating	13	2	21	4	4	2	11	1	20

RESERVES

Second-year men Derrick McKey and Olden Polynice give hope to the Sonics for improvement in 1988–89, no matter how well their rookies play.

Perhaps the most gifted of all the rookies to enter the NBA last season, McKey made the All-Rookie team and ranked No. 3 in TENDEX among rookies (.492). He did this at age 21, as a hardship draftee, when normally he would have been playing his senior season at Alabama. McKey is a tremendous leaper, runs well, shoots well from short and long range, and is potentially a fine defensive forward.

Polynice, a 6'11" center, did not play enough minutes (1,500) to be listed among the top ten rookies, but his rating of .448 would have been good enough for eighth place. He'll probably see a lot more action this year as a substitute for Alton Lister.

At 30, Lister can still play center in the NBA (TENDEX .540) but gets in foul trouble when he tries to play more than 24 or 25 minutes. He started 55 games in 1987–88 but was listed as a reserve because he played only 1,812 minutes. Was rated No. 10 on the NBA's list of 100 reserves who played between 1,000 and 2,000 minutes.

Danny Young (.438) is a pretty good replacement for Nate McMillan or Dale Ellis.

OUTLOOK

It's difficult to figure out what Seattle had in mind when it traded Hersey Hawkins and a future No. 1 draft choice for Michael Cage.

Assuming Cage is a better player than Hawkins, which is doubtful, all the Sonics did was add one more forward to a team that has plenty of cornermen but not enough centers and guards.

Maybe the Sonics were afraid of losing free agent Tom Chambers. But second-year man Derrick McKey was probably ready to challenge for Chambers's job anyway; and, as an alternative to the Cage trade, the Sonics could have drafted a forward and held on to the 1989 choice. Xavier McDaniel is a fixture at one forward position.

Now Seattle could find itself with three forwards of starting caliber and only backup-level players Alton Lister and Olden Polynice to alternate at center.

And the starting backcourt of Nate McMillan and Dale Ellis is essentially naked, the more so now that Miami has taken Kevin Williams in the expansion draft.

This is a team that always seems to have potential, but always comes up a player or two short.

Probable finish: Fourth in Pacific Division.

23

Utah Jazz

*T*he Jazz surprised everybody except TENDEX by their performance in the 1988 playoffs. Underdogs to Portland, they upset the Trail Blazers in the first round, then came within a few hotly disputed officials' whistles of eliminating the defending champion Los Angeles Lakers in the second round.

In the series against the Lakers, John Stockton established a present superiority over Laker superstar Magic Johnson, center Mark Eaton outplayed Kareem Abdul-Jabbar, Karl Malone dominated James Worthy, and the Jazz in general sent out signals that the Laker's dynasty might be nearing an end.

Even though Utah registered only the ninth best record (47–35) in the NBA last season, TENDEX ratings showed the Jazz to be almost even with the Lakers and Celtics as the most talented teams in the league in terms of player personnel. Boston was rated at 106.4 going into the playoffs, Utah at 105.8, and Los Angeles at 105.1.

Coach Frank Layden could perhaps be faulted for the fact that the Jazz didn't win more games during the 1987–88 regular season, but it seemed as if they gathered momentum late in the season when they really began to believe that the underrated Stockton was the best point guard in the league.

The Jazz rated among the top half of the NBA teams in 11 of 13 statistical categories, with highs of No. 1 in field goal percentage, No. 4 in BEST and Shootist, and No. 6 in rebounds and PAR.

They held their opponents to a league-low field goal percentage of .449, 16 points less than the percentage against the next best defensive team against the two-point shot. The top ratings in blocked shots and field goal defense again verified that shot-blocking intimidates opponents' shooting.

Worst categories for the Jazz were turnovers (No. 20) and free throw percentage (No. 18).

JOHN STOCKTON

AGE: 26
HEIGHT: 6-1
WEIGHT: 175
POSITION: Point Guard
EXPERIENCE: 4 Seasons
COLLEGE: Gonzaga
BIRTHPLACE: Spokane, WA
1987–88 TENDEX: .749

Stockton didn't exactly appear overnight, as if conjured by a sorcerer just to plague the Lakers. What happened was that, after three seasons of being used as a part-time player, he finally was given a chance to play full-time in 1987–88 and made the most of it, beating out Magic Johnson as the highest-rated point guard (.749 to .721 in regular season and .743 to .599 in seven head-to-head playoff games) . . . in playoffs Stockton's dominance of Johnson was evidenced by a 4-to-1 margin in steals (4.0 to 1.0 per game), by an edge of 6.1 assists (16.4 to 10.3 per game), and by playing 6.0 more minutes per game (44.6 to 38.6) . . . Stockton set a single-season NBA assists record with 1,128 and nearly became the first player ever to average two assists for every five minutes of court time; his percentage of .397 assists per minute also was a league record . . . was the only NBA player to score 20 points and hand out 20 assists in a game last season and then did it twice more in the playoffs against Johnson . . . tied a playoff record with 24 assists in a game . . . also had great stats in other facets of play in regular season, leading the NBA in steals per minute and having one of the best shooting seasons ever by a backcourtman . . . No. 2 Shootist in the league with 1.080 points per shot, No. 3 in two-point field goal percent-

age, and No. 16 in PAR percentage . . . ranked in the bottom ten in turnovers but made up for it with a No. 8 rating in ratio of steals to turnovers . . . among point guards was dominant with No. 1 ratings in six important categories: Shootist, Shootist percentage, field goal percentage, assists, steals, and TENDEX.

KARL MALONE

AGE: 25
HEIGHT: 6-9
WEIGHT: 250
POSITION: Power Forward
EXPERIENCE: 3 Seasons
COLLEGE: Louisiana State
BIRTHPLACE: Summerfield, LA
1987–88 TENDEX: .693

The Mail Man made frequent deliveries last season but missed joining the TENDEX 700 Club because of Utah's efficient game pace. Malone got more votes than he deserved in being named to the NBA All-Defensive second team, but less than he deserved in balloting for the All-NBA team . . . ranked No. 3 in the league in minutes played, No. 4 in PAR percentage, No. 4 in total points, No. 2 in total rebounds, and No. 10 in TENDEX . . . doubtfulness of defensive reputation was pinpointed by bottom ten ratings in BEST and ratios of blocked shots and steals to turnovers . . . among power forwards was prominent in most major categories, weak in some of the minor ones . . . high ratings were No. 1 in minutes, No. 2 in scoring and PAR percentage, No. 3 in steals and TENDEX, and No. 6 in rebounds and two-point field goal percentage . . . low ratings were No. 20 in turnovers and ratios of steals and blocked shots to turnovers, No. 19 in BEST, and No. 18 in free throw percentage.

STOCKTON

1987–88	2PFG	3PFG	F.T.	REB.	AST.	STL.	T.O.	BLK.	PTS.
Per Game	.594	.358	.840	2.9	13.8	3.0	3.2	0.2	14.7
Per Minute	.594	.358	.840	.083	.397	.085	.092	.006	.424
Rating	1	4	8	14	1	1	18	8	7

MALONE

1987–88	2PFG	3PFG	F.T.	REB.	AST.	STL.	T.O.	BLK.	PTS.
Per Game	.522	.000	.700	12.0	2.4	1.4	4.0	0.6	27.7
Per Minute	.522	.000	.700	.308	.062	.037	.102	.016	.709
Rating	6	18	18	6	9	3	20	15	2

THURL BAILEY

AGE: 27
HEIGHT: 6-11
WEIGHT: 222
POSITION: Small Forward
EXPERIENCE: 5 Seasons
COLLEGE: North Carolina State
BIRTHPLACE: Washington, DC
1987–88 TENDEX: .542

Bailey was eligible for the NBA's Sixth Man award last season because he started only ten games, but he actually played the most minutes of any non-starter in the league and more than most of the regulars (2,804) . . . last season was Bailey's best with personal highs in minutes, rebounds, blocked shots, and scoring average (19.6) . . . ranked No. 12 in the league in blocked shots . . . was in the bottom ten in steals . . . top ratings among small forwards were No. 3 in blocked shots, No. 5 in ratio of blocks to turnovers, No. 6 in minutes, No. 7 in Shootist percentage, No. 8 in free throw percentage, and No. 8 in BEST . . . poor ratings were No. 20 in steals, No. 19 in assists, and No. 20 in ratio of steals to turnovers . . . finished in middle of 22 small forwards with No. 11 TENDEX rating.

MARK EATON

AGE: 31
HEIGHT: 7-4
WEIGHT: 290
POSITION: Center
EXPERIENCE: 6 Seasons
COLLEGE: UCLA
BIRTHPLACE: Westminster, CA
1987–88 TENDEX: .419

Eaton is the most lopsided player in the NBA, ranking either among the leaders or among the losers in nearly every phase of play. In 1987–88, he led the league in blocked shots, ratio of blocks to turnovers, and BEST . . . ranked No. 11 in turnovers (although that could be misleading because he rarely had the ball on offense) and No. 19 in rebounds . . . conversely, finished last in the NBA in points, PAR percentage, and both Shootist statistics . . . in bottom ten in steals, assists, two-point field goal percentage, PAR, and TENDEX . . . but showed in the playoffs that poor TENDEX rating didn't prove much because, as long as he stuck to his shot-blocking role, he was an intimidating force . . . named to NBA All-Defensive second team, but probably should have been on first team . . . statistics among centers also were unbalanced with No. 1 ratings in three shot-blocking related categories, and No. 21 or No. 22 in nine other categories.

BAILEY

1987–88	2PFG	3PFG	F.T.	REB.	AST.	STL.	T.O.	BLK.	PTS.
Per Game	.493	.333	.826	6.5	1.9	0.6	2.3	1.5	19.6
Per Minute	.493	.333	.826	.189	.056	.017	.068	.045	.572
Rating	14	5	8	10	19	20	14	3	10

EATON

1987–88	2PFG	3PFG	F.T.	REB.	AST.	STL.	T.O.	BLK.	PTS.
Per Game	.418	.000	.623	8.7	0.7	0.5	1.6	3.7	7.0
Per Minute	.418	.000	.623	.263	.020	.015	.048	.111	.209
Rating	22	9	21	9	21	18	4	1	21

RESERVES

This is Utah's weak department. The Jazz have the top quartet of players in the NBA, but after that there isn't much left. There are some players who used to be standouts, but who are average or considerably below average now.

Aging Jazz reserves include guard Darrell Griffith (.400), center Melvin Turpin (.526), and forward Marc Iavaroni (.378).

Bob Hansen (.427) took over as the starting shooting guard last season, replacing Griffith, but he too is replaceable if the Jazz can find somebody better.

OUTLOOK

Utah stands between the Lakers and a third straight NBA championship.

With the addition of three players from the 1988 college draft who could turn the Jazz bench from one of the thinnest in the NBA to a very good one, this team won't have to use John Stockton and Karl Malone for 45 minutes per game should they face the Lakers again in the Western Conference playoffs in 1989.

Tired as they were, Stockton and Malone dominated the Lakers' Magic Johnson and James Worthy in the 1988 playoff series, and they have the physical ability and mental toughness to beat the Lakers in 1989.

Rookie center Eric Leckner will be able to spell Mark Eaton and make it less of a disaster for the Jazz if Eaton should foul out, as he did in two 1988 playoff games against the Lakers.

Second-round draft choice Jeff Moe could back up another former Iowa University player, Bob Hansen, at shooting guard.

Third-round draftee Ricky Grace could make the team as a substitute for Stockton.

Utah's major weakness is corner depth. Malone and Thurl Bailey may have to be iron men again in 1988–89, as they were in 1987–88. But Coach Frank Layden could use Leckner to substitute for both Eaton and Malone.

Probable finish: First in Midwest Division.

24

Washington Bullets

*I*t's hard to tell whether the Bullets are coming or going, but chances are they're going.

They have aging players (Frank Johnson, Bernard King), players in the prime of their careers (Jeff Malone, Terry Catledge), and young players who could begin to make a serious impact this season (John Williams, Harvey Grant).

The Bullets finished in a tie with New York and Indiana for the final two playoff berths and made the playoffs along with the Knicks because of tie-breaking statistics. They put up a struggle, pushing the Detroit Pistons to a fifth game, before bowing out in the first round, three games to two.

Statistically, the Bullets just about matched their opponents last season in every category except assists and field goal percentage. They were on the losing side of these two categories, which is why they were also on the losing side of the standings.

Offensively, Washington did not excel last season, with a top rating of No. 9 in free throw percentage. They ranked last in the league in three-point field goal percentage, Shootist, and assists. In scoring they were No. 19.

Defensively, they were better: No. 6 in blocked shots and No. 9 in BEST.

Their overall TENDEX rating was No. 16, which was precisely where they finished in the standings, although they definitely perked up when Wes Unseld took over the head coaching job. They were 30–25 (.545) under Unseld after being 8–19 (.296) under Kevin Loughery.

JEFF MALONE

AGE: 27
HEIGHT: 6-4
WEIGHT: 205
POSITION: Shooting Guard
EXPERIENCE: 5 Seasons
COLLEGE: Mississippi State
BIRTHPLACE: Mobile, AL
1987–88 TENDEX: .470

Jeff Malone fits in the classification of "pure shooter," meaning in loose translation that points are about the only things you can expect from him. He averaged 25.6 points per game in Bullets' playoff series against Detroit, better than league MVP Michael Jordan was able to do playing the same position against the same team in the next playoff round . . . during regular season ranked No. 7 in the NBA in free throw percentage and No. 14 in points per minute played . . . was in the bottom ten in rebounds . . . in competition with other shooting guards he had ratings of No. 4 in scoring, No. 4 in free throw percentage, No. 7 in Shootist percentage, and No. 9 in turnovers . . . was on the down side at No. 18 in steals, No. 16 in BEST, No. 16 in assists, No. 15 in rebounds, No. 14 in two-point field goal percentage, No. 14 in blocked shots, and No. 14 in PAR . . . TENDEX rating was No. 11 out of 18 regular shooting guards.

JOHN WILLIAMS

AGE: 22
HEIGHT: 6-9
WEIGHT: 235
POSITION: Forward
EXPERIENCE: 2 Seasons
COLLEGE: Louisiana State
BIRTHPLACE: Los Angeles
1987–88 TENDEX: .497

Williams began his NBA career before reaching his 20th birthday and now, at 22, is striving for star status. A small forward in skills, with a power forward's body, he played so well in replacement of the injured Bernard King last season that King was unable to regain his starting job after returning from the injury . . . had ratings of No. 19 in the NBA in steals (very high for a frontcourtman) and No. 13 in ratio of steals to turnovers . . . listed among the power forwards (although he could have been listed among small forwards), his ratings were No. 1 in steals, No. 1 in ratio of steals to turnovers, No. 2 in assists, No. 6 in PAR, No. 8 in BEST, No. 8 in turnovers, and No. 10 in points . . . needs to improve shooting accuracy as shown by ratings of No. 14 in free throw percentage, No. 16 in two-point field goal percentage, and No. 15 and No. 18 in the two Shootist statistics.

MALONE

1987–88	2PFG	3PFG	F.T.	REB.	AST.	STL.	T.O.	BLK.	PTS.
Per Game	.478	.417	.882	2.6	3.0	0.6	2.2	0.2	20.5
Per Minute	.478	.417	.882	.078	.089	.019	.065	.005	.618
Rating	14	2	4	15	16	18	9	14	4

WILLIAMS

1987–88	2PFG	3PFG	F.T.	REB.	AST.	STL.	T.O.	BLK.	PTS.
Per Game	.484	.132	.734	5.4	2.8	1.4	1.8	0.4	12.8
Per Minute	.484	.132	.734	.183	.096	.048	.060	.014	.431
Rating	16	9	14	19	2	1	8	18	10

BERNARD KING

AGE: 31
HEIGHT: 6-7
WEIGHT: 205
POSITION: Small Forward
EXPERIENCE: 10 Seasons
COLLEGE: Tennessee
BIRTHPLACE: Brooklyn, NY
1987–88 TENDEX: .482

King did amazingly well to come back at all from an extremely serious knee injury that sidelined him for two years . . . although he wasn't close to the 700 Club player he had been before the injury, he was still a threat to score any time he got his hands on the basketball . . . despite missing 287 games—nearly one-third of the total he could have played since entering the league in 1977—King has scored 14,104 points and could attain the 15,000 plateau this season . . . career scoring average is 22.9 . . . led NBA in scoring once, named to All-NBA first team twice . . . Comeback Player of the Year winner in 1981 . . . ranked last in the league in 1987–88 in BEST and ratio of blocked shots to turnovers and was in the bottom ten in turnovers . . . among small forwards had ratings of No. 7 in assists, No. 8 in Shootist percentage, No. 9 in two-point field goal percentage, No. 9 in points, No. 10 in PAR, and No. 10 Shootist; however, he was last in all four categories related to turnovers: No. 20 in blocked shots, No. 18 in rebounds, No. 18 in free throw percentage, and No. 17 in TENDEX.

RESERVES

Washington has an interesting set of substitutes, beginning with point guard Frank Johnson.

Johnson is a competent point guard, but in four seasons from 1984–85 through 1987–88 he played in only 153 games out of a possible 328. He did manage to get into 75 games in 1987–88, but that was perhaps because he was used so sparingly that he played only 1,258 minutes. His TENDEX rating was .430.

Steve Colter (.438) probably will share point-guard duties in 1988–89 with Johnson, now that Tyrone Bogues has been lost in the expansion draft.

Forwards Terry Catledge and Charles Jones started 89 games between them in 1987–88 and could compete for regular jobs in 1988–89 with Bernard King, John Williams, and rookie Harvey Grant. Catledge's rating was .494 and Jones's was .439.

KING

1987–88	2PFG	3PFG	F.T.	REB.	AST.	STL.	T.O.	BLK.	PTS.
Per Game	.503	.167	.762	4.1	2.8	0.7	3.1	0.1	17.2
Per Minute	.503	.167	.762	.137	.094	.024	.103	.005	.581
Rating	9	15	18	18	7	17	22	20	9

OUTLOOK

After giving up on last year's No. 1 choice, Tyrone Bogues, and losing him in the expansion draft, you'd think the Bullets would select a point guard in the 1988 college draft.

Rod Strickland and Gary Grant were available when they drafted, but instead they chose Harvey Grant of Oklahoma.

Nothing against Harvey Grant, but he's a small forward and the Bullets had a surplus at that position before the draft, even without adding one more.

Bernard King, John Williams, and Terry Catledge all are essentially small forwards, although one of them—Williams perhaps—could be asked to play the power forward position this season. But even if Williams is able to play power forward, the Bullets will still have too many small forwards.

And not enough centers or guards.

Having traded Manute Bol to Golden State and having lost free agent center Moses Malone to the Atlanta Hawks, there is no hope this year for the Washington Bullets.

Probable finish: Fifth in Atlantic Division.

25

Expansion Teams

On an appropriately hot day in the summer of 1988, the Miami Heat walked into NBA headquarters in broad daylight and held up the league's best teams without even flaunting a dangerous weapon.

Armed with nothing more than the right to select the existing teams' ninth best players (or in some cases, involving free agency, only the 10th or 11th best), the Heat somehow wrenched valuable choices in the college draft away from the Los Angeles Lakers, Boston Celtics, Seattle Supersonics, Cleveland Cavaliers, Dallas Mavericks, and Milwaukee Bucks.

The other new team, Charlotte, treated the expansion draft with more deference, picking warmed-over morsels out of the proffered pottage.

But then, five days later, in the college draft, the Hornets made almost as much out of their few choices as the suddenly cooled-down Heat did with their many.

Overall, it appears as if management of the two expansion teams made about as many mistakes in stocking their rosters as their new players will make on the court this season. Their ultimate wisdom won't be known for at least five years, however.

The Heat surrendered their rights to take the best of the players in the expansion draft in exchange for Dallas' first-round choice in the college draft. The Mavericks yielded this choice to order to protect Steve Alford, Uwe Blab, and Bill Wennington. This appeared to be a bad move for Dallas in protecting Blab (TENDEX rating .339) and Alford (.345), although Wennington (.631 in brief playing time) certainly was worth protecting.

With that choice from Dallas (No. 20 in the college draft), the Heat picked shooting guard Kevin Edwards of DePaul. Edwards probably does not have as much potential as Dell Curry, another shooting guard who was taken by the Hornets with their No. 1 choice in the expansion draft.

Both Edwards and Curry are good athletes, but Curry has better shooting range. Curry's TENDEX rating in 1987–88 was .473 for Cleveland, 23 percentage points above the average for the shooting guard position. He was the only above-average player available in the expansion draft. His rating was actually three points better than that of Washington's Jeff Malone, a 20-point scorer. Curry is similar to Malone and could become a 20-point man for the Hornets if he plays regularly.

Score one for the Hornets.

With its second choice in the expansion draft, Miami put the heat on the Los Angeles Lakers. The Heat had no interest in paying

41-year-old Kareem Abdul-Jabbar $2 million to play one more mediocre season; but the Lakers, who had not protected Abdul-Jabbar, were somehow talked out of a second-round draft choice (in either 1991 or 1992) in addition to losing Billy Thompson, who almost certainly would have been the Heat's choice even if the Lakers hadn't sweetened the pot.

Thompson missed all of the 1987–88 season because of a knee injury, but showed potential at small forward with a .488 TENDEX rating in 1986–87 after helping Louisville win an NCAA title the season before.

The Hornets used their second expansion pick for Dave Hoppen, a center with a history of injuries who played only about 600 minutes last season for Golden State with a .459 TENDEX rating.

Score one for the Heat.

Next, the Heat held up the Celtics the same way they had the Mavericks and Lakers. By declining to choose aging Dennis Johnson, whom the Celtics had left unprotected, they landed Fred Roberts and a second-round draft choice. They then traded Roberts to Milwaukee for yet another second-round pick. With one of those two picks they took Sylvester Gray, an excellent athlete who went into the hardship draft after being declared ineligible at Memphis State University. Gray had dealings with an agent following his freshman season.

Gray is an aggressive power forward, similar in style to backboard-breaker Jerome Lane of Pittsburgh.

No. 3 pick for the Hornets in the expansion draft was 5'3" point guard Tyrone Bogues, the NBA's No. 9 rated rookie (.431) in 1987–88. If Bogues improves as much as Curry did from his first season to his second (78 points), this will turn out to be an excellent choice and Bogues could become a popular player in Charlotte.

Score this round even.

The average age of Edwards, Curry, Thompson, Hoppen, Bogues, and Gray is 23, so it is evident that both the Heat and Hornets were looking for youth.

There was a big drop off in available talent after the third round of the expansion draft, although each team did land a name player. The Hornets got Kelly Tripucka by trading their fourth pick, Mike Brown, to Utah. Tripucka, 29, faltered during the 1986–87 and 1987–88 seasons. A .600 TENDEX player early in his career, Tripucka's rating was down to .527 in 1985–86 and fell even further to .454 in 1986–87 and to an abysmal .338 in 1987–88. He'll be a pre-season conversation piece in Charlotte, but don't expect him to help the Hornets much. He is at the stage of his career where he may still be able to score 15 points per game for an expansion team, but he won't do much else.

The Heat's name player is Pearl Washington, who was heralded as the savior of the New Jersey franchise when the Nets drafted him No. 1 (No. 13 overall) out of Syracuse in 1986. But Washington turned out to be a step slow for an NBA point guard. He registered two mediocre seasons in a row for New Jersey (TENDEX .411 and .417) before the Nets gave up on him.

Seattle inexplicably gave Miami a second-round draft choice to protect Danny Young. This was strange because the Heat chose Kevin Williams off Seattle's unprotected list. Williams (TENDEX .421) and Young (.438) are almost identical in age and ability and played about the same number of minutes in 1987–88.

The Heat also got a 1990 or 1992 second-rounder from Cleveland in exchange for Darnell Valentine, whom they drafted from the Los Angeles Clippers.

So the Heat wound up with four extra draft choices in the 1988 college draft and two more for the future.

Trouble is, Miami did not show much wisdom in the 1988 college draft. Except for Gray, the Heat's draft was undistinguished, and the Hornets' wasn't much better.

Both teams could have done better than they did for their No. 1 choices. The Hornets took Rex Chapman as the No. 8 overall player in the draft. Although a great athlete,

Chapman is at about the same level of development as Gray, whom Miami took in the middle of the second round. Chapman plays the same position as Curry, so the Hornets did not fill a need with this choice. After selecting Curry and Bogues in the expansion draft, it had been anticipated that the Hornets would take a big man with their No. 1 choice in the college draft.

The Heat didn't do any better, if as well. Miami took center–forward Rony Seikaly of Syracuse with the No. 9 pick overall. Of the players available in the college draft, counting hardship cases, Seikaly was rated No. 17 with a .605 TENDEX. He has several flaws in his game (notably, free throw shooting and physical strength) that could limit him to being a below-average NBA big man, or average at best.

By picking Seikaly, who was Syracuse's second-best 6'10" player (Derrick Coleman's rating was 40 points better), the Heat gave notice of things to come. Edwards, their other first-rounder, was DePaul's second-best 6'3" guard (behind Rod Strickland).

You don't build winning NBA teams with players who weren't even the standouts of their college teams.

The other players selected by the two expansion teams in the college draft were the type that might be expected to be picked by expansion teams—sluggish wide-bodies. These included small-college space-eaters Grant Long and Orlando Graham (Miami), as well as Auburn's Jeff Moore and Arizona's Tom Tolbert (Charlotte).

Barring additional trades and free-agent signings, probable starting lineups for these two teams going into the 1988–89 season are:

	MIAMI	CHARLOTTE
Center:	Scott Hastings	Dave Hoppen
Forward:	Rony Seikaly	Jeff Moore
Forward:	Bill Thompson	Kelly Tripucka
Guard:	Pearl Washington	Tyrone Bogues
Guard:	Kevin Edwards	Dell Curry

Five years from now, it is unlikely that any of these players will still be starters. Rex Chapman and Sylvester Gray—who are a long way from being ready to play effectively in the NBA—could be the only long-range survivors from the initial season of the Miami Heat and the Charlotte Hornets.

Probable 1988–89 finishes:
CHARLOTTE: Sixth in Atlantic Division.
MIAMI: Sixth in Midwest Division.

SECTION III

CHARTS

Introduction

This book is about statistics, and Section III is its soul and essence. It could be called an appendix, but that would be like referring to the final act of a three-act play as an epilogue.

This section consists of charts illustrating every statistical category mentioned in this book, including all-time individual leaders (Charts 1–31), outstanding members of the college class of 1988 (32), individual ratings for the 1987–88 season (33–51) and team ratings for 1987–88 (52–63).

Listing of Charts

Chart 1
TENDEX NBA 700 CLUB

1. Chamberlain 1961–62 . . . . 1.037
2. Abdul-Jabbar 1971–72 972
3. Elgin Baylor 1960–61 968
4. W. Bellamy 1961–62 929
5. Bob Pettit 1960–61 919
6. O. Robertson 1961–62 892
7. M. Jordan 1987–88 887
8. Boerwinkle 1970–71 865
9. C. Barkley 1987–88 829
10. Larry Bird 1983–84 824
11. Bob Lanier 1973–74 820
12. Mag. Johnson 1986–87 811
13. Mo. Malone 1981–82 810
14. Bob McAdoo 1974–75 806
15. B. Howell 1960–61 804
16. B. Russell 1961–62 801
17. Bill Walton 1976–77 799
18. Jerry Lucas 1964–65 792
19. A. Olajuwon 1986–87 789
20. Willis Reed 1968–69 788
21. J. Erving 1979–80 788
22. A. Gilmore 1977–78 784
23. Ewing 1987–88 760
24. R. Parish 1981–82 758
25. N. Thurmond 1967–68 751
26. Jerry West 1965–66 750
27. Cunningham 1969–70 750
28. Stockton 1987–88 749
29. Rick Barry 1966–67 747
30. M. Stokes 1957–58 747
31. Cliff Hagan 1959–60 746
32. Tree Rollins 1979–80 744
33. K. McHale 1986–87 742
34. N. Johnston 1956–57 742
35. Jack Sikma 1984–85 736
36. B. King 1984–85 .735
37. Dan Issel 1976–77 734
38. S. Haywood 1972–73 734
39. Gus Johnson 1970–71 728
40. Alvan Adams 1978–79 725
41. Dave Cowens 1975–76 724
42. Mar. Johnson 1978–79 721
43. Do. Schayes 1957–58 718
44. R. Sampson 1983–84 717
45. T. Cummings 1984–85 717
46. Walt Davis 1978–79 714
47. Archibald 1972–73 712
48. Jeff Ruland 1983–84 711
49. A. Dantley 1985–86 710
50. Larry Foust 1955–56 709
51. John Kerr 1961–62 708

Chart 1 *(cont.)*

52. Wes Unseld 1969–70 706
53. Tarpley 1987–88 .701
54. Geo. Mikan 1953–54 700
55. Drexler 1987–88 .700

Chart 1A
NEAR MISSES

1. Larry Nance 1985–86 699
2. A. English 1982–83 692
3. G. McGinnis 1976–77 692
4. Bobby Jones 1976–77 683
5. I. Thomas 1984–85 681
6. B. Laimbeer 1983–84 678
7. B. Williams 1982–83 676
8. L. Lever 1986–87 .665
9. Walt Frazier 1971–72 665
10. S. Moncrief 1982–83 665
11. M. Lucas 1981–82 662
12. G. Gervin 1979–80 661
13. J. Havlicek 1969–70 660
14. R. Williams 1979–80 660

Chart 2
ALL-TIME LEADERS

1. Chamberlain 1961–62 . . . . 1.037
2. Chamberlain 1962–63 . . . . 1.025
3. Chamberlain 1963–64 . . . . 1.022
4. Abdul-Jabbar 1971–72 972
5. Chamberlain 1965–66 971
6. Abdul-Jabbar 1970–71 971
7. Elgin Baylor 1960–61 968
8. Chamberlain 1966–67 963
9. Abdul-Jabbar 1972–73 954
10. Abdul-Jabbar 1977–78 936
11. Chamberlain 1960–61 933
12. W. Bellamy 1961–62 929
13. Chamberlain 1959–60 927
14. Abdul-Jabbar 1976–77 921
15. Bob Pettit 1960–61 919
16. Chamberlain 1967–68 901
17. Chamberlain 1964–65 897
18. O. Robertson 1961–62 892
19. M. Jordan 1987–88 887
20. Bob Pettit 1961–62 884
21. Abdul-Jabbar 1975–76 879
22. Abdul-Jabbar 1978–79 870
23. Boerwinkle 1970–71 865
24. Elgin Baylor 1962–63 863
25. O. Robertson 1963–64 860
26. Bob Pettit 1962–63 860

Chart 3
TENDEX SEASON-BY-SEASON LEADERS

1951–52 George Mikan .... .627
1952–53 George Mikan .... .672
1953–54 George Mikan .... .700
1954–55 Neil Johnston .... .714
1955–56 Bob Pettit...................... .778
1956–57 Bob Pettit...................... .773
1957–58 Bob Pettit...................... .813
1958–59 Bob Pettit...................... .837
1959–60 W. Chamberlain .... .927
1960–61 Elgin Baylor .... .968
1961–62 Chamberlain 1.037
1962–63 Chamberlain 1.025
1963–64 Chamberlain 1.022
1964–65 Chamberlain .... .897
1965–66 Chamberlain .... .971
1966–67 Chamberlain .... .963
1967–68 Chamberlain .... .901
1968–69 Jerry Lucas .... .790
1969–70 K. Abdul-Jabbar .... .782
1970–71 K. Abdul-Jabbar .... .971
1971–72 K. Abdul-Jabbar .... .972
1972–73 K. Abdul-Jabbar .... .954
1973–74 Bob Lanier..................... .820
1974–75 K. Abdul-Jabbar .... .836
1975–76 K. Abdul-Jabbar .... .879
1976–77 K. Abdul-Jabbar .... .921
1977–78 K. Abdul-Jabbar .... .936
1978–79 K. Abdul-Jabbar .... .870
1979–80 K. Abdul-Jabbar .... .834
1980–81 K. Abdul-Jabbar .... .823
1981–82 Moses Malone.................. .810
1982–83 Moses Malone.................. .805
1983–84 Larry Bird..................... .824
1984–85 Larry Bird..................... .820
1985–86 Larry Bird..................... .801
1986–87 Charles Barkley .... .828
1987–88 Michael Jordan .... .887

Chart 4
TENDEX LEADERS BASED ON POSITIONAL NORMS

1. M. Jordan 1987–88 .... 1.971
2. Chamberlain 1961–62................ 1.885
3. Robertson 1961–62................. 1.878
4. E. Baylor 1960–61 .... 1.844
5. Abdul-Jabbar 1971–72 .... 1.767
6. B. Pettit 1960–61 .... 1.750

Chart 4 *(cont.)*

7. Mag. Johnson 1986–87.............. 1.707
8. W. Bellamy 1961–62 .... 1.689
9. Jerry West 1965–66................. 1.667
10. L. Bird 1984–85 .... 1.648
11. W. Davis 1978–79 .... 1.587
12. Barkley 1987–88 .... 1.579
13. Stockton 1987–88.................. 1.577
14. J. Erving 1979–80 .... 1.576
15. Boerwinkle 1970–71................ 1.573
16. Drexler 1987–88................... 1.556
17. B. Howell 1960–61................. 1.531
18. I. Thomas 1984–85 .... 1.514
19. J. Lucas 1964–65.................. 1.505
20. Cunningham 1969–70............... 1.500
21. Archibald 1972–73................. 1.499
22. R. Barry 1966–67.................. 1.494
23. C. Hagan 1959–60................. 1.490
24. B. Lanier 1973–74 .... 1.491
25. Ber. King 1984–85 .... 1.486
26. Moncrief 1982–83 .... 1.478
27. M. Malone 1978–79................ 1.473
28. G. Gervin 1979–80................. 1.469
29. T. Cummings 1984–85 .... 1.468
30. Havlicek 1969–70.................. 1.467
31. Ray Williams 1979–80.............. 1.467
32. B. McAdoo 1974–75 .... 1.465
33. Russell 1961–62................... 1.456
34. Sam Jones 1965–66................ 1.456
35. Westphal 1977–78.................. 1.456
36. B. Walton 1976–77 .... 1.453
37. Mar. Johnson 1978–79 .... 1.442
38. Olajuwon 1986–87................. 1.435
39. W. Reed 1968–69.................. 1.433
40. Gilmore 1977–78 .... 1.425
41. M. Stokes 1957–58 .... 1.423
42. Dantley 1985–86 .... 1.420
43. K. McHale 1986–87................ 1.413
44. D. Thompson 1977–78 .... 1.407
45. L. Lever 1986–87.................. 1.400
46. W. Frazier 1971–72 .... 1.400
47. L. Nance 1985–86 .... 1.398
48. S. Haywood 1972–73 .... 1.398
49. Gus Johnson 1970–71.............. 1.387
50. English 1982–83................... 1.384
51. Ewing 1987–88.................... 1.382
52. R. Parish 1981–82................. 1.378
53. R. Guerin 1961–62................. 1.373
54. Schayes 1957–58.................. 1.368
55. Bob Jones 1976–77 .... 1.366
56. Thurmond 1967–68 .... 1.365

Chart 5
THE SHOOTISTS: POINTS PER SHOT

1. K. McHale 1986–87 .... 1.104
2. M. Guokas 1972–73.................. 1.096
3. Abdul-Jabbar 1979–80 .... 1.094
4. D. Ainge 1987–88................... 1.093
5. A. Gilmore 1981–82................. 1.092
6. Mo Cheeks 1984–85 .... 1.090
7. Donaldson 1984–85.................. 1.088
8. Stockton 1987–88................... 1.080
9. B. Davis 1982–83................... 1.079
10. J. Worthy 1984–85 .... 1.076
11. Bird 1987–88....................... 1.071
12. L. Nance 1984–85 .... 1.071
13. Parish 1987–88..................... 1.071
14. S. Nater 1978–79 .... 1.068
15. D. Dawkins 1980–81 .... 1.064
16. C. Natt 1983–84.................... 1.062
17. Dantley 1979–80 .... 1.061
18. Vandeweghe 1984–85............... 1.058
19. W. Davis 1978–79 .... 1.055
20. Ber. King 1980–81 .... 1.054
21. B. Scott 1987–88................... 1.053
22. B. Jones 1977–78 .... 1.048
23. K. Macy 1981–82................... 1.044
24. B. Taylor 1980–81 .... 1.044
25. Price 1987–88...................... 1.043
26. English 1981–82.................... 1.043
27. Barkley 1986–87 .... 1.042
28. McGlocklin 1970–71 .... 1.042
29. Sichting 1983–84 .... 1.041
30. Chamberlain 1972–73 .... 1.041
31. N. Nixon 1978-79 .... 1.038
32. G. Banks 1984–85.................. 1.037
33. Mag. Johnson 1983–84.............. 1.035
34. Maxwell 1979–80 .... 1.035
35. J. Wilkes 1979–80 .... 1.033
36. McMillian 1975–76.................. 1.031
37. Whitehead 1981–82................. 1.030
38. M. Turpin 1985–86.................. 1.029
39. Wittman 1985–86................... 1.027
40. R. Pierce 1985–86 .... 1.025
41. L. Lloyd 1985–86 .... 1.023
42. Mar. Johnson 1978–79 .... 1.023
43. Blackman 1983–84 .... 1.021
44. G. Gervin 1979–80.................. 1.021
45. Westphal 1978–79.................. 1.021
46. B. Lanier 1983–84 .... 1.020
47. M. Cooper 1982–83................. 1.019
48. Tomjanovich 1973–74 .... 1.019
49. Boswell 1979–80 .... 1.019
50. Jerry Lucas 1968–69................ 1.017

Chart 5 (cont.)

51. Rollins 1981–82 .... 1.017
52. B. McAdoo 1973–74 .... 1.016
53. D. Ellis 1986–87 .... 1.016
54. T. Owens 1978–79................... 1.015
55. G. Henderson 1983–84 .... 1.015
56. B. Knight 1979–80 .... 1.015
57. Mullin 1987–88 .... 1.014
58. Robinzine 1978-79 .... 1.014
59. S. Wedman 1978–79 .... 1.013
60. Woolridge 1984–85 .... 1.012
61. D. Snyder 1971–72 .... 1.012
62. Levingston 1987–88 .... 1.011
63. G. Gross 1976–77 .... 1.010
64. W. Unseld 1978–79 .... 1.010
65. M. Adams 1987–88 .... 1.010
66. Jim Paxson 1980–81 .... 1.010
67. Laimbeer 1983–84 .... 1.009
68. L. Hudson 1969–70 .... 1.008
69. Porter 1987–88...................... 1.007
70. Higgins 1987–88.................... 1.007
71. Cartwright 1980–81.................. 1.006
72. C. Murphy 1973–74 .... 1.006
73. A. Adams 1978–79 .... 1.005
74. D. Nelson 1974–75.................. 1.005
75. J. Erving 1981–82 .... 1.004
76. D. Harper 1985–86 .... 1.004
77. Jordan 1987–88 .... 1.003
78. Poquette 1980–81 .... 1.001

Chart 6
PERCENTAGE ALL SHOTS

1. A. Gilmore 1981–82.................. .698
2. C. Maxwell 1979–80 .... .685
3. A. Dantley 1983–84.................. .677
4. J. Donaldson 1984–85............... .677
5. K. McHale 1986–87 .... .670
6. Bobby Jones 1977–78................ .669
7. Schayes 1987–88.................... .665
8. R. Pierce 1986–87 .... .657
9. Mag. Johnson 1984–85............... .657
10. Barkley 1987–88 .... .657
11. Cartwright 1983–84.................. .654
12. Stockton 1987–88 .... .651
13. Gene Banks 1984–85 .... .651
14. Abdul-Jabbar 1979–80 .... .645
15. Calvin Natt 1983–84 .... .645
16. Brad Davis 1982–83 .... .643
17. D. Dawkins 1983–84................. .643
18. Swen Nater 1979–80................ .642
19. Vandeweghe 1985–86............... .642

Chart 6 *(cont.)*

20. Jeff Ruland 1983–84	.637
21. Mo Cheeks 1984–85	.635
22. Olberding 1984–85	.634
23. Dan Issel 1977–78	.634
24. S. Moncrief 1980–81	.633
25. Chamberlain 1972–73	.632
26. Ber. King 1983–84	.631

Chart 7
TWO-POINT FIELD GOAL PERCENTAGE

1. Chamberlain 1972–73	.727
2. A. Gilmore 1978–79	.670
3. C. Barkley 1986–87	.643
4. J. Donaldson 1984–85	.637
5. S. Johnson 1985–86	.632
6. C. Maxwell 1978–79	.609
7. D. Dawkins 1977–78	.607
8. Kevin McHale 1986–87	.606
9. Abdul-Jabbar 1976–77	.604
10. Mike McGee 1983–84	.604
11. Otis Thorpe 1984–85	.602
12. Brad Davis 1982–83	.595
13. J. Stockton 1987–88	.594
14. Calvin Natt 1983–84	.593
15. Buck Williams 1982–83	.590
16. R. Parish 1987–88	.590
17. Bern. King 1980–81	.589
18. John Green 1970–71	.587
19. Larry Nance 1984–85	.587
20. Woolridge 1982–83	.583
21. Mo Cheeks 1984–85	.582
22. Jeff Ruland 1983–84	.582
23. J. Worthy 1982–83	.581
24. Bobby Jones 1977–78	.578
25. Wes Unseld 1978–79	.577
26. A. Dantley 1979–80	.577
27. Bob Lanier 1983–84	.575
28. M. Kupchak 1976–77	.572

Chart 8
THREE-POINT FIELD GOAL PERCENTAGE

1. Craig Hodges 1987–88	.491
2. Mark Price 1987–88	.486
3. Dan Ainge 1986–87	.443
4. Byron Scott 1986–87	.436
5. Larry Bird 1984–85	.427
6. Chris Ford 1979–80	.427
7. Henderson 1987–88	.423
8. Trent Tucker 1986–87	.422

Chart 8 *(cont.)*

9. W. B. Free 1985–86	.420
10. K. McKenna 1986–87	.419
11. Dale Ellis 1987–88	.413
12. B. Winters 1981–82	.411
13. Brad Davis 1984–85	.409
14. Leon Wood 1987–88	.409
15. Kyle Macy 1985–86	.390
16. M. Cooper 1985–86	.387
17. Don Buse 1981–82	.386
18. E. Floyd 1986–87	.384
19. B. Taylor 1980–81	.380
20. John Roche 1979–80	.380
21. Mike McGee 1986–87	.376
22. T. Chambers 1986–87	.372
23. John Paxson 1986–87	.371
24. A. Toney 1984–85	.371
25. M. Adams 1987–88	.367
26. John Lucas 1986–87	.365
27. Mike Evans 1984–85	.363
28. D. Bradley 1987–88	.363
29. D. Griffith 1983–84	.361
30. D. Harper 1986–87	.358

Chart 9
FREE THROW PERCENTAGE

1. C. Murphy 1980–81	.958
2. R. Sobers 1980–81	.935
3. B. Sharman 1958–59	.932
4. Rick Barry 1977–78	.924
5. Jack Sikma 1987–88	.922
6. Larry Bird 1987–88	.916
7. M. Gminski 1987–88	.906
8. Bob Wanzer 1951–52	.904
9. D. Schayes 1956–57	.904
10. Adrian Smith 1966–67	.903
11. F. Robinson 1969–70	.898
12. Fred Brown 1977–78	.898
13. Vandeweghe 1984–85	.896
14. J. Dawkins 1987–88	.896
15. C. Mullin 1985–86	.896
16. Jack Marin 1971–72	.894
17. B. Laimbeer 1986–87	.894
18. Caz. Russell 1975–76	.892
19. B. Scott 1986–87	.892
20. John Long 1986–87	.890
21. Jim Paxson 1985–86	.889
22. Mike Newlin 1980–81	.888
23. J. Silas 1979–80	.887
24. W. Davis 1987–88	.887
25. Spanarkel 1980–81	.887

Chart 9 *(cont.)*

26. K. Tripucka 1984–85 885
27. Jeff Malone 1986–87 885
28. Jim Walker 1972–73 884
29. R. Blackman 1986–87 884
30. Bridgeman 1980–81 884
31. Alvan Adams 1984–85 883
32. Al Cervi 1951–52 .883

Chart 10
NBA ALL-TIME PAR-FIVE PLAYERS

1. O. Robertson 1961–62 . . . . PAR-11
2. Mag. Johnson 1981–82 . . . . PAR-9
3. Chamberlain 1967–68 . . . . PAR-8
4. L. Lever 1986–87 . . . . PAR-8
5. Larry Bird 1986–87 . . . . PAR-7
6. Havlicek 1970–71 . . . . PAR-7
7. Van Lier 1970–71 . . . . PAR-7
8. Richardson 1981–82 . . . . PAR-6
9. Bob Cousy 1955–56 . . . . PAR-6
10. Frazier 1970–71 . . . . PAR-6
11. A. Phillip 1951–52 . . . . PAR-6
12. G. Rodgers 1960–61 . . . . PAR-6
13. R. Guerin 1961–62 . . . . PAR-6
14. M. Stokes 1957–58 . . . . PAR-6
15. Drexler 1986–87 . . . . PAR-6
16. L. Wilkens 1968–69 . . . . PAR-6
17. J. West 1965–66 . . . . PAR-6
18. R. Barry 1973–74 . . . . PAR-6
19. Cunningham 1971–72 . . . . PAR-5
20. M. Jordan 1984–85 . . . . PAR-5
21. Sam Lacey 1979–80 . . . . PAR-5
22. A. Adams 1975–76 . . . . PAR-5
23. J. Mullins 1971–72 . . . . PAR-5
24. Tom Gola 1957–58 . . . . PAR-5
25. S. Wicks 1972–73 . . . . PAR-5
26. Costello 1959–60 . . . . PAR-5
27. A. Robertson 1985–86 . . . . PAR-5
28. Wilkerson 1977–78 . . . . PAR-5
29. Goodrich 1968–69 . . . . PAR-5
30. Abdul-Jabbar 1978–79 . . . . PAR-5
31. R. Smith 1976–77 . . . . PAR-5
32. E. Baylor 1968–69 . . . . PAR-5
33. Pressey 1984–85 . . . . PAR-5
34. R. McCray 1986–87 . . . . PAR-5
35. Maravich 1974–75 . . . . PAR-5
36. English 1981–82 . . . . PAR-5
37. J. White 1971–72 . . . . PAR-5
38. Russell 1964–65 . . . . PAR-5
39. H. Gilliam 1972–73 . . . . PAR-5
40. J. Johnson 1979–80 . . . . PAR-5

Chart 10 *(cont.)*

41. McGuire 1950–51 . . . . PAR-5
42. W. Unseld 1975–76 . . . . PAR-5
43. C. Hawkins 1973–74 . . . . PAR-5
44. Moncrief 1984–85 . . . . PAR-5
45. Kauffman 1972–73 . . . . PAR-5
46. Hal Greer 1968–69 . . . . PAR-5
47. Dave Bing 1968–69 . . . . PAR-5
48. C. Hagan 1960–61 . . . . PAR-5
49. R. Williams 1979–80 . . . . PAR-5

Chart 11
GROSS PAR TOTALS

1. Chamberlain 1961–62 . . . . 78.5
2. E. Baylor 1961–62 . . . . 61.5
3. Abdul-Jabbar 1971–72 . . . . 56.0
4. O. Robertson 1961–62 . . . . 54.7
5. Bob Pettit 1961–62 . . . . 53.5
6. W. Bellamy 1961–62 . . . . 53.3
7. B. McAdoo 1974–75 . . . . 50.8
8. Rick Barry 1966–67 . . . . 48.4
9. Archibald 1972–73 . . . . 48.2
10. M. Malone 1981–82 . . . . 47.6
11. B. Russell 1961–62 . . . . 47.0
12. M. Jordan 1986–87 . . . . 46.9
13. Larry Bird 1984–85 . . . . 45.8
14. G. Mikan 1950–51 . . . . 45.6
15. Havlicek 1970–71 . . . . 45.4
16. Jerry Lucas 1965–66 . . . . 45.3
17. Thurmond 1968–69 . . . . 44.8
18. Jerry West 1965–66 . . . . 44.5
19. Cunningham 1969–70 . . . . 44.0
20. Barkley 1987–88 . . . . 43.4
21. R. Guerin 1961–62 . . . . 42.8
22. Ber. King 1984–85 . . . . 42.4
23. Mag. Johnson 1986–87 . . . . 42.4
24. D. Schayes 1957–58 . . . . 42.2
25. Maravich 1976–77 . . . . 41.6

Chart 12
POINTS PER MINUTE

1. Chamberlain 1961–62 . . . . 1.038
2. M. Jordan 1986–87 927
3. G. Gervin 1981–82 906
4. Bernard King 1984–85 877
5. Rick Barry 1966–67 874
6. Elgin Baylor 1961–62 862
7. K. Tripucka 1981–82 853
8. Vandeweghe 1983–84 839
9. A. Dantley 1985–86 826

Chart 12 *(cont.)*

10. D. Wilkins 1987–88 .... .813
11. P. Westphal 1977–78................. .812
12. M. Aguirre 1983–84.................. .803
13. Bob McAdoo 1974–75................ .800
14. A. English 1985–86 .... .798
15. W. B. Free 1979–80................. .795
16. Abdul-Jabbar 1970–71 .... .790
17. J. Twyman 1959–60 .... .773
18. Jerry West 1965–66................. .769
19. Larry Bird 1987–88 .... .767
20. D. Thompson 1980–81 .... .751
21. Dan Issel 1981–82.................. .749
22. J. Erving 1979–80 .... .747
23. P. Maravich 1976–77................ .747
24. John Drew 1978–79................. .745
25. M. Malone 1981–82................. .742
26. Bob Pettit 1961–62 .... .740
27. M. Aguirre 1987–88................. .740

Chart 13
ASSISTS PER MINUTE

1. J. Stockton 1987–88................. .397
2. Isiah Thomas 1984–85 .... .364
3. Kevin Porter 1978–79 .... .359
4. Mag. Johnson 1985–86.............. .352
5. Johnny Moore 1981–82 .... .332
6. Glenn Rivers 1986–87............... .318
7. E. Whatley 1983–84 .... .307
8. Norm Nixon 1983–84................ .299
9. John Bagley 1985–86 .... .297
10. Guy Rodgers 1966–67.............. .296
11. McMillan 1987–88 .... .286
12. K. Porter 1987–88 .... .278
13. Eric Floyd 1986–87 .... .277
14. Bob Cousy 1959–60 .... .276
15. Richardson 1979–80 .... .272
16. R. Green 1983–84 .... .270
17. Reg. Theus 1985–86 .... .270
18. John Lucas 1985–86............... .269
19. Mark Jackson 1987–88............. .267
20. Mo Cheeks 1981–82 .... .267
21. T. Porter 1986–87 .... .263
22. Ray Williams 1982–83.............. .262
23. O. Robertson 1961–62 .... .257
24. Len Wilkens 1971–72 .... .256
25. Phil Ford 1980–81 .... .254
26. Foots Walker 1979–80 .... .251
27. N. Van Lier 1970–71 .... .250
28. Archibald 1981–82.................. .250

Chart 14
REBOUNDS PER MINUTE

1. B. Russell 1957–58 .... .592
2. Chamberlain 1959–60 .... .581
3. Bob Pettit 1960–61 .... .509
4. N. Thurmond 1967–68............... .505
5. Walter Dukes 1960–61 .... .503
6. Wes Unseld 1968–69............... .502
7. Boerwinkle 1970–71 .... .478
8. Jerry Lucas 1965–66................ .474
9. Gus Johnson 1970–71.............. .474
10. M. Stokes 1955–56 .... .471
11. E. Baylor 1960–61 .... .462
12. W. Bellamy 1961–62 .... .449
13. G. Mikan 1953–54 .... .435
14. M. Malone 1976–77................. .428
15. John Kerr 1961–62 .... .425
16. Clyde Lee 1971–72 .... .423
17. Ken Sears 1959–60................. .417
18. Tarpley 1987–88.................... .416
19. Ray Scott 1961–62 .... .414
20. Hap Hairston 1974–75 .... .414
21. Bill Walton 1976–77................. .413
22. W. Naulls 1959–60 .... .409
23. Abdul-Jabbar 1975–76 .... .409
24. H. Gallatin 1953–54................. .408
25. Elvin Hayes 1973–74................ .406

Chart 15
THE ALL-TIME BEST

1. Manute Bol 1985–86 .... +360
2. W. Rollins 1982–83 .... +297
3. Mark Eaton 1984–85................. +286
4. Mark Eaton 1983–84................. +278
5. Mark Eaton 1985–86................. +245
6. Mark Eaton 1986–87................. +222
7. Mark Eaton 1987–88................. +214
8. W. Rollins 1983–84 .... +211
9. W. Rollins 1979–80 .... +199
10. W. Rollins 1981–82 .... +180
11. Olajuwon 1985–86 .... +170
12. Olajuwon 1986–87 .... +166
13. T. Tyler 1978–79 .... +164
14. T. Tyler 1979–80 .... +152
15. W. Cooper 1985–86................. +152
16. Geo. Johnson 1978–79.............. +143
17. T. Tyler 1982–83 .... +143
18. M. Jordan 1987–88 .... +138
19. Olajuwon 1987–88 .... +133
20. Geo. Johnson 1977–78.............. +131

Chart 15 *(cont.)*

21. T. Tyler 1980–81 .... +129
22. L. Nance 1982–83 .... +126
23. Benjamin 1985–86 .... +125
24. T. R. Dunn 1985–86.................. +120
25. Poquette 1980–81 .... +119
26. Geo. Johnson 1979–80.............. +112
27. Gar Heard 1977–78.................. +110
28. Abdul-Jabbar 1978–79 .... +110
29. T. R. Dunn 1983–84.................. +108
30. R. Parish 1980–81 .... +104
31. Poquette 1979–80 .... +104
32. J. Williams 1987–88.................. +102

Chart 16
BEST: 100 STEALS AND BLOCKS

1. A. Olajuwon 1985–86 .... +170
2. A. Olajuwon 1986–87 .... +166
3. Terry Tyler 1978–79 .... +164
4. Terry Tyler 1979–80 .... +152
5. Terry Tyler 1982–83 .... +143
6. M. Jordan 1987–88 .... +138
7. Olajuwon 1987–88.................... +133
8. Terry Tyler 1980–81 .... +129
9. Gar Heard 1977–78 .... +110
10. M. Jordan 1986–87 .... +89
11. J. Erving 1981–82 .... +88
12. R. Parish 1978–79 .... +84
13. Abdul-Jabbar 1977–78 .... +80
14. Bobby Jones 1979–80............... +74
15. Bobby Jones 1977–78 .... +69
16. P. Ewing 1987–88 .... +62
17. J. Erving 1980–81 .... +54
18. J. Erving 1983–84 .... +50
19. J. Erving 1982–83 .... +47
20. Sam Lacey 1977–78 .... +42
21. J. Erving 1984–85 .... +36
22. J. Erving 1979–80 .... +26
23. Sam Lacey 1979–80 .... +9
24. Roundfield 1979–80.................. +7
25. Rich Kelley 1978–79 .... +4

Chart 17
MORE STEALS THAN TURNOVERS

1. T. R. Dunn 1985–86.................. +104
2. T. R. Dunn 1983–84.................. +76
3. T. R. Dunn 1984–85.................. +75
4. Don Buse 1981–82 .... +69
5. Don Buse 1977–78 .... +61

Chart 17 *(cont.)*

6. Don Buse 1978–79 .... +60
7. A. Robertson 1985–86 .... +45
8. D. Bradley 1979–80.................. +45
9. R. Green 1983–84 .... +43
10. L. Lever 1987–88.................... +41
11. Don Buse 1979–80 .... +41
12. T. R. Dunn 1982–83.................. +34
13. L. Lever 1986–87.................... +34
14. D. Harper 1986–87 .... +29
15. Mo Cheeks 1981–82 .... +25
16. M. Adams 1987–88 .... +24
17. L. Conner 1984–85 .... +23
18. D. Harper 1984–85 .... +21
19. L. Conner 1983–84 .... +19
20. Gus Williams 1979–80............... +19
21. Mo Cheeks 1980–81 .... +19
22. G. Ballard 1981–82 .... +18
23. A. Robertson 1986–87 .... +17
24. L. Lever 1982–83.................... +16
25. Mo Cheeks 1984–85 .... +14
26. L. Lever 1983–84.................... +10
27. R. Parker 1979–80................... +10
28. Gar Heard 1977–78 .... +9
29. D. Harper 1985–86 .... +9
30. Jim Paxson 1980–81 .... +9
31. M. Jordan 1987–88 .... +7
32. Mo Cheeks 1986–87 .... +7
33. Kyle Macy 1983–84 .... +7
34. Mo Cheeks 1987–88 .... +7
35. Brian Taylor 1980–81.................. +7
36. R. Parker 1977–78................... +7
37. Chris Ford 1979–80.................. +6
38. Brian Taylor 1979–80.................. +6
39. Mo Cheeks 1982–83 .... +5
40. G. Ballard 1980–81 .... +1

Chart 18
MORE BLOCKS THAN TURNOVERS

1. Manute Bol 1985–86 .... +332
2. Mark Eaton 1983–84.................. +253
3. Mark Eaton 1984–85.................. +250
4. W. Rollins 1982–83 .... +248
5. Mark Eaton 1985–86.................. +212
6. Mark Eaton 1986–87.................. +179
7. W. Rollins 1983–84 .... +176
8. Mark Eaton 1987–88.................. +173
9. W. Rollins 1979–80 .... +145
10. W. Rollins 1981–82 .... +145
11. W. Cooper 1985–86.................. +110

Chart 18 *(cont.)*

12. Geo. Johnson 1978–79 . . . . +75
13. B. Benjamin 1985–86 . . . . +61
14. Terry Tyler 1978–79 . . . . +60
15. T. Poquette 1979–80 . . . . +59
16. Geo. Johnson 1979–80 . . . . +59
17. Geo. Johnson 1977–78 . . . . +53
18. T. Poquette 1980–81 . . . . +52
19. W. Cooper 1984–85 . . . . +48
20. K. Nimphius 1983–84 . . . . +46
21. Terry Tyler 1979–80 . . . . +45
22. H. Williams 1981–82 . . . . +41
23. Terry Tyler 1982–83 . . . . +40
24. A. Olajuwon 1985–86 . . . . +36
25. Abdul-Jabbar 1978–79 . . . . +34
26. K. McHale 1982–83 . . . . +33
27. Donaldson 1986–87 . . . . +32
28. Sam Bowie 1984–85 . . . . +31
29. K. Nimphius 1984–85 . . . . +31
30. J. Williams 1986–87 . . . . +28
31. Bill Paultz 1977–78 . . . . +27
32. Larry Nance 1982–83 . . . . +27
33. A. Olajuwon 1986–87 . . . . +26
34. R. Parish 1980–81 . . . . +23
35. T. Bailey 1983–84 . . . . +17
36. John Salley 1987–88 . . . . +17
37. Terry Tyler 1980–81 . . . . +17
38. T. Poquette 1982–83 . . . . +16
39. Donaldson 1985–86 . . . . +16
40. Terry Tyler 1984–85 . . . . +14
41. Roy Hinson 1986–87 . . . . +12
42. A. Lister 1986–87 . . . . +11
43. Larry Nance 1987–88 . . . . +4
44. B. Benjamin 1986–87 . . . . +3
45. Roy Hinson 1984–85 . . . . +2
46. B. Benjamin 1987–88 . . . . +2
47. Cald. Jones 1978–79 . . . . +1

Chart 19
BLOCKED SHOTS PER MINUTE

1. Manute Bol 1985–86 190
2. Mark Eaton 1983–84 164
3. Tree Rollins 1982–83 139
4. Elmore Smith 1973–74 134
5. Geo. Johnson 1978–79 123
6. Wayne Cooper 1985–86 107
7. B. Benjamin 1987–88 104
8. Abdul-Jabbar 1974–75 100
9. Cald. Jones 1976–77 099
10. P. Ewing 1987–88 096
11. A. Olajuwon 1985–86 094
12. R. Parish 1980–81 093

Chart 19 *(cont.)*

13. Bill Walton 1976–77 093
14. Sam Bowie 1984–85 092
15. Terry Tyler 1979–80 082
16. K. McHale 1982–83 082
17. Bob Lanier 1973–74 081
18. Gar Heard 1973–74 080
19. A. Lister 1984–85 080
20. A. Gilmore 1981–82 079
21. Bill Paultz 1977–78 078
22. H. Williams 1981–82 078
23. Bob McAdoo 1973–74 077
24. Larry Nance 1982–83 074
25. Roy Hinson 1984–85 074
26. R. Sampson 1983–84 073
27. D. Dawkins 1982–83 073
28. Thurmond 1973–74 073
29. M. Malone 1976–77 072

Chart 20
STEALS PER MINUTE

1. A. Robertson 1985–86 105
2. Dud. Bradley 1979–80 104
3. Don Buse 1976–77 095
4. Slick Watts 1975–76 094
5. Q. Buckner 1976–77 092
6. Ed Jordan 1978–79 089
7. Richardson 1982–83 088
8. J. Stockton 1987–88 085
9. Johnny Moore 1984–85 085
10. Mo Cheeks 1981–82 084
11. Larry Steele 1973–74 082
12. Brian Taylor 1976–77 080
13. L. Lever 1984–85 079
14. R. Green 1982–83 079
15. M. Jordan 1987–88 078
16. G. Rivers 1984–85 077
17. C. Drexler 1985–86 076
18. Mike Gale 1977–78 076
19. L. Hollins 1976–77 075
20. Randy Smith 1973–74 074
21. Darwin Cook 1982–83 074
22. Ray Williams 1981–82 073
23. Gus Williams 1977–78 072
24. Steve Mix 1973–74 071
25. L. Conner 1984–85 071
26. P. Westphal 1975–76 071
27. Chris Ford 1976–77 071
28. Foots Walker 1977–78 071
29. Rick Barry 1974–75 070
30. Fred Brown 1974–75 070
31. A. Leavell 1981–82 070

Chart 21
LEAST TURNOVERS PER MINUTE

1. Manute Bol 1985–86 031
2. R. Wittman 1987–88 034
3. Don Buse 1979–80 036
4. T. R. Dunn 1983–84 036
5. B. Smith 1979–80 038
6. W. Rollins 1982–83 038
7. T. Tyler 1984–85 038
8. Ken Walker 1987–88 039
9. John Paxson 1986–87 039
10. Robisch 1980–81 039
11. Ballard 1981–82 040
12. Robert Reid 1986–87 040
13. J. Malone 1984–85 041
14. B. Sellers 1987–88 041
15. S. Wedman 1978–79 042
16. Laimbeer 1986–87 042
17. Nimphius 1983–84 043
18. Poquette 1980–81 043
19. Levingston 1987–88 044
20. Kyle Macy 1981–82 044
21. M. Cooper 1986–87 045
22. M. Mitchell 1981–83 045
23. A. C. Green 1987–88 045
24. Mark Eaton 1983–84 046
25. Vandeweghe 1984–85 046
26. Donaldson 1985–86 046
27. McDonald 1987–88 046

Chart 22A
UNDERRATED PLAYERS 1987–88

1. Bird, Boston 824
2. Stockton, Utah 749
3. Tarpley, Dallas 701
4. Nance, Phoe-Cle. 677
5. Rivers, Atlanta 652
6. Rodman, Detroit .618
7. Oakley, Chicago 611
8. Thorpe, Sacramento 603
9. Fleming, Indiana 572
10. Kersey, Portland 566
11. Benjamin, LA Clip. 562
12. Rasmussen, Denver 551
13. Scott, LA Lakers 550
14. Price, Cleveland 533
15. Brickowski, San Ant. 532
16. Breuer, Milwaukee 522
17. Floyd, Houston .501
18. West, Phoenix 500
19. Coleman, Phila .472

Chart 22A (cont.)

20. Battle, Atlanta 460
21. Dumars, Detroit 417

Chart 22B
OVERRATED PLAYERS 1987–88

1. Alford, Dallas 345
2. Griffith, Utah 400
3. Washington, N.J. 417
4. Bogues, Wash 431
5. D. Johnson, Boston 440
6. K. Walker, N.Y. 447
7. Schrempf, Dallas 462
8. Bol, Washington .482
9. Sampson, Golden St 508
10. Abdul-Jabbar, LAL 525
11. Worthy, LA Lakers 541
12. Chambers, Seattle 543
13. Vandeweghe, Port 557

Chart 23
UP AND COMING 1987–88

1. Stockton, Utah 749
2. Tarpley, Dallas 701
3. K. Malone, Utah .693
4. Rodman, Detroit .618
5. Mullin, Golden State 578
6. Daugherty, Cleveland 571
7. Kersey, Portland 566
8. Porter, Portland .561
9. Williams, Cleveland 559
10. Berry, San Antonio 557
11. Jackson, New York 545
12. Price, Cleveland 533
13. Harper, Cleveland 522
14. K. Johnson, Phoenix 517
15. Salley, Detroit 516
16. B. Johnson, Houston 498
17. Williams, Washington 497
18. Dawkins, San Antonio 495
19. McKey, Seattle .492
20. Anderson, San Ant. 490
21. Green, LA Lakers 487
22. Grant, Chicago .478
23. Lohaus, Boston .461
24. Battle, Atlanta 460
25. Garland, Golden State 453
26. Adams, Denver .452
27. Pippen, Chicago 451
28. Gilliam, Phoenix 445

Chart 23 *(cont.)*

29. Reynolds, Milwaukee .... .432
30. Miller, Indiana .... .419
31. K. Smith, Sacramento .... .408
32. Acres, Boston .... .383
33. Hopson, New Jersey .... .334
34. Williams, LA Clip .... .282
35. Wingate, Philadel .... .263

Chart 24
DOWN AND GOING 1987–88

1. Dawkins, Detroit .... −.124
2. Free, Houston .... .328
3. Birdsong, New Jersey .... .338
4. Gilmore, Boston .... .351
5. Tripucka, Utah .... .388
6. Drew, LA Clippers .... .388
7. Griffith, Utah .... .400
8. Tyler, Sacramento .... .409
9. Hubbard, Cleveland .... .410
10. Toney, Philadelphia .... .426
11. Maxwell, Houston .... .428
12. D. Smith, Sacramento .... .432
13. Johnson, Boston .... .440
14. Mitchell, San Ant .... .444
15. Woodson, LA Clip .... .448
16. Rollins, Atlanta .... .448
17. Natt, Denver .... .454
18. M. Lucas, Portland .... .461
19. Valentine, LA Clip .... .463
20. L. Smith, Golden St .... .467
21. Williams, Indiana .... .473
22. Donaldson, Dallas .... .474
23. Corzine, Chicago .... .482
24. Moncrief, Milwaukee .... .491
25. Dailey, LA Clip .... .495
26. Abdul-Jabbar, LAL .... .525

Chart 25
MID-CAREER CRISES 1987–88

1. Jordan, Chicago .... .887
2. Barkley, Philadelphia .... .829
3. Ewing, New York .... .760
4. McHale, Boston .... .665
5. Lever, Denver .... .642
6. Aguirre, Dallas .... .615
7. Thorpe, Sacramento .... .603
8. Benjamin, LA Clip .... .562
9. Thomas, Detroit .... .562

Chart 25 *(cont.)*

10. Vandeweghe, Portland .... .557
11. Scott, LA Lakers .... .550
12. Stipanovich, Ind .... .549
13. Chambers, Seattle .... .543
14. Bailey, Utah .... .542
15. Brickowski, San Ant .... .532
16. Breuer, Milwaukee .... .522
17. Harper, Cleveland .... .522
18. W. Davis, Phoenix .... .512
19. Sampson, Hou-G. St .... .508
20. B. King, Washington .... .482
21. Willis, Atlanta .... .479
22. Woolridge, N.J. .... .476
23. Leavell, Houston .... .448

Chart 26
THE MONEY MEN

1. Gus Williams 78–79 .... +.385
2. Mo Cheeks 85–86 .... +.351
3. Bernard King 83–84 .... +.323
4. Andrew Toney 81–82 .... +.321
5. D. Johnson 78–79 .... +.314
6. Abdul-Jabbar 76–77 .... +.313
7. Jerry West 64–65 .... +.310
8. Heinsohn 62–63 .... +.307
9. Rick Barry 76–77 .... +.303
10. Hal Greer 66–67 .... +.253
11. A. Olajuwon 86–87 .... +.248
12. J. Worthy 86–87 .... +.216
13. W. Frazier 68–69 .... +.211
14. Havlicek 73–74 .... +.199
15. B. Russell 61–62 .... +.185
16. I. Thomas 86–87 .... +.170
17. E. Hayes 73–74 .... +.109
18. W. Bellamy 64–65 .... −.157
19. B. Howell 68–69 .... −.239
20. Aguirre 83–84 .... −.254
21. G. Johnson 70–71 .... −.286
22. Chamberlain 61–62 .... −.306
23. Jerry Lucas 63–64 .... −.311
24. G. McGinnis 76–77 .... −.336
25. L. Foust 59–60 .... −.467

Chart 27
MOST SEASONS 3,000 MINUTES PLAYED

1. Wilt Chamberlain 13
2. Elvin Hayes 12
3. Bill Russell 9
4. Oscar Robertson 9

Chart 27 (cont.)

5.	Kareem Abdul-Jabbar	9
6.	Walt Bellamy	8
7.	Hal Greer	7
8.	John Havlicek	7
9.	Elgin Baylor	6
10.	Jerry Lucas	6
11.	Dave Bing	6
12.	Walt Frazier	6
13.	Jo Jo White	6
14.	Rick Barry	5
15.	Bob Love	5
16.	Dave Cowens	5
17.	Larry Bird	5
18.	Jerry West	4
19.	Nate Thurmond	4
20.	Bill Bridges	4
21.	Gail Goodrich	4
22.	Lou Hudson	4
23.	Nate Archibald	4
24.	Sidney Wicks	4
25.	Randy Smith	4
26.	Moses Malone	4
27.	Norm Nixon	4
28.	Alex English	4
29.	Bob Pettit	4
30.	Gene Shue	3
31.	Willis Reed	3
32.	Earl Monroe	3
33.	Archie Clark	3
34.	Tom Van Arsdale	3
35.	Billy Cunningham	3
36.	Dick Van Arsdale	3
37.	Wes Unseld	3
38.	Norm Van Lier	3
39.	Geoff Petrie	3
40.	Bob Lanier	3
41.	Chet Walker	3
42.	Spencer Haywood	3
43.	Bob McAdoo	3
44.	Rudy Tomjanovich	3
45.	Sam Lacey	3
46.	Micheal Ray Richardson	3
47.	Isiah Thomas	3
48.	Buck Williams	3
49.	Michael Jordan	3

Chart 28
3,000-MINUTE STREAKS

1.	Wilt Chamberlain	10
2.	Bill Russell	8

Chart 28 (cont.)

3.	Oscar Robertson	7
4.	John Havlicek	7
5.	Elvin Hayes	7
6.	Walt Bellamy	6
7.	Hal Greer	6
8.	Walt Frazier	6
9.	Jo Jo White	6
10.	Bob Love	5
11.	Kareem Abdul-Jabbar	5
12.	Bob Pettit	4
13.	Jerry Lucas	4
14.	Lou Hudson	4
15.	Randy Smith	4
16.	Moses Malone	4
17.	Larry Bird	4
18.	Gene Shue	3
19.	Elgin Baylor	3
20.	Earl Monroe	3
21.	Dave Bing	3
22.	Billy Cunningham	3
23.	Bob Lanier	3
24.	Spencer Haywood	3
25.	Sam Lacey	3
26.	Isiah Thomas	3
27.	Buck Williams	3
28.	Wilt Chamberlain	3

Chart 29
SEASONAL MINUTES LEADERS

1.	Wilt Chamberlain	8
2.	Elvin Hayes	4
3.	Neil Johnston	2
4.	Dolph Schayes	2
5.	Bill Russell	2
6.	John Havlicek	2
7.	Bob McAdoo	2
8.	Moses Malone	2
9.	Paul Arizin	2
10.	Michael Jordan	2
11.	Jack George	1
12.	Gene Shue	1
13.	Nate Archibald	1
14.	Kareem Abdul-Jabbar	1
15.	Leonard Robinson	1
16.	Norm Nixon	1
17.	Adrian Dantley	1
18.	Jeff Ruland	1
19.	Buck Williams	1
20.	Jeff Hornacek	1
21.	Maurice Cheeks	1

Chart 30
CONSECUTIVE SEASONS PLAYING EVERY GAME

1. Randy Smith 10
2. Dolph Schayes 9
3. John Kerr 9
4. Vern Mikkelsen 8
5. Jack Twyman 8
6. Jim Chones 6
7. Bill Laimbeer 6
8. Jo Jo White 5
9. Jack Sikma 5
10. Reggie Theus 5
11. Michael Cooper 5
12. Mel Hutchins 4
13. Bobby Wanzer 4
14. Harry Gallatin 4
15. Wilt Chamberlain 4
16. Satch Sanders 4
17. Walt Bellamy 4
18. Adrian Smith 4
19. Chet Walker 4
20. Jack Marin 4
21. Elvin Hayes 4
22. Bob Weiss 4
23. Dave Corzine 4
24. Ed Johnson 4
25. James Donaldson 4

Chart 31
BEST SIXTH MEN 1987–88

1. Tarpley, Dallas 701
2. Cartwright, New York 627
3. Rodman, Detroit 618
4. Vandeweghe, Portland 557
5. Rasmussen, Denver 551
6. Bailey, Utah 542
7. Hornacek, Phoenix 515
8. Pierce, Milwaukee 500
9. Williams, Washington 497
10. McKey, Seattle 492
11. Anderson, San Anton 490
12. Short, Houston 486
13. Curry, Cleveland 473
14. Coleman, Phila 472
15. Battle, Atlanta 460
16. Pippen, Chicago 451
17. Miller, Indiana 419
18. McGee, Sacramento 414
19. Cooper, LA Lakers 389
20. Teagle, Golden St .375

Chart 31 (cont.)

21. Paxson, Boston 345
22. Hopson, New Jersey 334
23. Williams, LA Clip 282

Chart 32
TOP 1988 DRAFTEES

1. Manning, Kansas 830
2. Perdue, Vanderbilt .812
3. Smits, Marist 756
4. Morris, Auburn 716
5. Smith, Pittsburgh 715
6. Hawkins, Bradley 713
7. Bryant, Seton Hall .691
8. Strickland, DePaul .663
9. Chievous, Missouri .661
10. Dembo, Wyoming .659
11. Garrett, Indiana 644
12. Richmond, Kansas St 642
13. Grayer, Iowa State .618
14. Leckner, Wyoming .610
15. Perry, Temple 607
16. Majerle, Cent. Mich 606
17. Seikaly, Syracuse .605
18. Grant, Michigan 597
19. Edwards, DePaul .595
20. Rivers, Notre Dame 579
21. Lane, Pittsburgh 577
22. Berry, San Jose St .577
23. Grant, Oklahoma 571
24. Jones, St. John's 562
25. Anderson, Georgia 560
26. Shaw, Santa Barbara 548
27. Chapman, Kentucky 504
28. Smart, Indiana 485
29. Taylor, Oregon 480
30. Stephens, Purdue .469

Chart 33
1987–88 TENDEX RATINGS

ALL-PURPOSE

1. Jordan, Chicago	.887	11. M. Malone, Wash.	.677
2. Barkley, Philadelphia	.829	12. Nance, Phoe-Cle.	.677
3. Bird, Boston	.824	13. McHale, Boston	.665
4. Olajuwon, Houston	.782	14. Rivers, Atlanta	.652
5. Ewing, New York	.760	15. Wilkins, Atlanta	.646
6. Stockton, Utah	.749	16. Schayes, Denver	.644
7. Johnson, LA Lakers	.721	17. Lever, Denver	.642
8. Tarpley, Dallas	.701	18. B. Williams, N.J.	.635
9. Drexler, Portland	.700	19. Rodman, Detroit	.618
10. K. Malone, Utah	.693	20. Aguirre, Dallas	.615

CENTERS

1. Olajuwon, Houston	.782
2. Ewing, New York	.760
3. M. Malone, Washington	.677
4. Schayes, Denver	.644
5. Laimbeer, Detroit	.583
6. Parish, Boston	.579
7. Daugherty, Cleveland	.571
8. Gminski, N.J.-Phila.	.568
9. Benjamin, LA Clippers	.562
10. Stipanovich, Indiana	.549

POWER FORWARDS

1. Barkley, Philadelphia	.829
2. Tarpley, Dallas	.701
3. K. Malone, Utah	.693
4. McHale, Boston	.665
5. B. Williams, N.J.	.635
6. Sikma, Milwaukee	.614
7. Oakley, Chicago	.611
8. Thorpe, Sacramento	.603
9. Cage, LA Clippers	.591
10. McDaniel, Seattle	.571

SMALL FORWARDS

1. Bird, Boston	.824
2. Nance, Phoe-Cle.	.677
3. Wilkins, Atlanta	.646
4. Rodman, Detroit	.618
5. Aguirre, Dallas	.615
6. English, Denver	.569
7. Dantley, Detroit	.569
8. Kersey, Portland	.566
9. Cummings, Milwaukee	.557
10. Worthy, LA Lakers	.541

POINT GUARDS

1. Stockton, Utah	.749
2. Johnson, LA Lakers	.721
3. Rivers, Atlanta	.652
4. Fleming, Indiana	.572
5. Pressey, Milwaukee	.567
6. Thomas, Detroit	.562
7. Porter, Portland	.561
8. McMillan, Seattle	.558
9. Jackson, New York	.545
10. Cheeks, Philadel.	.534

SHOOTING GUARDS

1. Jordan, Chicago	.887
2. Drexler, Portland	.700
3. Lever, Denver	.642
4. Mullin, Golden St.	.578
5. Robertson, San Anton.	.571
6. Ellis, Seattle	.552
7. Scott, LA Lakers	.550
8. Hornacek, Phoenix	.515
9. Floyd, GS-Houston	.501
10. Theus, Sacramento	.483

BOTTOM TEN

1. McDonald, Golden St.	.344
2. Sellers, Chicago	.349
3. Wittman, Atlanta	.354
4. Drew, LA Clippers	.388
5. K. Smith, Sacramento	.408
6. Bagley, New Jersey	.413
7. Long, Indiana	.415
8. Dumars, Detroit	.417
9. Eaton, Utah	.419
10. Pressley, Sacramento	.433

Chart 34
1987–88 SHOOTISTS: POINTS PER SHOT

ALL-PURPOSE

1.	Ainge, Boston	1.093	11. Levingston, Atlanta	1.011
2.	Stockton, Utah	1.080	12. Adams, Denver	1.010
3.	McHale, Boston	1.075	13. Worthy, LA Lakers	1.009
4.	Bird, Boston	1.071	14. Porter, Portland	1.007
5.	Parish, Boston	1.071	15. Higgins, Golden St.	1.007
6.	Scott, LA Lakers	1.053	16. Donaldson, Dallas	1.004
7.	Price, Cleveland	1.043	17. Jordan, Chicago	1.003
8.	Mullin, Golden St.	1.014	18. Ewing, New York	.996
9.	Barkley, Philadel.	1.013	19. Abdul-Jabbar, LAL	.994
10.	Ellis, Seattle	1.013	20. Hornacek, Phoenix	.989

CENTERS

1.	Parish, Boston	1.071
2.	Donaldson, Dallas	1.004
3.	Ewing, New York	.996
4.	Abdul-Jabbar, LAL	.994
5.	Schayes, Denver	.977
6.	Laimbeer, Detroit	.976
7.	McCormick, Pha.-N.J.	.975
8.	Brickowski, San Ant.	.970
9.	Stipanovich, Indiana	.945
10.	West, Cle.-Phoe.	.935

POWER FORWARDS

1.	McHale, Boston	1.075
2.	Barkley, Philadel.	1.013
3.	Levingston, Atlanta	1.011
4.	Salley, Detroit	.978
5.	Tisdale, Indiana	.966
6.	Sikma, Milwaukee	.962
7.	B. Williams, N.J.	.947
8.	Tarpley, Dallas	.938
9.	Willis, Atlanta	.935
10.	K. Malone, Utah	.930

SMALL FORWARDS

1.	Bird, Boston	1.071
2.	Worthy, LA Lakers	1.009
3.	Higgins, Golden St.	1.007
4.	Nance, Phoe.-Cle.	.977
5.	Dantley, Detroit	.962
6.	English, Denver	.960
7.	Rodman, Detroit	.960
8.	Ed Johnson, Phoenix	.959
9.	Bailey, Utah	.947
10.	B. King, Washington	.941

POINT GUARDS

1.	Stockton, Utah	1.080
2.	Price, Cleveland	1.043
3.	Adams, Denver	1.010
4.	Porter, Portland	1.007
5.	Fleming, Indiana	.985
6.	Dawkins, San Anton.	.973
7.	Cheeks, Philadelphia	.953
8.	Johnson, LA Lakers	.948
9.	K. Smith, Sacramento	.937
10.	Pressey, Milwaukee	.928

SHOOTING GUARDS

1.	Ainge, Boston	1.093
2.	Scott, LA Lakers	1.053
3.	Mullin, Golden St.	1.014
4.	Ellis, Seattle	1.013
5.	Jordan, Chicago	1.003
6.	Hornacek, Phoenix	.989
7.	Long, Indiana	.974
8.	Drexler, Portland	.964
9.	J. Malone, Washing.	943
10.	Wittman, Atlanta	.939

BOTTOM TEN

1.	Eaton, Utah	.780
2.	Green, New York	.828
3.	Cage, LA Clippers	.844
4.	Carroll, G.S.-Hou.	.849
5.	Rivers, Atlanta	.865
6.	Jackson, New York	.871
7.	Floyd, G.S.-Hou.	.873
8.	D. Johnson, Boston	.882
9.	Perkins, Dallas	.882
10.	Robinson, Philadel.	.883

Chart 35
1987–88 SHOOTISTS: PERCENTAGE ALL SHOTS

ALL-PURPOSE

1. McHale, Boston	.666		11. Salley, Detroit	.618
2. Schayes, Denver	.665		12. Johnson, LA Lakers	.611
3. Barkley, Philadelphia	.657		13. Bird, Boston	.610
4. Dantley, Detroit	.652		14. Porter, Portland	.606
5. Stockton, Utah	.651		15. Nance, Phoe.-Cle.	.604
6. Donaldson, Dallas	.631		16. Green, LA Lakers	.604
7. Jordan, Chicago	.627		17. M. Malone, Washing.	.604
8. Parish, Boston	.625		18. Ewing, New York	.601
9. Higgins, Golden St.	.615		19. Brickowski, San Ant.	.601
10. Levingston, Atlanta	.622		20. B. Williams, N.J.	.601

CENTERS

1. Schayes, Denver	.665
2. Donaldson, Dallas	.631
3. Parish, Boston	.625
4. M. Malone, Washing.	.604
5. Ewing, New York	.601
6. Brickowski, San Ant.	.601
7. Duckworth, Portland	.584
8. Abdul-Jabbar, LAL	.584
9. Stipanovich, Indiana	.582
10. Daugherty, Cleveland	.577

POWER FORWARDS

1. McHale, Boston	.666
2. Barkley, Philadel.	.657
3. Levingston, Atlanta	.622
4. Salley, Detroit	.618
5. Green, LA Lakers	.604
6. B. Williams, N.J.	.601
7. Sikma, Milwaukee	.594
8. Thorpe, Sacramento	.590
9. K. Malone, Utah	.578
10. Tisdale, Indiana	.577

SMALL FORWARDS

1. Dantley, Detroit	.652
2. Higgins, Golden St.	.615
3. Bird, Boston	.610
4. Nance, Phoe.-Cle.	.604
5. Worthy, LA Lakers	.586
6. McCray, Houston	.581
7. Bailey, Utah	.573
8. B. King, Washington	.568
9. Hinson, Pha.-N.J.	.566
10. Kersey, Portland	.556

POINT GUARDS

1. Stockton, Utah	.651
2. Johnson, LA Lakers	.611
3. Porter, Portland	.606
4. Pressey, Milwaukee	.595
5. Fleming, Indiana	.593
6. Price, Cleveland	.582
7. Cheeks, Philadelphia	.575
8. Dawkins, San Antonio	.571
9. K. Smith, Sacramento	.555
10. Leavell, Houston	.555

SHOOTING GUARDS

1. Jordan, Chicago	.627
2. Mullin, Golden State	.593
3. Scott, LA Lakers	.590
4. Drexler, Portland	.585
5. Hornacek, Phoenix	.580
6. Blackman, Dallas	.579
7. J. Malone, Washing.	.565
8. Ellis, Seattle	.557
9. Dumars, Detroit	.555
10. Theus, Sacramento	.551

BOTTOM TEN

1. Eaton, Washington	.471
2. Person, Indiana	.488
3. Green, New York	.495
4. Drew, LA Clippers	.496
5. Wilkins, New York	.499
6. Carroll, G.S.-Hou.	.500
7. Bagley, New Jersey	.503
8. Jackson, New York	.504
9. Wittman, Atlanta	.510
10. Garland, Golden St.	.513

Chart 36
1987–88: TWO-POINT FIELD GOAL PERCENTAGE

ALL-PURPOSE

1. Barkley, Philadel.	.630	11. West, Cle.-Phoe.	.552
2. McHale, Boston	.604	12. Jordan, Chicago	.546
3. Stockton, Utah	.594	13. Bird, Boston	.546
4. Parish, Boston	.590	14. Carr, Atlanta	.546
5. Rodman, Detroit	.568	15. Cartwright, New York	.544
6. Berry, San Antonio	.563	16. Schayes, Denver	.542
7. B. Williams, N.J.	.560	17. Humphries, Pho.-Mil.	.540
8. Levingston, Atlanta	.557	18. McCormick, Pha.-Mil.	.539
9. Ewing, New York	.556	19. Worthy, LA Lakers	.537
10. Scott, LA Lakers	.554	20. Ainge, Boston	.534

CENTERS

1. Parish, Boston	.590
2. Ewing, New York	.556
3. West, Cle.-Phoe.	.552
4. Cartwright, N.Y.	.544
5. Schayes, Denver	.542
6. McCormick, Pha.-Mil.	.539
7. Abdul-Jabbar, LAL	.532
8. Brickowski, San Ant.	.530
9. Olajuwon, Houston	.516
10. Thompson, LA Lakers	.515

POWER FORWARDS

1. Barkley, Philadel.	.630
2. McHale, Boston	.604
3. B. Williams, N.J.	.560
4. Levingston, Atlanta	.557
5. K. Malone, Utah	.522
6. Willis, Atlanta	.520
7. Tisdale, Indiana	.513
8. Thorpe, Sacramento	.510
9. Catledge, Washington	.508
10. Green, LA Lakers	.505

SMALL FORWARDS

1. Rodman, Detroit	.568
2. Berry, San Antonio	.563
3. Bird, Boston	.546
4. Carr, Atlanta	.546
5. Worthy, LA Lakers	.537
6. Nance, Phoe.-Cle.	.531
7. Higgins, Golden St.	.528
8. Dantley, Detroit	.516
9. King, Washington	.503
10. Kersey, Portland	.502

POINT GUARDS

1. Stockton, Utah	.594
2. Humphries, Pho.-Mil.	.540
3. Porter, Portland	.533
4. Fleming, Indiana	.531
5. Johnson, LA Lakers	.510
6. Price, Cleveland	.510
7. Pressey, Milwaukee	.508
8. Adams, Denver	.505
9. Cheeks, Philadelphia	.504
10. Dawkins, San Ant.	.499

SHOOTING GUARDS

1. Scott, LA Lakers	.554
2. Hansen, Utah	.553
3. Jordan, Chicago	.546
4. Ainge, Boston	.534
5. Hornacek, Phoenix	.528
6. Mullin, Golden St.	.526
7. Ellis, Seattle	.521
8. Drexler, Portland	.515
9. O. Smith, Golden St.	.502
10. Short, Houston	.486

BOTTOM TEN

1. Wingate, Philadel.	.412
2. Hopson, New Jersey	.416
3. Valentine, LA Clip.	.416
4. Eaton, Utah	.418
5. Williams, Indiana	.428
6. Frank, Golden State	.429
7. Carroll, G.S.-Hou.	.436
8. Dailey, LA Clippers	.439
9. Sampson, Hou.-G.S.	.443
10. Green, New York	.443

Chart 37
1987–88: FREE THROW PERCENTAGE

ALL-PURPOSE

1. Sikma, Milwaukee	.922	11. Leavell, Houston	.869
2. Bird, Boston	.916	12. Woodson, LA Clip.	.868
3. Gminski, N.J.-Pha.	.906	13. Jordan, Chicago	.860
4. Dawkins, San Antonio	.896	14. Dantley, Detroit	.860
5. W. Davis, Phoenix	.887	15. Scott, LA Lakers	.858
6. Mullin, Golden State	.885	16. Short, Houston	.858
7. J. Malone, Wash.	.882	17. D. Johnson, Boston	.856
8. Price, Cleveland	.877	18. Johnson, LA Lakers	.853
9. Laimbeer, Detroit	.874	19. Floyd, G.S.-Hou.	.850
10. Blackman, Dallas	.873	20. Ed Johnson, Phoenix	.850

CENTERS

1. Gminski, N.J.-Pha.	.906
2. Laimbeer, Detroit	.874
3. Schayes, Denver	.836
4. Stipanovich, Indiana	.809
5. Cartwright, New York	.798
6. M. Malone, Wash.	.788
7. Duckworth, Portland	.770
8. Brickowski, San Ant.	.768
9. Carroll, G.S.-Hou.	.764
10. Abdul-Jabbar, LAL	.762

POWER FORWARDS

1. Sikma, Milwaukee	.922
2. Perkins, Dallas	.822
3. J. Vincent, Denver	.805
4. McHale, Boston	.797
5. Tisdale, Indiana	.783
6. Green, LA Lakers	.773
7. Levingston, Atlanta	.772
8. McKey, Seattle	.772
9. Williams, Cleveland	.756
10. Thorpe, Sacramento	.755

SMALL FORWARDS

1. Bird, Boston	.916
2. Dantley, Detroit	.860
3. Ed Johnson, Phoenix	.850
4. Higgins, Golden St.	.848
5. Newman, New York	.841
6. English, Denver	.828
7. Wilkins, Atlanta	.826
8. Bailey, Utah	.826
9. Chambers, Seattle	.807
10. Worthy, LA Lakers	.796

POINT GUARDS

1. Dawkins, San Ant.	.896
2. Price, Cleveland	.877
3. Leavell, Houston	.869
4. D. Johnson, Boston	.856
5. Johnson, LA Lakers	.853
6. Porter, Portland	.846
7. Stockton, Utah	.840
8. K. Johnson, Cle.-Pho.	.839
9. Cheeks, Philadelphia	.825
10. K. Smith, Sacramen.	.819

SHOOTING GUARDS

1. W. Davis, Phoenix	.887
2. Mullin, Golden St.	.885
3. J. Malone, Washing.	.882
4. Blackman, Dallas	.873
5. Woodson, LA Clippers	.868
6. Jordan, Chicago	.860
7. Scott, LA Lakers	.858
8. Short, Houston	.858
9. Floyd, G.S.-Hou.	.850
10. Theus, Sacramento	.831

BOTTOM TEN

1. Rodman, Detroit	.535
2. S. Johnson, Portland	.586
3. West, Cle.-Phoe.	.596
4. Berry, San Antonio	.600
5. Anderson, San Ant.	.604
6. M. Thompson, LAL	.634
7. Willis, Atlanta	.649
8. Edwards, Phoe.-Det.	.654
9. Catledge, Washington	.655
10. Breuer, Milwaukee	.657

Chart 38
1987–88: PAR

ALL-PURPOSE

1. Lever, Denver	PAR-7	11. Rivers, Atlanta	PAR-4
2. Johnson, LA Lakers	6	12. Fleming, Indiana	4
3. Bird, Boston	6	13. Daugherty, Cleveland	4
4. Robertson, San Antonio	6	14. McMillan, Seattle	4
5. Drexler, Portland	5	15. Scott, LA Lakers	4
6. Jordan, Chicago	5	16. Person, Indiana	3
7. Pressey, Milwaukee	5	17. Worthy, LA Lakers	3
8. Jackson, New York	4	18. Floyd, G.S.-Houston	3
9. English, Denver	4	19. Brickowski, San Anton.	3
10. Porter, Portland	4	20. Aguirre, Dallas	3

CENTERS

		POWER FORWARDS	
1. Daugherty, Cleveland	4	1. Sikma, Milwaukee	3
2. Brickowski, San Anton.	3	2. McDaniel, Seattle	3
3. Benjamin, LA Clippers	2	3. Thorpe, Sacramento	3
4. Laimbeer, Detroit	2	4. Barkley, Philadelphia	3
5. Stipanovich, Indiana	2	5. Oakley, Chicago	3
6. Olajuwon, Houston	2	6. Williams, Washington	2
7. Corzine, Chicago	1	7. McHale, Boston	2
8. Gminski, N.J.-Pha.	1	8. K. Malone, Utah	2
9. Abdul-Jabbar, LA Laker	1	9. McDonald, Golden St.	1
10. McCormick, Pha.-N.J.	1	10. Perkins, Dallas	1

SMALL FORWARDS

		POINT GUARDS	
1. Bird, Boston	6	1. Johnson, LA Lakers	6
2. English, Denver	4	2. Pressey, Milwaukee	5
3. Person, Indiana	3	3. Jackson, New York	4
4. Worthy, LA Lakers	3	4. Porter, Portland	4
5. Aguirre, Dallas	3	5. Rivers, Atlanta	4
6. McCray, Houston	3	6. Fleming, Indiana	4
7. Nance, Phoe.-Cle.	3	7. McMillan, Seattle	4
8. Kersey, Portland	3	8. Thomas, Detroit	3
9. Wilkins, Atlanta	2	9. Garland, Golden St.	3
10. B. King, Washington	2	10. Cheeks, Philadelphia	3

SHOOTING GUARDS

		BOTTOM TEN	
1. Lever, Denver	7	1. Willis, Atlanta	0
2. Robertson, San Antonio	6	2. Eaton, Utah	0
3. Drexler, Portland	5	3. Donaldson, Dallas	0
4. Jordan, Chicago	5	4. Thompson, LA Lakers	0
5. Scott, LA Lakers	4	5. Duckworth, Portland	0
6. Floyd, G.S.-Houston	3	6. Levingston, Atlanta	0
7. Blackman, Dallas	3	7. West, Cle.-Phoe.	0
8. Mullin, Golden State	3	8. Walker, New York	1
9. G. Wilkins, New York	3	9. Tarpley, Dallas	1
10. Hornacek, Phoenix	3	10. Green, LA Lakers	1

Chart 39
1987–88: GROSS PAR PER MINUTE

ALL-PURPOSE

1. Bird, Boston	1.162	11. M. Malone, Wash. ... .965
2. Jordan, Chicago	1.148	12. Ewing, New York ... .965
3. Barkley, Phila.	1.096	13. Lever, Denver ... .933
4. K. Malone, Utah	1.079	14. Tarpley, Dallas. ... .926
5. Wilkins, Atlanta.	1.042	15. Thorpe, Sacramento ... .912
6. Drexler, Portland	1.041	16. Stockton, Utah ... .906
7. Olajuwon, Houston	1.034	17. McDaniel, Seattle ... .905
8. Johnson, LA Lakers	1.032	18. McHale, Boston ... .903
9. Aguirre, Dallas.	1.012	19. Rivers, Atlanta. ... .898
10. English, Denver	.977	20. Cummings, Milwaukee ... .895

CENTERS

1. Olajuwon, Houston	1.034
2. M. Malone, Washing.	.965
3. Ewing, New York	.965
4. Schayes, Denver	.876
5. Duckworth, Portland	.846
6. Brickowski, San Ant.	.840
7. Daugherty, Cleveland	.837
8. Carroll, G.S.-Hou.	.792
9. Parish, Boston.	.782
10. Gminski, N.J.-Pha.	.781

POWER FORWARDS

1. Barkley, Philadel.	1.096
2. K. Malone, Utah	1.079
3. Tarpley, Dallas.	.926
4. Thorpe, Sacramento	.912
5. McDaniel, Seattle	.905
6. McHale, Boston	.903
7. B. Williams, N.J.	.844
8. Oakley, Chicago	.828
9. Sikma, Milwaukee	.803
10. Cage, LA Clippers	.786

SMALL FORWARDS

1. Bird, Boston	1.162
2. Wilkins, Atlanta.	1.042
3. Aguirre, Dallas.	1.012
4. English, Denver	.977
5. Cummings, Milwaukee	.895
6. Chambers, Seattle	.886
7. Nance, Phoe.-Cle.	.879
8. Kersey, Portland	.836
9. Dantley, Detroit	.830
10. Rodman, Detroit	.828

POINT GUARDS

1. Johnson, LA Lakers	1.032
2. Stockton, Utah	.906
3. Rivers, Atlanta.	.898
4. Thomas, Detroit	.867
5. Porter, Portland	.812
6. Dawkins, San Antonio	.786
7. Pressey, Milwaukee	.757
8. D. Harper, Dallas	.749
9. Fleming, Indiana	.747
10. Price, Cleveland	.739

SHOOTING GUARDS

1. Jordan, Chicago	1.148
2. Drexler, Portland	1.041
3. Lever, Denver	.933
4. Robertson, San Anton.	.894
5. Ellis, Seattle.	.886
6. Theus, Sacramento	.857
7. Mullin, Golden State	.839
8. Scott, LA Lakers.	.797
9. Floyd, G.S.-Houston	.794
10. J. Malone, Wash.	.784

BOTTOM TEN

1. Eaton, Utah	.492
2. Sellers, Chicago	.530
3. McDonald, Golden St.	.532
4. Wittman, Atlanta.	.537
5. Donaldson, Dallas.	.550
6. Salley, Detroit	.607
7. Walker, New York.	.609
8. Bagley, New Jersey	.620
9. Drew, LA Clippers	.624
10. Leavell, Houston	.636

Chart 40
1987–88: POINTS PER MINUTE

ALL-PURPOSE

1. Jordan, Chicago	.866	11. Dantley, Detroit	.644
2. Wilkins, Atlanta	.813	12. Olajuwon, Houston	.639
3. Bird, Boston	.767	13. Chambers, Seattle	.625
4. Aguirre, Dallas	.740	14. J. Malone, Wash.	.618
5. Barkley, Philadelphia	.714	15. McDaniel, Seattle	.617
6. Drexler, Portland	.714	16. Cummings, Milwaukee	.617
7. English, Denver	.710	17. McHale, Boston	.605
8. K. Malone, Utah	.709	18. M. Malone, Wash.	.597
9. Ellis, Seattle	.695	19. Mullin, Golden St.	.597
10. Ewing, New York	.649	20. Ed Johnson, Phoenix	.594

CENTERS

1. Ewing, New York	.649
2. Olajuwon, Houston	.639
3. M. Malone, Wash.	.597
4. Duckworth, Portland	.554
5. Schayes, Denver	.521
6. Abdul-Jabbar, LAL	.505
7. Brickowski, San Ant.	.502
8. Daugherty, Cleveland	.501
9. Carroll, G.S.-Hou.	.487
10. Gminski, N.J.-Pha.	.461

POWER FORWARDS

1. Barkley, Phila.	.714
2. K. Malone, Utah	.709
3. McDaniel, Seattle	.617
4. McHale, Boston	.605
5. Thorpe, Sacramento	.555
6. Tisdale, Indiana	.533
7. B. Williams, N.J.	.485
8. Tarpley, Dallas	.474
9. Sikma, Milwaukee	.463
10. John Williams, Wash.	.431

SMALL FORWARDS

1. Wilkins, Atlanta	.813
2. Bird, Boston	.767
3. Aguirre, Dallas	.740
4. English, Denver	.710
5. Dantley, Detroit	.644
6. Chambers, Seattle	.625
7. Cummings, Milwaukee	.617
8. Ed Johnson, Phoenix	.594
9. King, Washington	.581
10. Bailey, Utah	.572

POINT GUARDS

1. Thomas, Detroit	.539
2. Johnson, LA Lakers	.534
3. Price, Cleveland	.487
4. Dawkins, San Anton.	.471
5. Harper, Dallas	.459
6. Rivers, Atlanta	.453
7. Stockton, Utah	.424
8. Porter, Portland	.409
9. Adams, Denver	.409
10. Fleming, Indiana	.407

SHOOTING GUARDS

1. Jordan, Chicago	.866
2. Drexler, Portland	.714
3. Ellis, Seattle	.695
4. J. Malone, Wash.	.618
5. Mullin, Golden St.	.597
6. Theus, Sacramento	.593
7. Scott, LA Lakers	.575
8. Woodson, LA Clippers	.567
9. Robertson, San Anton.	.541
10. G. Wilkins, New York	.522

BOTTOM TEN

1. Eaton, Utah	.209
2. Donaldson, Dallas	.226
3. McMillan, Seattle	.254
4. McDonald, Golden St.	.300
5. Green, New York	.313
6. Wittman, Atlanta	.341
7. Jackson, New York	.343
8. Corzine, Chicago	.345
9. Hornacek, Phoenix	.348
10. Salley, Detroit	.350

Chart 41
1987–88: ASSISTS PER MINUTE

ALL-PURPOSE

1. Stockton, Utah	.397	11. Dawkins, San Anton.	.220
2. Johnson, LA Lakers	.325	12. Floyd, G.S.-Houston	.216
3. Rivers, Atlanta.	.299	13. Pressey, Milwaukee	.211
4. McMillan, Seattle	.286	14. Lever, Denver	.209
5. Porter, Portland	.278	15. D. Harper, Dallas	.209
6. Jackson, New York	.267	16. Fleming, Indiana	.208
7. Hornacek, Phoenix	.241	17. Garland, Golden St.	.202
8. Thomas, Detroit	.232	18. K. Smith, Sacramento	.200
9. D. Johnson, Boston	.224	19. Drew, LA Clippers	.189
10. Cheeks, Philadel.	.221	20. Leavell, Houston	.188

CENTERS

1. Brickowski, San Ant.	.119
2. Daugherty, Cleveland	.113
3. Benjamin, LA Clip.	.079
4. Laimbeer, Detroit	.069
5. Stipanovich, Indiana	.068
6. Corzine, Chicago	.066
7. Olajuwon, Houston	.058
8. Abdul-Jabbar, LAL	.058
9. McCormick, Pha.-N.J.	.056
10. Carroll, G.S.-Hou.	.056

POWER FORWARDS

1. McDaniel, Seattle	.097
2. John Williams, Wash.	.096
3. Sikma, Milwaukee	.095
4. Oakley, Chicago	.088
5. Thorpe, Sacramento	.087
6. Barkley, Philadelphia	.080
7. McHale, Boston	.072
8. McDonald, Golden St.	.068
9. K. Malone, Utah	.062
10. Salley, Detroit	.056

SMALL FORWARDS

1. Bird, Boston	.158
2. English, Denver	.134
3. Person, Indiana	.110
4. Worthy, LA Lakers	.109
5. Aguirre, Dallas.	.107
6. McCray, Houston	.098
7. King, Washington	.094
8. Pressley, Sacramento	.091
9. Nance, Phoe.-Cle.	.087
10. Higgins, Golden St..	.086

POINT GUARDS

1. Stockton, Utah	.397
2. Johnson, LA Lakers	.325
3. Rivers, Atlanta.	.299
4. McMillan, Seattle	.286
5. Porter, Portland	.278
6. Jackson, New York	.267
7. Thomas, Detroit	.232
8. D. Johnson, Boston	.224
9. Cheeks, Philadelphia	.221
10. Dawkins, San Antonio	.220

SHOOTING GUARDS

1. Hornacek, Phoenix	.241
2. Floyd, G.S.-Houston	.216
3. Lever, Denver	.209
4. Robertson, San Anton.	.187
5. Theus, Sacramento	.175
6. Ainge, Boston	.167
7. Drexler, Portland.	.153
8. Jordan, Chicago	.146
9. Mullin, Golden St.	.143
10. Dumars, Detroit	.142

BOTTOM TEN

1. Willis, Atlanta	.013
2. Eaton, Utah	.020
3. Donaldson, Dallas.	.026
4. Duckworth, Portland	.030
5. Thompson, LA Lakers	.033
6. Levingston, Atlanta	.033
7. West, Cle.-Phoenix.	.035
8. Green, LA Lakers	.035
9. Tarpley, Dallas.	.037
10. Hinson, Pha.-N.J.	.038

Chart 42
1987–88: REBOUNDS PER MINUTE

ALL-PURPOSE

1.	Tarpley, Dallas	.416	11.	Barkley, Phila.	.300
2.	Oakley, Chicago	.379	12.	Donaldson, Dallas	.299
3.	Cage, LA Clippers	.353	13.	Laimbeer, Detroit	.287
4.	Olajuwon, Houston	.339	14.	Gminski, N.J.-Pha.	.275
5.	Rodman, Detroit	.333	15.	Thorpe, Sacramento	.272
6.	M. Malone, Wash.	.328	16.	Parish, Boston	.272
7.	B. Williams, N.J.	.316	17.	Green, LA Lakers	.269
8.	S. Green, New York	.313	18.	Ewing, New York	.266
9.	K. Malone, Utah	.308	19.	Eaton, Utah	.263
10.	Schayes, Denver	.306	20.	Willis, Atlanta	.262

CENTERS

1.	Olajuwon, Houston	.339
2.	M. Malone, Wash.	.328
3.	Schayes, Denver	.306
4.	Donaldson, Dallas	.299
5.	Laimbeer, Detroit	.287
6.	Gminski, N.J.-Pha.	.275
7.	Parish, Boston	.272
8.	Ewing, New York	.266
9.	Eaton, Utah	.263
10.	Duckworth, Portland	.259

POWER FORWARDS

1.	Tarpley, Dallas	.416
2.	Oakley, Chicago	.379
3.	Cage, LA Clippers	.353
4.	B. Williams, N.J.	.316
5.	S. Green, N.Y.	.313
6.	K. Malone, Utah	.308
7.	Barkley, Phila.	.300
8.	Thorpe, Sacramento	.272
9.	Green, LA Lakers	.269
10.	Willis, Atlanta	.262

SMALL FORWARDS

1.	Rodman, Detroit	.333
2.	Nance, Phoe.-Cle.	.255
3.	Bird, Boston	.237
4.	McCray, Houston	.235
5.	Kersey, Portland	.227
6.	Cummings, Milwaukee	.210
7.	Hinson, Pha.-N.J.	.199
8.	Robinson, Phila.	.192
9.	Person, Indiana	.191
10.	Bailey, Utah	.189

POINT GUARDS

1.	Johnson, LA Lakers	.170
2.	Pressey, Milwaukee	.151
3.	Rivers, Atlanta	.146
4.	McMillan, Seattle	.138
5.	Fleming, Indiana	.133
6.	Porter, Portland	.126
7.	Jackson, New York	.122
8.	Garland, Golden St.	.107
9.	Thomas, Detroit	.095
10.	Dawkins, San Anton.	.094

SHOOTING GUARDS

1.	Lever, Denver	.217
2.	Drexler, Portland	.174
3.	Robertson, San Anton.	.167
4.	Jordan, Chicago	.136
5.	Ellis, Seattle	.122
6.	Floyd, G.S.-Hou.	.118
7.	Hornacek, Phoenix	.117
8.	Long, Indiana	.113
9.	Scott, LA Lakers	.109
10.	Mullin, Golden St.	.101

BOTTOM TEN

1.	Drew, LA Clippers	.059
2.	K. Smith, Sacramento	.064
3.	Adams, Denver	.066
4.	Leavell, Houston	.069
5.	Price, Cleveland	.069
6.	Wittman, Atlanta	.070
7.	Dumars, Detroit	.073
8.	Woodson, LA Clippers	.075
9.	J. Malone, Wash.	.078
10.	D. Harper, Dallas	.081

Chart 43
1987–88: BEST PER MINUTE

ALL-PURPOSE

1. Eaton, Utah	+.078	11. Lever, Denver	+.020
2. J. Williams, Cleve.	+.048	12. Levingston, Atl.	+.020
3. Olajuwon, Houston	+.047	13. Walker, New York	+.018
4. Jordan, Chicago	+.042	14. Hinson, Pha.-N.J.	+.015
5. Salley, Detroit	+.035	15. Adams, Denver	+.014
6. Nance, Phoe.-Cle.	+.028	16. Donaldson, Dallas	+.012
7. Benjamin, LA Clip.	+.024	17. McMillan, Seattle	+.011
8. Ewing, New York	+.023	18. Kersey, Portland	+.011
9. Robertson, San Ant.	+.021	19. Cheeks, Phila.	+.010
10. Breuer, Milwaukee	+.020	20. West, Cle.-Phoe.	+.010

CENTERS

		POWER FORWARDS	
1. Eaton, Utah	+.078	1. J. Williams, Cleve.	+.048
2. Olajuwon, Houston	+.047	2. Salley, Detroit	+.035
3. Benjamin, LA Clip.	+.024	3. Levingston, Atl.	+.020
4. Ewing, New York	+.023	4. Tarpley, Dallas	+.007
5. Breuer, Milwaukee	+.020	5. Sikma, Milwaukee	+.006
6. Donaldson, Dallas	+.012	6. Green, LA Lakers	+.005
7. West, Cle.-Phoe.	+.010	7. Perkins, Dallas	+.004
8. Corzine, Chicago	+.010	8. J. Williams, Wash.	+.002
9. Laimbeer, Detroit	+.003	9. Cage, LA Clippers	−.004
10. Thompson, LAL	+.002	10. McHale, Boston	−.009

SMALL FORWARDS

		POINT GUARDS	
1. Nance, Phoe.-Cle.	+.028	1. Adams, Denver	+.014
2. Walker, New York	+.018	2. McMillan, Seattle	+.011
3. Hinson, Pha.-N.J.	+.015	3. Cheeks, Phila.	+.010
4. Kersey, Portland	+.011	4. D. Harper, Dallas	+.004
5. Sellers, Chicago	+.009	5. Leavell, Houston	+.001
6. Pressley, Sacra.	+.002	6. Stockton, Utah	−.001
7. Higgins, Golden St.	−.005	7. Rivers, Atlanta	−.012
8. Bailey, Utah	−.006	8. Jackson, New York	−.015
9. Bird, Boston	−.011	9. Fleming, Indiana	−.018
10. Worthy, LA Lakers	−.011	10. Garland, G.S.	−.021

SHOOTING GUARDS

		BOTTOM TEN	
1. Jordan, Chicago	+.042	1. B. King, Wash.	−.074
2. Robertson, San Ant.	+.021	2. Theus, Sacramento	−.060
3. Lever, Denver	+.020	3. Daugherty, Cleve.	−.055
4. Scott, LA Lakers	+.007	4. Johnson, LA Lakers	−.054
5. Drexler, Portland	+.006	5. Oakley, Chicago	−.052
6. Mullin, Golden St.	−.005	6. Duckworth, Port.	−.051
7. Wittman, Atlanta	−.006	7. Floyd, G.S.-Hou.	−.051
8. Ainge, Boston	−.007	8. K. Malone, Utah	−.049
9. Long, Indiana	−.016	9. Person, Indiana	−.046
10. Hornacek, Phoenix	−.018	10. Ed Johnson, Phoe.	−.045

Chart 44
1987–88: BLOCKED SHOTS PER MINUTE

ALL-PURPOSE

1. Eaton, Utah	.111	11. Breuer, Milwaukee	.047
2. Benjamin, LA Clippers	.104	12. Bailey, Utah	.045
3. Ewing, New York	.096	13. Schayes, Denver	.042
4. Olajuwon, Houston	.076	14. Donaldson, Dallas	.041
5. West, Cle.-Phoe.	.070	15. Corzine, Chicago	.041
6. J. Williams, Cleve.	.069	16. Jordan, Chicago	.040
7. Salley, Detroit	.068	17. Gminski, N.J.-Pha.	.040
8. Nance, Phoe.-Cle.	.067	18. Abdul-Jabbar, LAL	.040
9. Hinson, Pha.-N.J.	.054	19. Levingston, Atlanta	.039
10. Carroll, G.S.-Hou.	.053	20. Thompson, LA Lakers	.039

CENTERS

1. Eaton, Utah	.111		**POWER FORWARDS**	
2. Benjamin, LA Clip.	.104	1. J. Williams, Cleve.	.069
3. Ewing, New York	.096	2. Salley, Detroit	.068
4. Olajuwon, Houston	.076	3. Levingston, Atlanta	.039
5. West, Cle.-Phoe.	.070	4. McHale, Boston	.039
6. Carroll, G.S.-Hou.	.053	5. Tarpley, Dallas	.037
7. Breuer, Milwaukee	.047	6. Barkley, Phila.	.033
8. Schayes, Denver	.042	7. Sikma, Milwaukee	.027
9. Donaldson, Dallas	.041	8. Cage, LA Clippers	.022
10. Corzine, Chicago	.041	9. Perkins, Dallas	.022
		10. Willis, Atlanta	.020

SMALL FORWARDS   ### POINT GUARDS

1. Nance, Phoe.-Cle.	.067	1. McMillan, Seattle	.019
2. Hinson, Pha.-N.J.	.054	2. Rivers, Atlanta	.016
3. Bailey, Utah	.045	3. Pressey, Milwaukee	.014
4. Sellers, Chicago	.030	4. D. Harper, Dallas	.012
5. Walker, New York	.028	5. D. Johnson, Boston	.011
6. Pressley, Sacramento	.027	6. Cheeks, Phila.	.008
7. Kersey, Portland	.023	7. Thomas, Detroit	.006
8. Aguirre, Dallas	.022	8. Stockton, Utah	.006
9. Worthy, LA Lakers	.021	9. Adams, Denver	.006
10. Rodman, Detroit	.021	10. Porter, Portland	.005

SHOOTING GUARDS   ### BOTTOM TEN

1. Jordan, Chicago	.040	1. Drew, LA Clippers	.000
2. Robertson, San Anton.	.023	2. Dawkins, San Anton.	.001
3. Drexler, Portland	.017	3. Jackson, New York	.002
4. Mullin, Golden St.	.016	4. Garland, Golden St.	.003
5. Woodson, LA Clip.	.010	5. Person, Indiana	.003
6. Scott, LA Lakers	.009	6. McDonald, Golden St.	.004
7. G. Wilkins, New York	.008	7. Leavell, Houston	.004
8. Lever, Denver	.007	8. K. Smith, Sacramento	.004
9. Blackman, Dallas	.007	9. Ed. Johnson, Phoenix	.004
10. Wittman, Atlanta	.007	10. Hornacek, Phoenix	.004

Chart 45
1987–88: STEALS PER MINUTE

ALL-PURPOSE

1. Stockton, Utah	.085	11. Leavell, Houston .058
2. Robertson, San Anton.	.082	12. Rivers, Atlanta .056
3. Jordan, Chicago	.078	13. Mullin, Golden St. .056
4. Lever, Denver	.073	14. D. Harper, Dallas .055
5. McMillan, Seattle	.069	15. Garland, Golden St. .055
6. Drexler, Portland.	.066	16. Scott, LA Lakers. .051
7. Jackson, New York	.063	17. Porter, Portland .050
8. Adams, Denver	.060	18. Thomas, Detroit .048
9. Cheeks, Philadelphia	.058	19. J. Williams, Wash. .048
10. Olajuwon, Houston	.058	20. Hornacek, Phoenix .048

CENTERS

1. Olajuwon, Houston	.058
2. Ewing, New York	.041
3. Stipanovich, Indiana	.033
4. Brickowski, San Ant.	.033
5. Schayes, Denver	.028
6. Carroll, G.S.-Hou.	.025
7. Parish, Boston.	.024
8. Laimbeer, Detroit	.023
9. Benjamin, LA Clip.	.023
10. West, Cle.-Phoe.	.022

POWER FORWARDS

1. J. Williams, Wash.	.048
2. Tarpley, Dallas.	.045
3. K. Malone, Utah	.037
4. McDaniel, Seattle	.036
5. Cage, LA Clippers	.034
6. Green, LA Lakers	.033
7. Willis, Atlanta	.033
8. Sikma, Milwaukee	.032
9. Green, New York	.032
10. Barkley, Phila.	.032

SMALL FORWARDS

1. Kersey, Portland	.044
2. Bird, Boston	.042
3. Pressley, Sacra.	.041
4. Robinson, Phila.	.037
5. Wilkins, Atlanta.	.035
6. Rodman, Detroit	.035
7. Chambers, Seattle	.032
8. Higgins, Golden St.	.032
9. Cummings, Milwaukee	.030
10. Walker, New York	.029

POINT GUARDS

1. Stockton, Utah	.085
2. McMillan, Seattle	.069
3. Jackson, New York	.063
4. Adams, Denver	.060
5. Cheeks, Phila.	.058
6. Leavell, Houston	.058
7. Rivers, Atlanta.	.056
8. D. Harper, Dallas	.055
9. Garland, Golden St.	.055
10. Porter, Portland	.050

SHOOTING GUARDS

1. Robertson, San Ant.	.082
2. Jordan, Chicago	.078
3. Lever, Denver	.073
4. Drexler, Portland.	.066
5. Mullin, Golden St.	.056
6. Scott, LA Lakers.	.051
7. Hornacek, Phoenix	.048
8. Woodson, LA Clip.	.043
9. Long, Indiana.	.042
10. Ainge, Boston	.038

BOTTOM TEN

1. McHale, Boston	.011
2. Duckworth, Portland	.014
3. Sellers, Chicago	.015
4. Ed Johnson, Phoenix	.015
5. Corzine, Chicago	.015
6. McCormick, Pha.-N.J.	.015
7. Eaton, Utah	.015
8. Donaldson, Dallas.	.016
9. Daugherty, Cleve	.016
10. Bailey, Utah	.017

Chart 46
1987–88: TURNOVERS PER MINUTE

ALL-PURPOSE

1. Wittman, Atlanta	.034	11. Eaton, Utah	.048
2. Walker, New York	.039	12. Donaldson, Dallas	.049
3. Sellers, Chicago	.041	13. J. Williams, Cleve.	.049
4. Levingston, Atlanta	.044	14. Ainge, Boston	.051
5. Green, LA Lakers	.045	15. Higgins, Golden St.	.051
6. McDonald, Golden St.	.046	16. Adams, Denver	.052
7. Corzine, Chicago	.047	17. Scott, LA Lakers	.053
8. Laimbeer, Detroit	.047	18. McCormick, Pha.-N.J.	.053
9. Breuer, Milwaukee	.047	19. Sikma, Milwaukee	.054
10. Perkins, Dallas	.048	20. McCray, Houston	.054

CENTERS

1. Corzine, Chicago	.047
2. Laimbeer, Detroit	.047
3. Breuer, Milwaukee	.047
4. Eaton, Utah	.048
5. Donaldson, Dallas	.049
6. McCormick, Pha.-N.J.	.053
7. Thompson, LA Lakers	.056
8. Stipanovich, Indiana	.058
9. Gminski, N.J.-Pha.	.060
10. Parish, Boston	.067

POWER FORWARDS

1. Levingston, Atlanta	.044
2. Green, LA Lakers	.045
3. McDonald, Golden St.	.046
4. Perkins, Dallas	.048
5. J. Williams, Cleve.	.049
6. Sikma, Milwaukee	.054
7. McHale, Boston	.059
8. J. Williams, Wash.	.060
9. Salley, Detroit	.060
10. Cage, LA Clippers	.060

SMALL FORWARDS

1. Walker, New York	.039
2. Sellers, Chicago	.041
3. Higgins, Golden St.	.051
4. McCray, Houston	.054
5. Kersey, Portland	.056
6. Worthy, LA Lakers	.058
7. Dantley, Detroit	.063
8. English, Denver	.064
9. Ed. Johnson, Phoe.	.064
10. Nance, Phoe.-Cle.	.065

POINT GUARDS

1. Adams, Denver	.052
2. Cheeks, Phila.	.056
3. Leavell, Houston	.060
4. D. Harper, Dallas	.063
5. Fleming, Indiana	.064
6. Price, Cleveland	.070
7. Dawkins, San Antonio	.071
8. Bagley, New Jersey	.072
9. D. Johnson, Boston	.073
10. Drew, LA Clippers	.075

SHOOTING GUARDS

1. Wittman, Atlanta	.034
2. Ainge, Boston	.051
3. Scott, LA Lakers	.053
4. Blackman, Dallas	.056
5. Lever, Denver	.059
6. Ellis, Seattle	.062
7. Long, Indiana	.063
8. Dumars, Detroit	.063
9. J. Malone, Wash.	.065
10. Hornacek, Phoenix	.070

BOTTOM TEN

1. Ewing, New York	.113
2. B. King, Washington	.103
3. Benjamin, LA Clip.	.103
4. Johnson, LA Lakers	.102
5. K. Malone, Utah	.102
6. Barkley, Phila.	.096
7. Brickowski, San Ant.	.093
8. Thomas, Detroit	.093
9. M. Malone, Wash.	.092
10. Stockton, Utah	.092

Chart 47
1987–88: COMPARING BLOCKED SHOTS WITH TURNOVERS

ALL-PURPOSE

1. Eaton, Utah	+.063	11. Hinson, Pha.-N.J.	−.011
2. J. Williams, Cleve.	+.020	12. Walker, New York	−.011
3. Salley, Detroit	+.009	13. Sellers, Detroit	−.011
4. Nance, Phoe.-Cle.	+.002	14. West, Cle.-Phoe.	−.012
5. Benjamin, LA Clip.	+.001	15. Ewing, New York	−.017
6. Breuer, Milwaukee	.000	16. Thompson, LAL	−.017
7. Donaldson, Dallas	−.004	17. Gminski, N.J.-Pha.	−.020
8. Levingston, Atlan.	−.005	18. Laimbeer, Detroit	−.020
9. Corzine, Chicago	−.006	19. McHale, Boston	−.021
10. Olajuwon, Houston	−.010	20. Perkins, Dallas	−.026

CENTERS

1. Eaton, Utah	+.063
2. Benjamin, LA Clip.	+.001
3. Breuer, Milwaukee	.000
4. Donaldson, Dallas	−.004
5. Corzine, Chicago	−.006
6. Olajuwon, Houston	−.010
7. West, Cle.-Phoe.	−.012
8. Ewing, New York	−.017
9. Thompson, LAL	−.017
10. Gminski, N.J.-Pha.	−.020

POWER FORWARDS

1. J. Williams, Cleve.	+.020
2. Salley, Detroit	+.009
3. Levingston, Atl.	−.005
4. McHale, Boston	−.021
5. Perkins, Dallas	−.026
6. Sikma, Milwaukee	−.026
7. Green, LA Lakers	−.029
8. Tarpley, Dallas	−.031
9. Cage, LA Clippers	−.038
10. McDonald, G. St.	−.042

SMALL FORWARDS

1. Nance, Phoe.-Cle.	+.002
2. Hinson, Pha.-N.J.	−.011
3. Walker, New York	−.011
4. Sellers, Chicago	−.011
5. Bailey, Utah	−.023
6. Kersey, Portland	−.033
7. McCray, Houston	−.035
8. Higgins, Golden St.	−.037
9. Worthy, LA Lakers	−.038
10. Pressley, Sacra.	−.039

POINT GUARDS

1. Adams, Denver	−.046
2. Cheeks, Phila.	−.048
3. D. Harper, Dallas	−.051
4. Leavell, Houston	−.058
5. McMillan, Seattle	−.058
6. Fleming, Indiana	−.060
7. D. Johnson, Boston	−.062
8. Price, Cleveland	−.066
9. Pressey, Milwaukee	−.066
10. Rivers, Atlanta	−.068

SHOOTING GUARDS

1. Wittman, Atlanta	−.027
2. Jordan, Chicago	−.037
3. Scott, LA Lakers	−.044
4. Ainge, Boston	−.045
5. Blackman, Dallas	−.049
6. Lever, Denver	−.053
7. Long, Indiana	−.057
8. Dumars, Detroit	−.058
9. Ellis, Seattle	−.058
10. J. Malone, Wash.	−.060

BOTTOM TEN

1. King, New York	−.098
2. Johnson, LA Lakers	−.097
3. Thomas, Detroit	−.088
4. Stockton, Utah	−.087
5. K. Malone, Utah	−.086
6. Floyd, G.S.-Hou.	−.084
7. Theus, Sacramento	−.082
8. Oakley, Chicago	−.082
9. K. Smith, Sacra.	−.081
10. Brickowski, S.A.	−.077

Chart 48
1987–88: COMPARING STEALS WITH TURNOVERS

ALL-PURPOSE

1. Lever, Denver	+.013	11. Walker, New York	−.009
2. Adams, Denver	+.009	12. Drexler, Portland	−.011
3. Cheeks, Philadel.	+.002	13. J. Williams, Wash.	−.012
4. Jordan, Chicago	+.002	14. Kersey, Portland	−.012
5. Scott, LA Lakers	−.002	15. Green, LA Lakers	−.013
6. Robertson, San Ant.	−.003	16. Ainge, Boston	−.013
7. Leavell, Houston	−.003	17. Wittman, Atlanta	−.013
8. Stockton, Utah	−.007	18. Jackson, New York	−.016
9. D. Harper, Dallas	−.007	19. Perkins, Dallas	−.018
10. McMillan, Seattle	−.008	20. Higgins, Golden St.	−.019

CENTERS

		POWER FORWARDS	
1. Laimbeer, Detroit	−.024	1. J. Williams, Wash.	−.012
2. Stipanovich, Ind.	−.025	2. Green, LA Lakers	−.013
3. Breuer, Milwaukee	−.027	3. Perkins, Dallas	−.018
4. Olajuwon, Houston	−.029	4. Levingston, Atl.	−.020
5. Donaldson, Dallas	−.029	5. J. Williams, Cleve.	−.020
6. Corzine, Chicago	−.031	6. Sikma, Milwaukee	−.022
7. Eaton, Utah	−.033	7. Cage, LA Clippers	−.026
8. Thompson, LA Lakers	−.037	8. McDonald, Golden St.	−.027
9. McCormick, Pha.-N.J.	−.037	9. Tarpley, Dallas	−.030
10. Gminski, N.J.-Pha.	−.038	10. Salley, Detroit	−.033

SMALL FORWARDS

		POINT GUARDS	
1. Walker, New York	−.009	1. Adams, Denver	+.009
2. Kersey, Portland	−.012	2. Cheeks, Phila.	+.002
3. Higgins, Golden St.	−.019	3. Leavell, Houston	−.003
4. Pressley, Sacra.	−.025	4. Stockton, Utah	−.007
5. Sellers, Chicago	−.026	5. D. Harper, Dallas	−.007
6. Bird, Boston	−.030	6. McMillan, Seattle	−.008
7. Worthy, LA Lakers	−.031	7. Jackson, New York	−.016
8. McCray, Houston	−.032	8. Fleming, Indiana	−.022
9. Cummings, Milwaukee	−.035	9. Garland, G. St.	−.024
10. Rodman, Detroit	−.038	10. Rivers, Atlanta	−.028

SHOOTING GUARDS

		BOTTOM TEN	
1. Lever, Denver	+.013	1. Benjamin, LA Clip.	−.080
2. Jordan, Chicago	+.002	2. King, Washington	−.079
3. Scott, LA Lakers	−.002	3. Daugherty, Cleve.	−.074
4. Robertson, San Ant.	−.003	4. M. Malone, Wash.	−.071
5. Drexler, Portland	−.011	5. K. Malone, Utah	−.068
6. Ainge, Boston	−.013	6. Theus, Sacramento	−.066
7. Wittman, Atlanta	−.013	7. Duckworth, Port.	−.066
8. Mullin, Golden St.	−.021	8. Barkley, Phila.	−.064
9. Long, Indiana	−.021	9. Oakley, Chicago	−.061
10. Hornacek, Phoenix	−.022	10. West, Cle.-Phoe.	−.060

Chart 49
1987–88: COMPARING ASSISTS WITH TURNOVERS

ALL-PURPOSE

1. Stockton, Utah	+.305	11. Lever, Denver	+.149
2. Johnson, LA Lakers	+.223	12. D. Harper, Dallas	+.146
3. Rivers, Atlanta.	+.215	13. Fleming, Indiana	+.144
4. McMillan, Seattle	+.209	14. Thomas, Detroit	+.138
5. Porter, Portland	+.196	15. Pressey, Milwau.	+.131
6. Jackson, New York	+.188	16. Adams, Denver	+.129
7. Hornacek, Phoenix	+.171	17. Leavell, Houston	+.128
8. Cheeks, Phila.	+.165	18. Floyd, G.S.-Hou.	+.128
9. D. Johnson, Boston	+.151	19. Garland, G. St.	+.123
10. Dawkins, San Ant.	+.150	20. Ainge, Boston	+.116

CENTERS

		POWER FORWARDS	
1. Brickowski, San Ant.	+.027	1. Sikma, Milwaukee	+.042
2. Daugherty, Cleve.	+.022	2. J. Williams, Wash.	+.036
3. Laimbeer, Detroit	+.022	3. McDonald, G. St.	+.022
4. Corzine, Chicago	+.019	4. McDaniel, Seattle	+.015
5. Stipanovich, Ind.	+.010	5. McHale, Boston	+.013
6. McCormick, Pha.-N.J.	+.003	6. Thorpe, Sacramento	+.012
7. Breuer, Milwaukee	−.002	7. Oakley, Chicago	+.003
8. Abdul-Jabbar, LAL	−.010	8. Perkins, Dallas	0.000
9. Gminski, N.J.-Pha.	−.013	9. J. Williams, Cle.	0.000
10. Parish, Boston.	−.017	10. Salley, Detroit	−.003

SMALL FORWARDS

		POINT GUARDS	
1. Bird, Boston	+.086	1. Stockton, Utah	+.305
2. English, Denver	+.070	2. Johnson, LA Lakers	+.223
3. Worthy, LA Lakers	+.051	3. Rivers, Atlanta.	+.215
4. McCray, Houston	+.045	4. McMillan, Seattle	+.209
5. Person, Indiana	+.035	5. Porter, Portland	+.196
6. Higgins, Golden St.	+.035	6. Jackson, New York	+.188
7. Aguirre, Dallas.	+.029	7. Cheeks, Phila.	+.165
8. Kersey, Portland	+.028	8. D. Johnson, Boston	+.151
9. Pressley, Sacra.	+.025	9. Dawkins, San Ant.	+.150
10. Sellers, Chicago	+.023	10. D. Harper, Dallas	+.146

SHOOTING GUARD

		BOTTOM TEN	
1. Hornacek, Phoenix	+.171	1. Ewing, New York	−.064
2. Lever, Denver	+.149	2. Willis, Atlanta	−.053
3. Floyd, G.S.-Hou.	+.128	3. M. Malone, Wash.	−.051
4. Ainge, Boston	+.116	4. Duckworth, Portland	−.050
5. Robertson, San Ant.	+.103	5. West, Cle.-Phoe.	−.047
6. Wittman, Atlanta.	+.091	6. K. Malone, Utah	−.039
7. Theus, Sacramento	+.086	7. Tarpley, Dallas.	−.037
8. Dumars, Detroit	+.079	8. B. Williams, N.J.	−.030
9. Drexler, Portland.	+.075	9. Olajuwon, Houston	−.028
10. Jordan, Chicago	+.070	10. Eaton, Utah	−.028

Chart 50
1987–88: MINUTES PLAYED

ALL-PURPOSE

1. Jordan, Chicago	3311	11. Porter, Portland	2991
2. Jackson, New York	3249	12. Robertson, San Ant.	2978
3. K. Malone, Utah	3198	13. Bird, Boston	2965
4. Barkley, Phila.	3170	14. Gminski, N.J.-Pha.	2961
5. Thorpe, Sacramento	3072	15. Daugherty, Cleve.	2957
6. Lever, Denver	3061	16. Wilkins, Atlanta	2948
7. Drexler, Portland	3060	17. Thomas, Detroit	2927
8. Scott, LA Lakers	3048	18. Sikma, Milwaukee	2923
9. D. Harper, Dallas	3032	19. Laimbeer, Detroit	2897
10. Ainge, Boston	3018	20. Kersey, Portland	2888

CENTERS

1. Gminski, N.J.-Pha.	2961
2. Daugherty, Cleve.	2957
3. Laimbeer, Detroit	2897
4. Olajuwon, Houston	2825
5. Eaton, Utah	2731
6. M. Malone, Wash.	2692
7. Stipanovich, Ind.	2692
8. Ewing, New York	2546
9. Donaldson, Dallas	2523
10. Corzine, Chicago	2328

POWER FORWARDS

1. K. Malone, Utah	3198
2. Barkley, Phila.	3170
3. Thorpe, Sacramento	3072
4. Sikma, Milwaukee	2923
5. Oakley, Chicago	2816
6. McDaniel, Seattle	2703
7. Cage, LA Clippers	2660
8. B. Williams, N.J.	2637
9. Green, LA Lakers	2636
10. Perkins, Dallas	2499

SMALL FORWARDS

1. Bird, Boston	2965
2. Wilkins, Atlanta	2948
3. Kersey, Portland	2888
4. English, Denver	2818
5. Person, Indiana	2807
6. Bailey, Utah	2804
7. McCray, Houston	2689
8. Chambers, Seattle	2680
9. Worthy, LA Lakers	2655
10. Cummings, Milwaukee	2629

POINT GUARDS

1. Jackson, New York	3249
2. D. Harper, Dallas	3032
3. Porter, Portland	2991
4. Thomas, Detroit	2927
5. Cheeks, Phila.	2871
6. Stockton, Utah	2842
7. Adams, Denver	2778
8. Bagley, New Jersey	2774
9. Fleming, Indiana	2733
10. D. Johnson, Boston	2670

SHOOTING GUARDS

1. Jordan, Chicago	3311
2. Lever, Denver	3061
3. Drexler, Portland	3060
4. Scott, LA Lakers	3048
5. Ainge, Boston	3018
6. Robertson, San Ant.	2978
7. Ellis, Seattle	2790
8. Dumars, Detroit	2732
9. G. Wilkins, N.Y.	2703
10. J. Malone, Wash.	2655

AVERAGE PER GAME

1. Jordan, Chicago	40.4
2. Jackson, New York	39.6
3. Barkley, Phila.	39.6
4. K. Malone, Utah	39.0
5. Bird, Boston	39.0
6. Drexler, Portland	37.8
7. Wilkins, Atlanta	37.8
8. B. Williams, N.J.	37.7
9. Thorpe, Sacramento	37.5
10. Daugherty, Cleve.	37.4

Chart 51
1987–88: TOP RESERVES

ALL-PURPOSE

1. Cartwright, New York .... .627	11. Turpin, Utah........................ .526
2. Thompson, Sacramento .... .586	12. R. Harper, Cleve. .... .522
3. A. Carr, Atlanta..................... .558	13. R. Anderson, Ind. .... .518
4. Berry, San Antonio.................. .557	14. S. Vincent, Chicago .... .518
5. Vandeweghe, Portland............... .557	15. K. Johnson, Cle.-Phoe. .... .517
6. O. Smith, Den.-G.S. 553	16. W. Davis, Phoenix .... .512
7. Rasmussen, Denver.................. .551	17. Sampson, Hou.-G.S. .... .508
8. Mahorn, Detroit..................... .546	18. Webb, Atlanta .... .507
9. Gudmundsen, San Ant................ .543	19. Kleine, Sacramento .... .503
10. Lister, Seattle .... .540	20. A. Adams, Phoenix.................. .502

CENTERS

1. Cartwright, New York .... .627	
2. Thompson, Sacramento .... .586	
3. Rasmussen, Denver.................. .551	
4. Gudmundsen, San Ant............... .543	
5. Lister, Seattle .... .540	
6. Turpin, Utah........................ .526	
7. Sampson, Hou.-G.S. .... .508	
8. Kleine, Sacramento .... .503	
9. S. Johnson, Portland .... .500	
10. Bol, Washington .... .482	

POWER FORWARDS

1. Mahorn, Detroit..................... .546	
2. Adams, Phoenix .... .502	
3. Catledge, Washington .... .494	
4. G. Anderson, San Ant................ .490	
5. H. Grant, Chicago................... .478	
6. H. Williams, Ind. .... .473	
7. Coleman, N.J.-Pha.................. .472	
8. Petersen, Houston .... .463	
9. M. Lucas, Portland.................. .461	
10. Whitehead, G. St.................... .447	

SMALL FORWARDS

1. A. Carr, Atlanta..................... .558	
2. Vandeweghe, Portland............... .557	
3. Berry, San Antonio.................. .557	
4. Ron Anderson, Ind. .... .518	
5. J. Vincent, Denver .... .497	
6. McKey, Seattle .... .492	
7. Pinckney, Sacramento............... .463	
8. Schrempf, Dallas .... .462	
9. Corbin, Cle.-Phoe. .... .450	
10. Mitchell, San Ant................... .444	

POINT GUARDS

1. S. Vincent, Sea.-Chi. .... .518	
2. K. Johnson, Cle.-Pho. .... .517	
3. Webb, Atlanta .... .507	
4. J. Lucas, Milwaukee................. .500	
5. Humphries, Pho.-Mil. .... .486	
6. B. Davis, Dallas..................... .464	
7. Valentine, LA Clip. .... .463	
8. R. Green, Utah .... .452	
9. Colter, Pha.-Wash. .... .438	
10. Bogues, Washington .... .431	

SHOOTING GUARDS

1. O. Smith, Den.-G.S. .... .553	
2. R. Harper, Cleveland .... .522	
3. W. Davis, Phoenix .... .512	
4. Threatt, Chi.-Sea.................... .502	
5. Dailey, LA Clippers.................. .495	
6. Moncrief, Milwaukee .... .491	
7. Short, Houston .... .486	
8. Curry, Cleveland .... .473	
9. Battle, Atlanta...................... .460	
10. Pippen, Chicago .... .451	

BOTTOM TEN

1. Wingate, Phila. .... .263	
2. A. King, Phila. .... .287	
3. Sparrow, Chicago.................... .294	
4. Dunn, Denver........................ .298	
5. Hanzlik, Denver..................... .319	
6. Hopson, New Jersey .... .334	
7. Birdsong, New Jersey .... .338	
8. Wolf, LA Clippers .... .340	
9. Sundvold, San Ant. 367	
10. Hodges, Mil.-Phoe................... .368	

Chart 52
TEAM SHOOTIST RATINGS

1. Boston Celtics...................... 1.012
2. Los Angeles Lakers .... .968
3. Indiana Pacers..................... .939
4. Chicago Bulls .... .938
5. Utah Jazz.......................... .937
6. Portland Blazers.................... .937
7. Phoenix Suns .... .936
8. San Antonio Spurs.................. .934
9. Denver Nuggets .... .934
10. Cleveland Cavaliers .... .932
11. Detroit Pistons .... .930
12. Atlanta Hawks...................... .927
13. Seattle Supersonics................. .924
14. Dallas Mavericks.................... .924
15. Milwaukee Bucks .... .921
16. Sacramento Kings .... .917
17. Golden St. Warriors .... .913
18. Philadelphia 76ers.................. .911
19. Houston Rockets .... .908
20. New York Knicks .... .907
21. New Jersey Nets .... .899
22. Washington Bullets .... .898
23. Los Angeles Clippers............... .853

Chart 53
TEAM TWO-POINT
FIELD GOAL PERCENTAGE

1. Boston Celtics...................... .537
2. Los Angeles Lakers .... .520
3. Utah Jazz.......................... .502
4. Portland Blazers.................... .501
5. San Antonio Spurs.................. .500
6. Detroit Pistons .... .499
7. Chicago Bulls .... .499
8. Cleveland Cavaliers .... .496
9. Phoenix Suns .... .494
10. Atlanta Hawks...................... .492
11. Indiana Pacers..................... .490
12. Dallas Mavericks.................... .489
13. Seattle Supersonics................. .488
14. Philadelphia 76ers.................. .485
15. Milwaukee Bucks .... .485
16. Denver Nuggets .... .484
17. Sacramento Kings .... .481
18. Houston Rockets .... .481
19. New Jersey Nets .... .480
20. New York Knicks .... .478
21. Golden St. Warriors .... .476
22. Washington Bullets .... .473
23. Los Angeles Clippers............... .452

Chart 54
TEAM THREE-POINT
FIELD GOAL PERCENTAGE

1. Boston Celtics...................... .384
2. Cleveland Cavaliers .... .378
3. Seattle Supersonics................. .346
4. Denver Nuggets .... .342
5. Indiana Pacers..................... .336
6. Phoenix Suns .... .331
7. Milwaukee Bucks .... .324
8. San Antonio Spurs.................. .323
9. Philadelphia 76ers.................. .323
10. Sacramento Kings .... .320
11. Utah Jazz.......................... .319
12. New York Knicks .... .316
13. Portland Biazers.................... .308
14. Atlanta Hawks...................... .301
15. New Jersey Nets .... .301
16. Los Angeles Lakers .... .297
17. Dallas Mavericks.................... .293
18. Golden St. Warriors .... .292
19. Detroit Pistons .... .287
20. Los Angeles Clippers................ .249
21. Houston Rockets .... .237
22. Chicago Bulls .... .230
23. Washington Bullets .... .210

Chart 55
TEAM FREE THROW PERCENTAGE

1. Denver Nuggets .... .804
2. Boston Celtics...................... .803
3. Golden St. Warriors .... .796
4. Dallas Mavericks.................... .789
5. Los Angeles Lakers .... .789
6. Indiana Pacers..................... .780
7. Houston Rockets .... .780
8. Milwaukee Bucks .... .775
9. Washington Bullets .... .773
10. Sacramento Kings .... .772
11. Portland Blazers .... .770
12. Atlanta Hawks...................... .767
13. Philadelphia 76ers.................. .764
14. Phoenix Suns .... .764
15. New York Knicks .... .759
16. Chicago Bulls .... .759
17. Detroit Pistons .... .757
18. Utah Jazz.......................... .750
19. Seattle Supersonics................. .748
20. Cleveland Cavaliers .... .744
21. San Antonio Spurs.................. .733
22. New Jersey Nets .... .729
23. Los Angeles Clippers............... .713

Chart 56
TEAM PAR RATINGS

1.	Portland Blazers	3.945
2.	Denver Nuggets	3.913
3.	San Antonio Spurs	3.832
4.	Los Angeles Lakers	3.828
5.	Boston Celtics	3.826
6.	Utah Jazz	3.787
7.	Seattle Supersonics	3.754
8.	Dallas Mavericks	3.741
9.	Phoenix Suns	3.732
10.	Houston Rockets	3.720
11.	Sacramento Kings	3.707
12.	Detroit Pistons	3.699
13.	Atlanta Hawks	3.669
14.	Milwaukee Bucks	3.626
15.	Chicago Bulls	3.623
16.	Gol. St. Warriors	3.582
17.	Indiana Pacers	3.576
18.	New York Knicks	3.572
19.	Philadelphia 76ers	3.540
20.	Washington Bullets	3.535
21.	Cleveland Cavs.	3.524
22.	Los Angeles Clips.	3.416
23.	New Jersey Nets	3.379

Chart 58
TEAM ASSISTS/MINUTE

1.	Boston Celtics	.619
2.	Utah Jazz	.611
3.	Los Angeles Lakers	.593
4.	San Antonio Spurs	.592
5.	Phoenix Suns	.591
6.	Portland Blazers	.585
7.	Denver Nuggets	.582
8.	Milwaukee Bucks	.555
9.	Chicago Bulls	.541
10.	Seattle Supersonics	.541
11.	Sacramento Kings	.535
12.	Cleveland Cavaliers	.524
13.	Atlanta Hawks	.521
14.	Detroit Pistons	.509
15.	New York Knicks	.508
16.	Golden St. Warriors	.507
17.	Dallas Mavericks	.502
18.	Indiana Pacers	.502
19.	Houston Rockets	.492
20.	Philadelphia 76ers	.477
21.	Los Angeles Clips.	.476
22.	Washington Bullets	.472
23.	New Jersey Nets	.454

Chart 57
TEAM POINTS/MINUTE

1.	Denver Nuggets	2.420
2.	Portland Blazers	2.412
3.	Boston Celtics	2.355
4.	San Antonio Spurs	2.352
5.	Los Angeles Lakers	2.336
6.	Seattle Supersonics	2.301
7.	Houston Rockets	2.270
8.	Dallas Mavericks	2.268
9.	Detroit Pistons	2.264
10.	Utah Jazz	2.258
11.	Phoenix Suns	2.256
12.	Sacramento Kings	2.239
13.	Atlanta Hawks	2.236
14.	Gol. St. Warriors	2.217
15.	Milwaukee Bucks	2.199
16.	New York Knicks	2.185
17.	Indiana Pacers	2.178
18.	Philadelphia 76ers	2.177
19.	Washington Bullets	2.177
20.	Chicago Bulls	2.168
21.	Cleveland Cavs.	2.166
22.	New Jersey Nets	2.082
23.	Los Angeles Clips.	2.046

Chart 59
TEAM REBOUNDS/MINUTE

1.	Dallas Mavericks	.971
2.	Houston Rockets	.958
3.	Portland Blazers	.949
4.	Sacramento Kings	.934
5.	Detroit Pistons	.926
6.	Utah Jazz	.919
7.	Chicago Bulls	.914
8.	Seattle Supersonics	.914
9.	Atlanta Hawks	.912
10.	Denver Nuggets	.912
11.	Los Angeles Lakers	.900
12.	Indiana Pacers	.897
13.	Los Angeles Clippers	.894
14.	San Antonio Spurs	.889
15.	Washington Bullets	.887
16.	Philadelphia 76ers	.886
17.	Phoenix Suns	.885
18.	New York Knicks	.879
19.	Milwaukee Bucks	.873
20.	Golden St. Warriors	.857
21.	Boston Celtics	.852
22.	New Jersey Nets	.844
23.	Cleveland Cavaliers	.835

Chart 60
TEAM 'BEST' RATINGS

1. Denver Nuggets .... +0.573
2. Atlanta Hawks..................... −0.646
3. Chicago Bulls .... −0.927
4. Utah Jazz......................... −1.012
5. Houston Rockets .... −1.866
6. Seattle Sonics..................... −1.878
7. Dallas Mavericks.................. −2.024
8. Cleveland Cavs. .... −2.195
9. Washington Bullets .... −2.244
10. San Antonio Spurs................. −2.573
11. Milwaukee Bucks .... −2.732
12. Los Angeles Lakers .... −2.951
13. Boston Celtics.................... −3.280
14. Portland Blazers.................. −3.390
15. New York Knicks .... −3.463
16. Los Angeles Clips................. −3.573
17. Philadelphia 76ers................ −3.610
18. Indiana Pacers.................... −4.317
19. Detroit Pistons .... −4.463
20. Gol. St. Warriors................. −4.524
21. Sacramento Kings .... −4.658
22. Phoenix Suns .... −4.695
23. New Jersey Nets .... −4.768

Chart 61
TEAM BLOCKS/MINUTE

1. Utah Jazz......................... .159
2. Atlanta Hawks..................... .136
3. Cleveland Cavaliers .... .133
4. Los Angeles Clippers.............. .132
5. Houston Rockets .... .128
6. Washington Bullets .... .127
7. Sacramento Kings .... .125
8. Chicago Bulls .... .120
9. San Antonio Spurs................. .118
10. Philadelphia 76ers................ .117
11. Dallas Mavericks.................. .113
12. New York Knicks .... .113
13. Seattle Supersonics............... .113
14. Boston Celtics.................... .105
15. Los Angeles Lakers .... .102
16. Denver Nuggets .... .102
17. Detroit Pistons .... .100
18. New Jersey Nets .... .098
19. Milwaukee Bucks .... .096
20. Phoenix Suns .... .090
21. Portland Blazers.................. .088
22. Indiana Pacers.................... .088
23. Golden St. Warriors............... .072

Chart 62
TEAM STEALS/MINUTE

1. Denver Nuggets .... .211
2. New York Knicks .... .199
3. Utah Jazz......................... .196
4. Seattle Supersonics................ .195
5. Golden St. Warriors .... .188
6. San Antonio Spurs................. .187
7. Cleveland Cavaliers .... .186
8. New Jersey Nets .... .184
9. Portland Blazers.................. .184
10. Los Angeles Clippers.............. .182
11. Houston Rockets .... .181
12. Chicago Bulls .... .180
13. Washington Bullets .... .176
14. Phoenix Suns .... .171
15. Los Angeles Lakers .... .170
16. Milwaukee Bucks .... .170
17. Philadelphia 76ers................ .169
18. Dallas Mavericks.................. .163
19. Atlanta Hawks..................... .161
20. Indiana Pacers.................... .157
21. Boston Celtics.................... .157
22. Detroit Pistons .... .149
23. Sacramento Kings .... .147

Chart 63
TEAM TURNOVERS/MINUTE

1. Denver Nuggets .... .300
2. Atlanta Hawks..................... .310
3. Dallas Mavericks.................. .318
4. Chicago Bulls .... .318
5. Milwaukee Bucks .... .323
6. Boston Celtics.................... .330
7. Los Angeles Lakers .... .333
8. Indiana Pacers.................... .335
9. Detroit Pistons .... .341
10. Portland Blazers.................. .343
11. Seattle Supersonics............... .347
12. Houston Rockets .... .348
13. Washington Bullets .... .348
14. Golden St. Warriors .... .353
15. San Antonio Spurs................. .358
16. Phoenix Suns .... .358
17. Philadelphia 76ers................ .360
18. Celveland Cavaliers .... .364
19. Sacramento Kings .... .369
20. Utah Jazz......................... .376
21. New Jersey Nets .... .380
22. New York Knicks .... .383
23. Los Angeles Clippers.............. .388